Out on a Limb

Out on a Limb

My own story

Martin Crowe

REED

First published 1995 by Reed Publishing (NZ) Ltd,
39 Rawene Road, Birkenhead, Auckland 10. Associated
companies, branches and representatives throughout
the world.

Copyright © Reed Publishing (NZ) Ltd 1995

ISBN 0 7900 0387 2

Printed in Australia

Contents

Dedicated to

Wally Lees, Mark Greatbatch, John Wright, Andrew Jones, Ian Smith, Rod Latham, Ken Rutherford, Chris Harris, Dipak Patel, Gavin Larsen, Chris Cairns, Danny Morrison, Willie Watson, Murphy Su'a, Ian Taylor, Mark Plummer — the Young Guns from the New Zealand World Cup squad who all but took us to the grand final, and helped lift a nation in the most amazing month's cricket I was privileged to play in.

And to Simone, who inspired and encouraged me to lead the team with courage and skill.

Finally to my family, Audrey and Dave, Jeff and Debbie, for their constant loving support.

Acknowledgements

My sincere thanks to everyone who has helped in the preparation of this book:

To Bryce Courtenay, who wrote the Foreword; to Anthony Boswell, who compiled the statistics; to Anna Rogers, who edited the text; and to Alan Smith, Ian Watt and the staff of Reed Publishing.

To my Winning Ways business team: Jeff Crowe, Dave Howman and Lyall Bunt.

To my friends and team mates.

To my family, and especially to Simone, thank you so much.

Lyrics from 'Brothers in Arms', 'On Every Street' and 'Private Investigations' are copyright © Mark Knopfler Chariscourt Ltd/Rondor Music (London) Limited, and are reprinted by permission of Rondor Music (Australia) Pty Ltd.

Extracts from *From Sammy to Jimmy*, copyright © Peter Roebuck 1991, are reprinted by permission of Transworld Publishers Ltd.

Thanks to Patrick Eagar, Photosport, Fotopacific, Visual Impact Pictures and Allsport Photographic for their assistance with photographs.

Foreword

by Bryce Courtenay

It was late afternoon on 22 September 1962 at Eden Park when the crowd exploded on the final whistle and the All Blacks had beaten John Thornett's Wallabies 16–8. At that very same moment, to the jubilation of the large crowd, Martin Crowe was born in a hospital up the road.

For a New Zealander the omens don't get any better than that.

Martin Crowe is tall and powerful, and that's not a bad start for almost anything in life. He attracts attention, often cruel and unjust criticism, but that's to be expected in the shitty world we live in, where the tall poppy is soon enough chopped down. But that's the strength in Martin Crowe, who long ago realised that when you chop down the tall poppies only the weeds remain, and so he has kept his head high, his roots firmly planted in solid earth and has continued to grow and to blossom, season after season, to the enormous chagrin of his would-be detractors.

While most of us walk down the centre of the road, Martin has always dared his genius to walk the wildest unknown way. This makes him different and better at what he does, and that's how it should be, or we would have no genius on the roll-call of humankind.

He is one of only seven players in the game of cricket to have scored over 4,000 runs in a calendar year. With an average in the mid-fifties in first class cricket, he is among only 20 players in the history of the game. When you realise that this average is higher than that of Viv Richards, Barry Richards, Greg Chappell and Graeme Pollock, you begin to perceive his stature in the cricketing world.

He is to the pull shot what Grant Fox was to the penalty kick. He makes this prince of strokes look effortless when it is truly the shot most likely to bring down the greatest in the game. Add one more statistic and you begin to have some measure of the man: Martin Crowe also has the highest and fastest run-rate in one-day internationals of any New Zealander.

Comparisons are usually thought to be odious, but I don't think New Zealanders begin to understand that if Crowe were a rugby player he would perhaps be among the finest footballers ever to run onto a paddock. What's more, he has the height and the strength, and certainly the temperament, to have been the greatest of all locks.

There have been, in my opinion, only three truly great New Zealand batsmen: John Reid, who could bludgeon almost any attack to death; Glenn Turner, who could defend his end until the moon turned to green cheese; and Martin Crowe, who brings a new meaning to the word 'elegance', for he is perhaps the finest stroke-player the game of cricket has ever seen. If you think I am laying it on too thick, I have talked to some of the most knowledgeable people in the game and I have heard this from them all.

This leaves one more factor to consider — the totally disastrous New Zealand pitches on which a Kiwi cricketer must learn the game. The only hallowed turf in New Zealand is terminally punctured with the stud marks of the All Blacks. The New Zealand cricket pitch, even at some of the major venues, is often an off-duty rugby ground come through a hard, wet winter. It is built in haste, is lacking in love and it repays its hapless groundsman by being on the slow side with an uneven bounce. Great batsmen simply do not evolve from pitches that have done winter battle with the boot and have had the living shit kicked out of them. So the advent of a Martin Crowe is a very large miracle indeed.

A man is more than the sum of what he does well. Martin Crowe, who walks to the beat of a different drum, has transcended the bungling, officious running dogs who have yapped so furiously at his heels or those few team-mates who have tried on occasion to undo him. He is a fine man, a gentle man and a gentleman, possessed of a great inner spirit, and he is also, but perhaps less importantly, one of the greatest players in the history of history's greatest game. In Martin, New Zealand really does have something and someone to Crowe about.

Prologue

Don't be afraid to go out on a limb. That's where the fruit is.
— H. JACKSON BROWN, JR

9 February 1992

I knocked and entered the room. As I moved to the far end I could see them seated, waiting. I felt good. Hadn't been that way for a while, but the confidence was returning.

It was the end of the fourth day of the third test against England at the Basin Reserve in Wellington, where finally we had moved into a winning position. The agony of the first test, which we had lost so incredibly, was now distant. I was the one who had made the final mistake as we went down by an innings and four runs. We had lost six wickets in the last session of the match while I stood at the non-striker's end, and then had number 11 Chris Pringle join me for the final half-hour to help save the match. We batted until 12 minutes remained, but still needed four runs to make England bat again; the required 10 minutes between innings would finish the game, and give us a draw. I gambled on hitting the four to ensure the draw there and then, but I failed, and the loss came down heavily on me. Instead of being the hero, I became the villain.

In the second test we performed better, despite four changes to the team, but in the end England were too good on a result pitch. Going into the third test, having lost a home series for the first time in 12 years, we needed to restore pride. More important, at the end of the test a World Cup squad of 14 was to be named. Eighteen months of planning was catching up on us and it would not be long before the World Cup opened at Eden Park, Auckland, with New Zealand taking on the world champions, Australia. This test was everyone's last chance for selection.

As I approached the large windows of the family viewing room in the pavilion I could see on the huge scoreboard across the ground that New Zealand was in a good position. England in their second innings had a lead of only 44 with three wickets down. A quick breakthrough in the morning would give us a chance of pulling off a welcome win.

The selectors had called me to a meeting, obviously, I thought, because they wanted my final views on the make-up of the squad. After many meetings over 18 months about the World Cup and our players, I also thought this was merely a tidying up process. But when I received no greeting of any kind and there was no casual chat, I tensed.

We sat in a semi-circle around the window-ledge with me in the middle. Don Neely, the convenor, was on my left, his chair, oddly, facing away from the others and towards the window. He kept his head down, concentrating on a folder in his lap. In front of me was Bruce Taylor. The likeable former test allrounder, always so chirpy and positive, was definitely edgy. On my right was Ross Dykes, a newcomer to the panel. Ross had played for Auckland in the 1970s as an effective wicketkeeper, and had selected for the city over the past few years. I liked Ross, who was always approachable and great to talk cricket to, yet he too looked pale and under stress. He sat on the window-ledge right beside me but hardly looked up from his feet.

Don spoke first. Reading directly from the folder, glasses on, eyes down, he proceeded to issue a statement from his notes rather than addressing me directly, eye to eye. He began by saying that the selectors felt I wasn't enjoying the captaincy and, because of that, the players weren't performing under my leadership. There was obvious doubt about my fitness, although they could see that my batting form was coming right. Don said that they were very concerned going into the World Cup, and that, after discussing the situation with a few people, they had to ask whether everyone would be better off if I weren't captain. Don then asked, 'Will you play under John Wright?'

He finished speaking, but continued to look down at his folder, as if searching for something he'd missed. I looked around, but not one of the selectors would meet my eye. I was stunned.

Naturally, as it seemed to be my turn to speak, I reacted strongly. 'You've got to be joking! What's the problem? We're on the verge of winning this test match, and you want me to resign? You say the guys aren't performing because of my captaincy? Get real! We are coming right, if you haven't noticed — in fact we could win this match. You guys have made all these changes lately, which makes nearly 30 players since the Pakistan tour. What's the problem? I mean, what are you on about? I've spent 18 months planning this World Cup campaign and you want me to throw it all away? Are you kidding me?

'Forget it. I won't resign. If you sack me as captain then forget about picking me as a batsman. I'm not available. I'd sooner go and play in Australia or South Africa if I'm not captain. I can't believe this!'

Don Neely just kept staring at his notes, giving the impression he wasn't in control. Although he had been a selector for 13 years and convenor for six, he had never played for New Zealand and had no idea what playing at the top level was like. He was speechless. Ross Dykes spoke out, suggesting that I wasn't putting my arm around the bowlers enough. Bruce Taylor then said that I'd looked on edge in Christchurch when I had a blow-up with the bowlers at practice, because they kept bowling no balls.

'You don't know, do you? You don't know what this is all about! Eighteen months into this and you want to throw it all away! You can stick it. *No resignation.*'

With that, I stood and walked out. As I reached the door I turned and said, 'Hey, good luck.' I felt they needed some help.

I was shattered. Maybe my reaction didn't help my cause, but I felt I was fighting for my professional life. I wasn't going to give up, so I said what I felt was needed to stay in charge, even though deep down I knew I would still play if I was sacked as captain. Anyway, since when did you get asked if you were available just because you might not be captain. I was under contract and therefore available for anything. In other words, they either picked you or they didn't. If they didn't want me as captain, then I should have been sacked. It was weird. I suppose they were making a gesture by giving me a chance to resign first, but they underestimated how I felt about all the work that had gone in. What did they expect me to say?

I caught up immediately with Andrew Jones, who was waiting to grab a lift back home to Eastbourne. 'Pick the team okay?' he said casually. I just sat there, gripping the wheel hard, then turned and replied, 'I don't think so, because I can't even be sure I'm in it!'

'What happened?'

'They wanted me to resign. They want Wrighty to take over! I just told them to stick it. If they sack me, I said I wouldn't play just as a batter.'

'Jeez,' Andrew announced, 'that's ridiculous, to change everything now. How stupid.'

I dropped Andrew off, as he lived only a few minutes away. Simone's father, Rodger, was down for the test so I told him what had happened,

13

and then Simmy herself when she came in. We comforted ourselves with some red wine, and discussed how this could have happened.

Maybe John Wright could have wanted the job back, after giving it up in 1990. Perhaps there were a few who had been working behind my back? Maybe they were taking notice of Henry 'my dear old thing' Blofeld, who, during the test series, had called for my head as captain. Taking any notice of him was like subscribing to the Saddam Hussein fan club! I had been relieved to see that Andrew seemed bewildered by it all.

Then the phone rang. It was John Wright, who stressed immediately that he didn't want the job unless I wanted him to take it. I repeated what I told the selectors, that I wasn't giving it up and if they sacked me then I wasn't available at all.

'I'll talk to them tomorrow, Hogan, and we'll sort it out. I'm right behind you.'

Andrew had phoned John to tell him of the meeting so I appreciated that they had both acted quickly and supportively. It just seemed so stupid that all this was going on during a test match; it was a ridiculous time to start head-bashing. Maybe there were things I needed to work on, to improve, to be told quietly that something wasn't working. But to come straight out with a written statement basically asking me to hand over the captaincy in the middle of a critical test match?

I knew that Wally Lees was concerned about the way certain things were going, including how I was coping. He had seen me very stressed out after my first innings knock of 30 at the Basin and was really worried that I was losing control of my focus. He knew that the Christchurch loss was a huge blow to me and that the pressure was starting to mount. But Wally wasn't the sort to panic. I knew he would confront the issues in a team gathering after the test, just as he'd done on a number of occasions. So I didn't ring him, preferring to talk to him the next day about why the selectors wanted me to give up the captaincy. In the meantime I tried to forget it, but it was impossible. I didn't sleep well, and woke next morning realising that, although the selectors wanted me out, I was in fact leading a team on the verge of winning a test match. I had work to do.

I was in the bathroom when Simmy handed me the phone. It was Jeff, my brother, who had been phoned by Ross Dykes after the meeting and asked to get me to back down. So Jeff, being the eternal diplomat, did just that. He suggested I step down for a while and let John Wright take over until he retired, then I could come back in. I told Jeff that I wasn't going to give up all the hard work and that I didn't appreciate him doing the selectors' dirty work, especially as I didn't know exactly what it was I was supposed to have done wrong. He agreed and suggested I stick with my gut instincts, then finished by wishing me luck for the test.

My head was spinning, but it was time to get organised, pick up Andrew and drive to the ground, 10 kilometres away. In the dressing room, before play began, I told the team that prospects were good, and that we could win if we worked hard and made things happen. I stressed the need to remove Allan Lamb.

We filed out onto the field and began aggressively, plenty of chat, plenty of encouragement. Standing at first slip next to Ian Smith, I couldn't help mentioning the dilemma. It was so much on my mind and I needed to talk it out. We hadn't broken through after 20 minutes, so Ian and I started to discuss the situation between deliveries. He was astonished.

Just as we were in the middle of our chat Chris Cairns delivered a superb leg-cutter and Allan Lamb edged between Ian and me. The ball was coming more towards me so I threw myself left, flung out one hand and, to my delight, came up with it after diving and rolling. We had him!

Next I saw Allan standing his ground, expressing doubt, so the umpires conferred and the square-leg umpire ruled in our favour. As we raced up to congratulate Chris, I heard Ian say, 'Sorry Hogan, it didn't carry.'

'Truly?' My heart sank.

'Bounced first, I'm sure of it,' he said.

'Fair enough. Stay where you are, Lamby,' I offered.

I walked back to first slip, shrugging my shoulders. Great gesture, but this was a test match. So we missed our chance. I was still shrugging my shoulders when, hours later, Lamb cruised past 100.

Before tea, John Wright trotted off the field for a leak, only to be spotted talking for 10 minutes with the selectors, obviously explaining where he stood. I'd have loved to be a fly on the wall.

England saved the test and, with only a session left, Graham Gooch declared, just to be a nuisance. Straightaway John, in what could be his last test, was out to Ian Botham for a duck. Maybe his mind wasn't on the job either!

I'd already decided to relieve Andrew of the number three spot and go in myself — to get out of the dressing room, and for some practice in the middle. Then Syd Lawrence, England's fast bowler, snapped his kneecap in two while bowling to me and I thought to myself that Graham Gooch was to blame for a pointless declaration. I've never seen anyone in so much pain.

The test ended in horrific circumstances. As poor Syd was stretchered off in agony he was hassled by insensitive media people striving for sensational footage. England coach Mickey Stewart was supposed to have pushed a journalist out of the way, and apologies were demanded. The press conference was buzzing by the time I replaced Gooch and Stewart in the hot seat. Bryan Waddle of Radio New Zealand opened the questioning as usual, with a straightforward: 'Are you happy with the World Cup squad?'

'Uh, to be honest, I don't know, I haven't seen it yet.'

'Oh,' Bryan said wryly, 'you'd better have a look then, hadn't you?'

First name: 'M.D. Crowe, Captain'. Phew! I glanced quickly through the rest, noticing that all the test side except Blair Hartland had made it, plus Gavin Larsen, Mark Greatbatch and Chris Harris. I also noticed that, Chris Pringle, our best one-day bowler last year, had been omitted in favour of newcomer Murphy Su'a.

'Yes, I'm fairly happy, and pleased to be selected.'

They hadn't axed me. Somehow, within 24 hours they had backed off; thankfully, I felt sanity had been restored. Still, I wondered how it had all come about.

Wally told me that he had set up a meeting with the selectors to discuss the problems and find solutions to improving the team's performance, and mine. The meeting, however, was also attended by the chairman, Peter McDermott, and the deputy chairman, Cran Bull. In what Wally described as an initially productive meeting, they discussed the various issues and my situation in particular. Wally knew that he had to talk to me, along with the team, and that together we would sort out how we could improve. Then, towards the end, Peter McDermott apparently shocked everyone by stating that the best solution would be to get rid of me as captain. Don Neely responded by suggesting that it would be better to ask me if I would step down — hence the infamous meeting. The situation had got out of hand, and especially out of Wally's control. The big boys had moved in.

After the press conference I returned to the dressing room to hear Peter McDermott tell everyone, except Blair Hartland, that they were in the squad. We would leave for Dunedin very early next morning, to begin our final build-up for the cup. We were to play the last two one-dayers against England, and look for some more encouraging results.

Next morning when we gathered at the airport I was confronted immediately by Ian Taylor, our team manager, and John Wright, who insisted we have an urgent meeting. On the plane, it was in fact John and Andrew who sat on either side of me.

'You've got to be more consistent,' Wrighty told me. 'You must show the same attitude every morning, not this moody stuff one day and then all right the next. Just keep in touch more with the lads, and for heaven's sake stop talking to the media about that damned knee.'

I apologised, and assured him I understood, and would respond.

Finally someone had spoken, and spoken in a fair and constructive way. Why hadn't Don Neely taken the time to do what John had just done? Everyone needs professional advice from time to time and I welcomed any direction that would help to improve my game. Wrighty had always offered me assistance and I really appreciated this advice. To be asked to resign the week before the World Cup began was senseless.

It was all so bloody strange. Don had known me since I could walk. The Neelys and the Crowes had shared many times together, as Dave, my father, and Don's wife, Paddianne, were first cousins. I used to stay with Paddianne and Don often and really enjoyed their company. Don and I always discussed cricket and although we didn't see eye to eye at times, he had been very supportive towards me. So I was staggered by this lack of communication.

In Dunedin I called a meeting. I spoke to the team about working together, without distraction or selectorial changes, so that all 17 members of the group could focus positively on the five weeks ahead. John Wright went around the room and told each of us where we should be heading. It was just the meeting we needed. I sensed that now the team was finally settled, that we were at last on track, with nothing in our way.

I decided to stay away from the selectors and, with Wally, concentrate on what we thought was the way to go. There was no question in my mind that I should receive some direction from them at this point of the campaign, but it was also potentially stupid that the captaincy be called into question so late.

One thing was certain, however. I was now really fired up to prove the selectors and the chairman wrong. My motivation and determination were at fever pitch. I was going to lead by example in New Zealand cricket's most important hour.

Part One
The Cup Campaign

CHAPTER 1

Winning Ways

22 February 1992: Eden Park

To me this was what it was all about — playing for New Zealand, everyone on their feet, singing 'God Defend New Zealand'. I couldn't stop my eyes watering, or my chest heaving, let alone my body shaking, as I looked across at my opposite number, Allan Border of Australia, and sang the final words: 'Make her praises heard afar, God defend New Zealand.' This is what it must be like, lining up for the All Blacks: total adrenalin, pride and emotion. You keep sucking in deep breaths, huge gulps of air, just to stop yourself from breaking down. This is the emotion that really gets me going, the atmosphere that makes me rise to the challenge.

Australia, the yellow team, world-beaters. As usual they didn't expect a contest. They had sunk everyone in the last three months while we struggled to stay afloat. Now, opening day of the World Cup and the ceremony had set the scene, the weather was on cue and the 23,000-strong crowd waited, I suppose, for the inevitable. 'C'mon lads, we've got to compete, give them a game, shake them up somehow.'

On winning the toss we batted, for no particular reason except that the pitch looked flat and might get lower as the day wore on. We surprised a few people by leaving out Danny, but on this track Dipak was a must and Chris Cairns' all-round ability had him coming in at number seven. We needed a big score for our medium pacers to bowl at, so we talked of going for it, using the first 15 overs to attack, and then pinning our ears back to give them something beyond 220. In the past we had usually worried about wickets in hand and would struggle to 200 as our run rate never accelerated. This time, as underdogs, we had to get out there and show some courage and display some skill.

John Wright went third ball after two wides were called from Craig McDermott, so the crowd, understandably, began to sigh, especially when Andrew Jones got a shocking lbw from the Pakistan umpire, Khizar Hayat. It was his umpiring that had finished us off in 1984 at Hyderabad in the second test, when he gave out six wickets in the first

20

innings and four in the second. The local paper had congratulated him on reaching 100 test wickets for Pakistan in his 19th test, a Pakistani record! He wasn't highly rated and he confirmed it here. With Wright and Jones gone, and the score only 13, we were off to the worst possible start.

Rod Latham did look positive, however, and he started to go for his shots as planned, while I settled in. I was pleased for Rod; he always showed a good temperament, if not always the best technique, but this time he had both. He raced to 26 and took the team score to 53 by the end of 15 overs. To this point I had mainly played straight, working on moving my feet. 'Courage and skill', I would say to myself with every ball as I settled down at my stance. Then 'Soft hands', as I prepared to watch the bowler approach. 'Watch the ball', as the bowler released and soon I was middling the ball and working it around. Then at 53, Rod aimed a big slash through point only to see Ian Healy, the little Aussie keeper, not only save four but send our boy back for a shower, with a blinding catch.

Tom Moody was operating at this stage and this was where I began to feel I could dominate. Twice he banged it in short for me to swivel and find the square-leg fence. Then, as if my World Cup depended on it, I had some luck. Pulling another long hop from Moody I caught it high on the bat and the ball sailed high and deep to mid-wicket where Dean Jones, making ground to his left, lunged acrobatically to finger-tip the ball on towards the boundary. An escape!

Peter Taylor, the off-spinner, replaced Moody but the short balls kept coming. Finding my feet moving quicker sideways rather than forward, I found I could pick up most of my runs square on the leg-side. As it happened, I took Taylor, Australia's key one-day bowler, out of the attack and Border resorted to Mark Waugh. Now we had them worried as Ken Rutherford began to hit top gear and our partnership soared.

For years I had thought that this was the guy with all the ability, all the shots. Inexplicably he was thrown to the slaughter back in 1985 when we toured the West Indies. Ken had no chance. At the age of 19, he was asked to open the batting on debut against the might of Marshall, Holding and Garner. It was a suicidal selection, and the worst possible start for a young player.

As he fought for respect and recognition he seemed, on occasions, to forget that the only way to respond was to prepare better, work harder and discipline himself to be consistent with the bat. But Ken was from the deep south and he prided himself on being a team man, one of the boys. Sometimes that affected his preparation and discipline and he still hadn't fashioned a record worthy of his huge talent. He had scored many runs for Otago and in doing so was always in contention for a batting spot in the New Zealand team.

He reached a crisis point during the World Cup campaign. To succeed in the cup, Wally and I wanted to transform our middle-ranked players into performers with 30-plus averages. Ken, for example, was averaging only 18 in test cricket and in the mid-20s in one dayers, and he would be the first to admit that there needed to be a change for the better. So, for the development tour to Adelaide, the selectors decided to try out some new young players and drop some regular middle rankers. Ken was one of them, and he was very upset and very angry. They wanted him to address his preparation for internationals, as that was their assessment of what was preventing him from becoming a top-class player. Wally and I felt he was not fit enough, or certainly one of the least fit in the squad, and that he had to improve this aspect immeasurably so that he could turn in the big scores of which he was capable.

When he returned to the side after an intensive 'Bring back Ken' campaign by the media and supporting public, he was ready to deliver. For months there was speculation that Ken and I had fallen out, but in fact we never exchanged words at all. This was probably a mistake. As captain, I should have spoken to him personally but as we were never close mates I didn't take the initiative and explain why he needed time to sort out how to take the step up in his career. So, once he was told by New Zealand Cricket why he was being left out for a period, he reacted badly, and I felt his anger was directed largely at me. Ken probably never really forgot this.

So now, on this important day, Ken and I were batting together and enjoying it. Ken showed admirable poise as we began to attack the Australians. For the first time in ages the old arrogance returned, and I could see the Aussies were aware that our body language was changing, to our advantage. Bruce Reid came back and I stroked him once through mid-off, down on one knee, and then shimmied to hook him one bounce into the No. 4 stand. I was racing into the 70s as the 40-over mark approached but my legs, especially the right knee, were tiring. For weeks I had sought advice from Barry Tietjens, the knee surgeon, about why my knee wasn't settling after I'd had a cartilage trimmed. Less strain and more rest were diagnosed. If he went back in to look at the cartilage I would miss the first weeks of the cup, so I headed to the gym each day and hoped I could play to maximum effort.

With the score approaching 160 and the Aussies on the back foot, I knew I needed to bat through to the finish, at least to support the big hitters coming in. I calculated that we could reach 230 if we completed the full 50 overs.

After Ken departed for a superb 57, Chris Harris and then Ian Smith played cameo innings, but when Chris Cairns came in there were more surprises. He not only laid into their bowlers, smashing 16 in 11 balls, but began talking back to them as well, which the Aussies hated. With an over to go I was also in full charge, requiring just one more to reach a magical century. Off the only ball I faced in the 50th over, I managed a quick single, running through to meet a crowd invasion, with hundreds of kids everywhere. At the end of the innings, Chris and I ran off to a marvellous ovation and the important feeling that we could take out the game.

I lunched in the dressing room and, as Mark Plummer attended to my aching legs, I began to work out a plan to defend our 248. Chris Cairns would definitely open the bowling from one end, but we were uncertain who would bowl at the other end. I decided to bowl Dipak Patel, the right arm off-spinner.

The idea to open with Dipak had come from a meeting with Wally before the match.

'I think Dipak should definitely play on this pitch and even bowl quite early on,' I said.

'What about opening with him,' Wally suggested. 'We've got nothing to lose. We've got to try something different against Australia.'

I agreed, but we both knew we had to be flexible if it didn't work, and stay open-minded.

I also suggested we try the 'Hunt shuffle', a scheme developed by the late Otago selector, Ray Hunt, whereby he rotated the bowlers, giving each of them one over at a time. It was another unorthodox idea, but we needed to be innovative.

So with 248 to defend, I felt the time was perfect to play a trump card. I told Dipak to prepare to bowl the second over. But I had to work out a field for him, and that wasn't easy. In the first 15 overs two catchers had to be placed and that was the first problem. I decided on a short cover and a short mid-wicket. The outfielders? Well, you have to have a backward square leg and I decided also on a straight long-on. Mid-wicket was on his own with no protection behind and I placed a short fine leg for the turn, tickle or sweep. Three men at mid-off, extra cover and point completed the field placing. He had to bowl off-stump or outside, and not too slowly. The new ball helped his pace.

So out we went and Chris Cairns started. He soon had to finish: four overs, 30 costly runs. He wasn't chatting with anyone now. But Dipak, surprising all and sundry, kept Geoff Marsh and David Boon in check with only 19 from seven overs. Then Gavin followed him and snaffled Marsh. At last. Sixty-two was up and we needed to keep chipping in with the wickets.

Dean Jones began to dominate immediately and it looked ominous until we showed our other major weapon, our fielding. Cairns, fielding as sweeper on the leg-side, fired a return so flat and so fast that Jones, thinking of stealing another base, fell short and we danced!

Immediately I summoned Dipak again, this time to attack Allan Border. Twelve runs later Cairnsy screamed around to snatch a skyer and Dipak had his man. Then came the Hunt shuffle: Chris Harris for two overs, Rod Latham for two, Chris for two, Rod for two again until Moody spooned and Rod threw himself left. It stuck ... bingo!

Now we began to enjoy ourselves. I started to get a big kick out of seeing the shuffle confuse and frustrate the Aussies. David Boon, who was progressing, stabilising the yellow team, got bogged down at times by the constant changes and the lower, slower bounce of the wearing pitch. From this point the crowd could easily see on the big scoreboard the required run rate climb drastically upward to eight an over. Mark Waugh came and went and only his brother Steve was able to counter the attack and throw out a challenge. The Aussies were falling too far behind when Gavin got the Waugh double with a superb diving caught and bowled that lifted the roof off Eden Park.

One run later came the best piece of fielding of the cup. Chris Harris, lurking with quiet assurance and now obviously enjoying himself, seized on a 'run two' instruction from Healy and in one motion took out the single stump from side on, 60 metres away, on the full to send back century-maker Boon. We were ecstatic.

Everything was clicking. All that hard work, fielding practice and more fielding practice were paying off, on the very day we aimed for. The last three wickets went quickly for 11 runs and, just as Andrew took the last catch in front of the North Stand, the astonished crowd had already poured onto the ground, running anywhere and everywhere in a total frenzy, announcing to the 1992 World Cup that New Zealand had arrived. We had just knocked out the world champions.

It seemed amazing that what we had worked for over 18 months had actually happened. We celebrated that night, knowing at last that we could believe in ourselves. Our tactics had come off; as Allan Border admitted, we threw them completely with our unorthodox methods.

Now came the questions, especially 'Whose idea was it to open with Dipak?' I said nothing, but winked at Wally, pleased that we had had the imagination to tune into the unorthodox. I was proud of myself too for showing the courage to see out the idea. This sort of successful strategy confirmed that no one was going to interfere, that having achieved this victory we could go on to create more on our own. I was also privately overjoyed with my own batting performance, and my captaincy. After all the negativity surrounding my place as captain, in one match I had shown what I was capable of, and told them, in the best way I could, that I was not prepared to give up.

In our second match against Sri Lanka, who are dangerous on their day, we played well throughout, always in control and winning by six wickets. This time, bowling first, I elected to use Watson and Morrison, in for Cairns, with the new ball. The conditions were greasy and Dipak assumed the more orthodox role of bowling in the middle innings. Then amazingly, but mainly because of their long list of left-handers, I was able to bowl Dipak at the death in the last 10 overs, in which we conceded only 34 runs. One time he opened, the next he finished, and both times spot on.

Again we fielded well, and restricted the blue team to a minimal score. Ken continued to show great maturity in steering us home but this time I played very negatively, conscious that I'd hit 100 in the previous game and that there was some pressure to repeat it. In other words, I didn't back myself to play all those shots again in my very next innings.

After the game I sat down and remembered a very important meeting I'd had with a sports psychologist, Jenny Oakley. Jenny, who had been involved in our build-up camps in Christchurch, was also assigned to the Cricket Academy, helping cricketers to understand mental skills such as goal setting and autogenic training. I was in touch with my goals but also became interested in this other aspect.

My understanding of it is that if you are in an emotional state, high positive or low negative, then you should become neutral or 'grounded' to start again. After the Australian match I was high and entered the Sri Lankan game so high that I became scared of not reaching that standard again. Therefore I became negative and I played accordingly. If I had been grounded, however, I could have forgotten the past and approached the game in a neutral frame of mind. From that point I employed a simple technique. At the end of each match I would sit quietly in the dressing room and calm myself down by saying such things as 'It's over, now for the next match.' I would also start thinking immediately of the colour of the next opponent.

Mark Greatbatch and I had decided, after reading *Born to Win* by John Bertrand, the story of Australia beating the United States for the America's Cup, that we, too, would dehumanise our opposition. Every side we played during the World Cup would therefore be known by its colour, not its country. Australia would be known to us as yellow, Zimbabwe as red, and so on. Every side had to be beaten, so we took them all on equally, not differentiating them by nationality. I also decided that every night would be a quiet night, with no celebrating. I focused on the next match or innings, not on the last one. It began to work.

Our next match against South Africa at Eden Park was to be one of the great occasions. The atmosphere was probably the most fervent and passionate I had experienced with a home crowd.

John Wright had opened the batting in the first two games, but then a shoulder injury suffered in the field against Sri Lanka sidelined him for a week or two. So Mark (Paddy) Greatbatch came into the 11 for the match; we were meeting South Africa for the first time in 20 years. Logic suggested we put Paddy at three and open up with Andrew. But Jonesy didn't like moving around the order, and when I mentioned to Wally that Paddy could be at three, he was adamant that we retain our middle: Jones, Crowe, Rutherford. That was our strength and he didn't want to touch it.

Paddy had to open and he had to be positive. He had been given one chance against England in the series before the cup and then was dumped, despite his excellent career record. We had lost the second test because we didn't have someone like Paddy to take it to them, as we had done so often before. Fortunately he was included in the Cup squad, but his confidence and form had been crushed. He was hurt, but as fiercely determined as I was. Wally had a long chat with him at practice and something clicked. Going in first, not having to wait, walking out with his mate Rod Latham — the two big men together — made him feel important. Almost 30,000 packed the park to see that encounter and, after restricting South Africa to 190, we watched the two Sherman tanks move out to the middle. The next 15 overs threw the whole World Cup wide open.

After a couple of sighters Paddy suddenly launched into a huge swing off Brian McMillan, and the ball came off his bat like a gunshot. It sailed high into the stands, and you could see the adrenalin starting to pump in Paddy's system. Then the South Africans started to backchat, getting up Paddy's nose, and before long the ball was sailing everywhere. This was batting straight out of the top drawer. The white ball raced across the lushness of Eden Park, climbed up into the stands and, to add icing to this delicious cake, Paddy cleared the No. 4 (north) stand, one of the very few ever to do so. The crowd was on fire. The terraces, packed to capacity, were on their feet, cheering and rooting for their local hero.

In the end he got out of control. The adrenalin had reached its maximum and the big fellow was swinging at everything, determined to put his opponents on the canvas once and for all. There was a defiant 'I'll show you' attitude about him and when he was finally bowled by Peter Kirsten he'd scored 68 in 60 balls, with three huge sixes. With Rod Latham he had put on 114 in 17 overs and blown the Springboks off the park.

As he returned to the pavilion the whole park rose, but there was no smile, just defiance and determination. This was only the beginning. Mark Greatbatch was sick of being stuffed around.

To finish off the party, I sent in Ian Smith at number four, and he kept the crowd in raptures by hitting his first four balls for four! We completed the historic victory in the 35th over, enough time for me to join Andrew Jones and score three not out. Hitting the winning run was a very proud moment, and I was over the moon about the way the whole team had shown their skills and attitude. The Eden Park crowd was sending the rest of the country a message that this World Cup and this New Zealand team were something to get excited about. If the Australian match had filled us with hope and belief, then the South African game gave us the special confidence to take on every team and beat them with a style that was not only exciting to watch but also incredibly effective. At the end of the game I spent some time on my own, to focus on our next encounter. Despite the frenzy in the dressing room I managed to stay grounded and began to work on the red team, Zimbabwe.

We travelled to Napier for this fourth match and settled into a quiet hotel in Tamatea away from everyone. Naturally we were starting to enjoy the whole experience of being top of the table in the World Cup and that showed in our off-field activities. We had some classic fines meetings, led by John Wright and Ian Smith. Wrighty, with his sore shoulder healed, but without a place in the side because of Paddy's emergence, came into his own with his superb motivational and man management skills. He continually rallied the team, making them laugh, advising the younger ones, binding the side more closely every day. Wally and I, aware of the importance of this role, encouraged it, particularly as we had to keep telling Wrighty that he wasn't playing. He understood and still enjoyed it.

On the day of the Zimbabwe match the weather packed in. We couldn't get a start and when we finally did it was spasmodic. Batting first, we led off with 52 for two off 11 overs in a 30-over match, but rain stopped play again. Returning to play a match further reduced to 24 overs, Andrew and I cut loose. We had to. Never before have I managed to let myself go to this extent, lashing out at everything within reach, mainly hitting balls through or over the leg-side. I raced to the fastest ever World Cup 50 in 31 balls.

Dave Houghton, the opposing skipper, covered his leg-side, which left no off-side sweeper, so I stepped to leg repeatedly to send the white ball high and wide over cover and into the new Centenary Stand. With the score 162 for three off 20.5 overs, rain again drove us from the field. I ran off for the last time with the bat, unbeaten on 74 from 44 balls. Another three overs and I might have scored one-day cricket's fastest century.

With the match reduced to 18 overs the target for the red team was

153. It was vital at this stage that we complete at least 15 overs as we really needed maximum points from a match we were expected to win. This time I chose not to bowl Dipak Patel at all. The ball was damp and with the field up for the first seven overs I decided, for the only time in the cup, to use our fastest bowlers, Cairns and Morrison. Danny bowled well but Cairnsy was everywhere and I wondered if he would soon settle down in international cricket. Still, time is on his side and he's sure to become one of our finest allrounders.

All the other bowlers bowled so straight that the red team were soon in trouble with four out for 63. But it was drizzling again and I got our part-timers Chris Harris and Rod Latham to run through their overs quickly to ensure a total of 15. Chris bowled the 15th and, with two balls remaining and heavier rain falling, Campbell sliced a ball straight up, which soon veered toward me. My immediate reaction was to get under the ball to take the catch and then I thought that a dismissal could give the umpires time to confer and possibly take us from the field. To hell with it — I took the catch and threw it straight to Chris, saying, 'Get back to your mark, quick!'

To Zimbabwe's credit they got on with it, sending their next man in immediately, and as the rain eased slightly we won the game after completing the revised 18 overs. We now had four wins from four games. One more victory would secure a place in the semi-finals.

Our major goal now was to pick up as many wins as possible to secure a semi-final berth at Eden Park. That would depend on Australia, for if we both qualified to meet in the semis we would play at Sydney, no matter if we topped the table with eight wins and Australia were last to qualify. This was the trade-off between boards for New Zealand having the opening match at home. After four games Australia were second to last, with only one win, just ahead of Zimbabwe. We needed to keep our winning ways.

CHAPTER 2

Hogan's Heroes

You gain strength, courage and confidence by every
experience which you must stop and look fear in
the face … You must do the thing you think you
cannot do.

— ELEANOR ROOSEVELT

It was back to Eden Park for our fifth match of the preliminaries, back
to the very ground I had first visited as a six-year-old. Dad had taken me
to the test match where New Zealand were playing the West Indies in
1968–69. As I had begun playing cricket just one year before, this was a
huge thrill. To see the world's greatest player, Garfield Sobers, was
something I would never forget. I loved watching the Windies, as they
had so much flair and fun, but playing them was a completely different
story. Now we were due to meet these mighty men in a match that I
thought would be incredibly tough. Eden Park was described as one of
our secret weapons, but for this match a new pitch was prepared, green-
er and more moist than before.

As I tossed with Richie Richardson, their captain, I quickly came to
the conclusion that it might suit their fast bowlers, especially if they
bowled first. My lucky 1962 penny (the year I was born) came up
trumps and I asked the maroons to pad up. I marched straight into the
dressing room, turned to Dipak and said, 'You're bowling, Dip.' Without even acknowledging me, he was preparing himself for one of the
greatest bowling spells by a spinner in a one-day international.

In 10 priceless overs he conceded only 19 runs and completely shut
down the Haynes-Lara combination. For the only time in the series,
Gavin looked in trouble, with Lara taking 14 off his first over. I had to
shift him to the other end immediately and bring on the slower bowler
in Chris Harris. He obliged my decision when he expertly caught and
bowled Haynes while Gavin settled into the other end.

By now, in this tournament, I knew just what we were capable of,
when to change the bowling, where the fielders should be — and that it
was a glorious feeling leading this New Zealand side. We simply closed

in on our opposition, pressured them with straight bowling and straight fields and, best of all, electric groundwork.

It wasn't until the last four overs, with a tired-looking Willie Watson and Danny Morrison suffering a groin strain, that we conceded too many runs; the West Indies reached 203 when they shouldn't have scored 190. This was the only time, in the last four to five overs, when I felt Willie was not strong or quick enough to bowl in the blockhole, and we suffered because of it. Someone like Chris Pringle was more suited to bowling at the death but he hadn't been included in the squad.

With all due respect to Murphy Su'a, selecting someone so inexperienced in one-day cricket instead of Chris Pringle, who had been our best bowler 12 months before, was surprising. Willie had a huge workload in every game and I felt Pringle would have been handy at the end, particularly with improvising stroke-makers like the Windies or the Pakistanis. He'd proven he was a match winner, he had the temperament to cope under pressure and he could also bowl a brilliant slower ball, a delivery vital to bowling well at the death. This was something I thought could make all the difference if we were to go all the way to winning the World Cup.

Now, though, we had to combat the best bowling attack in the world. Would those 30-odd runs off the last overs make the difference? Not to Mark Greatbatch. He may have struggled for the first three overs from Curtly Ambrose, scarcely putting bat on ball, but it was only temporary. As soon as the cage opened Paddy was down the wicket to Malcolm Marshall, hitting him clean out of the park. That shot from Marshall will remain the stroke of the World Cup. Having gone down the wicket to a good length ball, Paddy made some room and slapped the white missile on the up over cover and into the top tier of the new West Stand. Unbelievable!

Malcolm Marshall turned, hands on hips, watching in astonishment. So when Paddy did it to Ambrose next over and the ball flew over point for six, the 2-metre (6 foot 9 inch) fast bowler followed the 187-centimetre (6 foot 2) opening batsman out to square leg with ball in hand, threatening: 'If you want to bat out of your crease, man, I'll bowl out of mine, from 15 yards!' So Paddy went back this time and pulled him high into the delirious terraces for six more. His astonishing, bewildering 63 shook the maroons to the core. He was out when the score was 100 and I was in on one. We needed another 104 and I knew then, as Paddy walked off to an explosive ovation, that I had to be there at the end if we were to triumph and secure our place in the semi-finals of the World Cup.

Winston Benjamin and Carl Hooper were operating together when I arrived at the crease, but the only runs on offer were quick singles as the Windies bowled straight and with purpose. Ken was with me by now, but struggling, so I decided to counter-attack just as Paddy had done. First, I glanced a four to deep fine leg and then launched into a front-foot sweep-pull off Hooper, and the ball climbed up and over the deep square-leg fielder by only a metre for four more.

Then a vicious cut, again off Hooper, had me on top and, with the ball coming off the bat so sweetly, I had no doubts about continuing the onslaught. Ken went to Curtly Ambrose when the giant bowler came back into the attack, and I needed to keep Chris Harris away from the strike while hooking and straight driving Ambrose to the fence.

Finally Richardson threw the ball to one of the all-time greats, Malcolm Marshall. I had faced 'Macho' many times before and we had had shared success against each other, so this was to be our last battle. He knew the importance of the contest and began charging in with that fast arm action, wheeling the ball angrily into the pitch. I defended, and waited.

With Chris I could take short singles as he was fast between the wickets, and this gave me the chance to attack at the other end. After three overs from Malcolm I finally got the ball I'd waited for. It was slightly short of a length and I pressed off the front foot onto the back and swung the ball one bounce over square leg. Macho just stood and grinned, for it was my best shot of the game. Then, to his annoyance, I pulled out my other signature shot — a flowing straight drive down the on-side of the pitch for four. Malcolm retired from the crease with one of his 10 overs left unbowled, for he knew now that the game was over. To finish I smashed my 12th boundary, a straight drive through bowler Benjamin and down to the fence for the victory.

I turned to shake the hands of Richardson and Marshall, both good friends, and then looked up to see Wally and the boys punch the air now that we had qualified. To score 81 in the same number of balls, out of 109 runs while I was in the middle, against the best bowlers, suggested to me that I couldn't play any better than this. This was my finest one-day innings, played under pressure, one to remember forever.

Reaching 100 against Australia at Eden Park in the opening match of the 1992 World Cup was the best reply I could give my doubters. It pleased the kids watching as well.

Mark Greatbatch, a best mate and a fighting spirit. He turned the 1992 World Cup and many other games with a ferocious swing of the bat. Here he is playing against the West Indies.

Securing a win over England during the World Cup was another sweet moment to savour. Here at the Basin Reserve, in front of a packed crowd, I play a controlled shot through point during an innings of 73 not out.

Things started to go wrong in our semi-final against Pakistan at Eden Park when I pulled my left hamstring while batting.

When Inzamam capitalised on our changed tactics, Wally came out to the boundary line to give visible support.

The painful walk around Eden Park after the semi-final loss to Pakistan. The emotion began to affect the team as we acknowledged the amazing ovation.
Left to right: Willie Watson, Wally Lees, Rod Latham, I and Chris Harris show the strain.

With Robin Smith, a fine opponent and a great friend. Here we share a bottle of 1966 Chateau Lafitte Rothschild, which he bought after our bet for most runs in the 1992 World Cup.

It was a marvellous feeling to have qualified already. So much pressure had come off us and we all felt elated. I was particularly pleased for Wally, who had put so much time and energy into worrying about the state of the players' minds, working out how to get the best from his men. He had become so close to the team, because he was warm, caring, happy to talk to anyone about anything. He was the core of our performance, a man who'd always achieved a lot as the underdog, and he deserved the highest praise. It was fitting that our next match was to be in Dunedin, Wally's home town.

The question everyone seemed to be asking me was whether we would give all the squad members a game. Murphy Su'a hadn't played yet, Chris Cairns was out of form and John Wright was keen to have a go. Initially I'd said we would, but during training at Carisbrook the thought occurred to me that we must keep playing our best side, win every game and qualify top, so that we could play the semi-final at Auckland. We had to keep that high standard and absorb as much pressure as possible, so we would be ready for the final confrontation. I apologised to the media for misleading them initially and announced my intention to keep the best side playing.

The day before the India match, the squad jogged the ground and then I called them in, as I had before each game, away from the public and even away from Wally. 'What we've done is special,' I said. 'An incredible performance in anyone's book, and you can all be proud of contributing beyond all expectations. We're ahead of schedule, we've qualified.

'But I want you to understand that the pressure isn't off. I want this team to go further by taking on and absorbing every pressure situation we come across. We want all our matches to be hard, to be the toughest challenge, so that when the time comes we'll be ready. This is why we'll continue to select the best side for each match. It's tough on some but we must continue to do everything together, to do it for each other. Just we 14 players, plus the other three, of course. We're capable now of going on to win the World Cup. I honestly believe that. Good luck.'

The next day we knocked off the useful total of 230 so comfortably that you would have thought we'd been doing it all our lives. Paddy went berserk once more, hitting five sixes in his 73 off 77 balls. The ground just wasn't big enough. Andrew Jones played the steady hand this time and saw us through to the end with a splendidly paced innings. I'd felt in great form again and had raced to 26 in 28 balls when Kiran More, the wicketkeeper, grabbed a ball with his back to the stumps as I was regaining my ground and, from the short gully area, flicked the ball behind his back, onto the stumps. It was a freak dismissal.

But I knew that I was due for some misfortune, so with this game already all but won I strolled off quite content. Six wins out of six. The plan was working. The boys were learning fast, with everyone now believing that if we beat England next then yes, we were capable of winning the World Cup.

I quickly put the India match out of my mind and concentrated on England. They had smashed us a month earlier and I was determined to wreak revenge. So I announced to the media that we had a few more tricks up our sleeves for the England match — I just had to think of some!

First look at the Basin Reserve pitch and I thought to myself, I hope it lasts. It was patchy and dry and looked as though it would take a lot of turn. The trick we had was to open the bowling with Dipak, of course, and Chris Harris. It was totally illogical, which was why I tried it. Against England in the previous month we had been too orthodox, too predictable; as with the Aussie match, I felt we needed to do everything differently.

First, we dropped Rod Latham for John Wright, as Rod hadn't scored since the South Africa match and his bowling had become unreliable. But we stuck with Cairns until Danny's groin had improved further. These, in fact, were logical decisions. Second, we won the toss and chose to bowl first on a pitch that would get worse, and certainly take spin. I elected to chase because I saw that as the hardest challenge; we had been chasing successfully and, amazingly, England left out Tufnell, playing the one spinner in Illingworth with Hick as back-up.

Upon hearing my decision our Wellingtonian, Andrew Jones, nearly went through the roof. I suggested to him we should play the game and wait and see the result. Then we might judge. He was in one of his stubborn moods, which was a good sign. It suggested that his motivation was high and that he really believed we could win this tournament. Andrew didn't say much at the best of times, so when he did it shook the whole dressing room. I wasn't that happy with his outburst, but quickly forgot it and prepared for the game. Patel and Harris to open: it hardly sent shivers up your spine.

To be fair, it didn't work either, as Chris was easy to hit with the field up and he was off after two overs. Dipak, however, was going from strength to strength. Just as, against India, he had removed the big-hitting Srikanth, so now did he dispose of a certain I.T. Botham.

From the other end the bowlers struggled. Too many times Willie dropped short and I wondered if perhaps he needed a game off. But he came back well later and, as usual, was very reliable. Cairns also struggled to find direction and by now he wasn't worth risking with the ball. Gavin was as outstanding as ever but, with Rod not playing, I was running out of bowlers. Remembering vividly his earlier comments, I tossed the ball to Andrew and suggested he might have a point to prove with some spin. He did. For his first bowl of the season he produced nine superb flat overs of off-spin, took two wickets and conceded just 42. All this in the last 20 overs!

England went from 135 for two to 200 for eight in total, completely stuffing up the last 20 overs thanks to the local lads, Larsen and Jones.

The pitch was taking enormous turn so I was conscious of needing a fast start against the new ball. Paddy gave us one, but not before Wrighty got bowled around his legs again in the second over. It only meant that Andrew could get out of the dressing room and out of everyone's earshot! He played an excellent knock of 78 and Paddy gave us a quickfire 35 in as many balls before I walked in to add 108 with Andrew in 23 overs. I was really enjoying myself, playing all sorts of shots — cuts, sweeps, backing away — and also having some luck. The win was assured as we knocked off the runs in only 40 overs with just three wickets down. I punched the air in victory, registering revenge over England.

This was sweet, and with seven wins from seven we had broken the World Cup record for successive wins and equalled our own New Zealand record for one-day internationals. Andrew picked up the man of the match award and as I congratulated him I asked, tongue in cheek, if he had any complaints about the tactics? He smiled and threw me a can of DB.

With at least 14 points from the preliminary matches we would top the qualifiers no matter what happened in the final round against Pakistan. If Pakistan beat us, however, they would advance and Australia, even with a late rally, would miss out. This would mean a Pakistan semi-final with us at Eden Park. But if the Windies beat Australia at Melbourne, then the Windies would qualify, not Pakistan, which meant that we would play South Africa at Auckland. The first thought was, shall we throw the game against Pakistan to ensure we play at Auckland? Or beat Pakistan and run the risk of Australia winning and forcing a semi-final with them at Sydney? We slept on it.

I was hoping the West Indies would win so we could meet the South Africans at Eden Park again. At the next team meeting we pondered the question. 'No way,' said Wally. 'Ten thousand fans aren't turning up to watch you throw a match!' I agreed. But there were some who said going to Sydney would defeat all our hard work. I agreed with that too, but we all knew in our hearts that we had to go out to win. To prove this we again selected our best team to play. We were thrashed!

Certainly Pakistan were desperate to win to stay alive, while over the Tasman Australia learned early in their match that their World Cup was over. We settled down in the evening to watch on TV as the Windies chased 216 to win, on a good pitch, and tried to take third place. I was rooting for the Calypsos but they froze on the night and, in doing so, let Pakistan in the back door to the semi-finals. Pakistan, as Imran said, were now playing like cornered tigers. The semis read: England (2) v. South Africa (3) at Sydney; New Zealand (1) v. Pakistan (4) at Auckland.

We had achieved our first goal, a goal set 18 months before. Now we knew we had the World Cup in our sights. The boys were playing like superheroes, showing that we could achieve anything. For me it was to be the greatest honour, leading those heroes into the semi-finals against Pakistan at Eden Park in three days' time.

CHAPTER 3
Showtime!

The adrenalin was pumping. I raced out the door and down the hall-way, passed three rooms and ducked right, through an open doorway into Wally Lee's room, high up in Auckland's Centra Hotel. Sitting by the window, stirring his coffee, Wally was expecting me, and he was happy. Every morning of every match during the World Cup I had marched into Wally's room for our pre-game chat. But, this was more than a game — 21 March 1992 was the biggest single day in New Zealand's cricket history. This was showtime!

Over the last month Wally and I had become inseparable. I would relay all my thoughts to him so that we kept working closely, and with trust.

'How are you feeling?' he asked.

'Not bad, just a bit concerned about this weather. It's forecast to rain heavily around two this afternoon. Naturally we want to bat last but, under these stupid rules, if there's any sign of rain we must bat first. We can't risk it in this one-off game. What do you think?'

'Sure, I agree, but whatever we do we're going to win! I just know it,' he cried, with a cheeky, boyish grin on his face.

I chuckled. Wally had really turned around from the England series. Then he had struggled at times, as I had, to concentrate on the games in hand, thinking always of the World Cup. Now he was in his element, confident, strong, believing totally that we would play at Melbourne for the World Cup.

I couldn't afford that sort of thinking. I was more focused on the small things — the weather, the toss, our tactics, my innings — to free my thoughts for the big picture. I concentrated on creating strong, clear ideas of us seeing off Pakistan on a pitch we had grown to appreciate. During our World Cup campaign, the Eden Park pitch had become our winged keel. It seemed to baffle and confuse the opposition, frustrating them and psyching them out to the extent that we were never really test-ed during our matches there.

Pakistan, though, never worried about where they played, unless it was really cold, for they were used to any conditions, often poor ones, in their own country. In fact, they had always performed well in Auckland. It was warmer for them, and the slow pitch was much to their liking, as it was to ours.

We discussed the line-up we had selected, noting that, since John Wright had come in to replace Rod Latham, we needed to warn Andrew Jones that he would be called upon to bowl a few overs. It was important to talk to him in advance, as, in my experience, he was never that keen on bowling. As I walked back down the corridor I could see the huge Melbourne Cricket Ground clearly in my mind, full to the brim, loud, alive — the World Cup final. We had to be there! I also thought how amazing these last 40 days had been, ever since I was asked to give up our campaign. We had come a long way and I knew it was because we had planned ahead and had sewn some very fertile seeds.

I gathered up my bag, had a quick chat to Simone, who pleaded with me to bowl first, then stood on the edge of the bed and gave me a big hug, as she had done before every match, and raced downstairs.

As we drove along Reimers Avenue we could see the long queues lining up at the turnstiles. The atmosphere, the excitement of the day suddenly struck us — the New Zealand flags, the banners, the smiling faces all wishing us well.

Walking into the dressing room brought us back to reality. We had work to do. 'Five minutes on the other side of the ground, all together,' Wally announced. There was a slight murmuring in the room, not a nervous silence, just a nice, let's-get-cracking kind of hum. Everyone walking past each other, patting on the back, winking, nodding, 'You okay?' Then we were one, striding as a unit out onto the park. Already there were thousands in, walking the ground, inspecting the pitch. This doesn't happen elsewhere in the world, and it makes it difficult to concentrate properly on your warm-up and fielding routines, yet the crowd seemed to appreciate that we were not to be bothered.

We all headed for the pitch. It looked in good order, flat, brown, even, easy-paced. Yes, there should be a few runs in this one. Batting second wouldn't be a problem, but the weather forecast had got worse. Thunderstorms by 1 pm and the game possibly heading for a washout. But if 25 overs had been bowled in the second innings, the game would be over. Whoever batted first in a rain-interrupted match would almost certainly win. We had to bat and post a good total, so I set a score of 225 to 230 as a realistic target, something we could defend, just as we did against Australia in the opening match.

We began our warm-ups, jogging a few laps, receiving huge applause and cheers from the terraces. We lined up on the No. 1 stand fence side by side, stretching our calves and Achilles' tendons, then our hamstrings and quads. 'Onto your backs,' shouted Mark Plummer, our outstanding physiotherapist. He had kept the team fit, and made sure we had a full squad to choose from. He was at his best in the World Cup, motivating the guys, working them in practice, looking after everyone, inspirational. 'Rocking back and forth,' he commanded.

The team were responding professionally, going through their exercises, concentrating, keeping busy, never stopping to glance at the Pakistanis, who had been scattered everywhere when they walked out, some with arms around each other, some even holding hands, some in different tracksuits. Imran was on his own. They were such a dangerous side, fighting among themselves one minute, playing highly skilled cricket the next. Today the only thing we noticed was that they wore green.

The greens were unpredictable, though. They had sneaked in the back door to the semi-finals after winning only one game of their first five. After five matches we had qualified. But I hadn't forgotten a recent TV interview with Imran Khan. He had talked passionately about winning the World Cup so he could build a cancer hospital in Pakistan in memory of his mother, who died of the disease. It was obvious that he was a motivated man. I have huge respect for Imran as a leader and a player; he is an all-time great. I knew that today I had to take him on, one on one, and match him in leadership.

As we were finishing our stretching I saw Ian Taylor striding over. Dressed in the splendid pin-striped blazer, especially made for the World Cup, he looked really good. (Everyone loved to wear their new number ones, unlike the old black blazer, which had become outdated and uncomfortable.) Our team looked smart; it was proud of the way it represented New Zealand, and Ian was as proud as anyone. Beaming he simply told me to go and collect my prize.

I looked across in the direction he indicated, to see, parked on the ground, a shining red Nissan Sports 300ZX, surrounded by cameramen, frontmen and sponsors. It was being announced that I had won the World Cup Champion award. This was a huge honour, especially on my home ground, before family and friends. But, as I took the keys to the car, I realised that it was time to refocus. I excused myself as quickly as possible and ran back to the team to begin our fielding routine. I was pleased that no one mentioned anything as I returned, although Chris Harris whispered that he'd love to drive it back to the hotel tonight, after we'd won. Anything that went fast, and Harry was on to it.

The boys looked good — sharp, alert, ready. Eighteen months of planning and practising, of working and wanting to be in this semi-final, and now the day had come.

Back in the dressing room I changed my uniform, and then walked out to toss for innings. On the way TV presenter Keith Quinn met me with a note I'd asked him to organise. I read as I walked: 'Weather forecast 21st March. Heavy thunderstorms by 12.30 pm. Rain all afternoon, worsening.'

I won the toss and told Imran, 'We'll bat.'

There wasn't much chat as Paddy Greatbatch and John Wright padded up. Everyone knew their job. The only thing to remind the lads was to believe in themselves, to let go of any doubts and anxiety, to go out and play. Play hard.

Paddy was our key man early on. He had had the most amazing month, but now, at 10.20 am on 21 March, Paddy was padding up for his most important assignment yet. He was up against one of the best attacking bowlers in the world, Wasim Akram. We needed Wright to survive the first 15 overs and Paddy to give us a run rate. We reckoned Akram had five overs in him for his first spell, so I suggested that Paddy try to take Aaqib Javed and John Wright, Akram.

The boys filed out at 10.25 for the national anthems and as we lined up the atmosphere was electric. Thirty-three thousand people stood to sing 'God Defend New Zealand' and, as I struggled to get out the words, emotion filling me, I looked over to see Paddy, his right hand clutching his heart, singing away, tears rolling openly. Playing for New Zealand right then was the greatest feeling, and when the whole nation joined in to share your devotion, your pride and your passion, it was almost overwhelming.

But we were ready and, as I settled into my seat, pads at my side, to watch the first over, I noticed Paddy walk straight to the far end to take first strike from Akram. So much for my suggestion!

Within three overs he had hit both Akram and Aaqib into the stands for six. Wright unleashed a full-blooded square cut off Akram, and the openers climbed to 35 in quick time before Paddy was confused by a superb slower ball from Aaqib that bowled him. The bowler's gesture as Paddy departed was disgraceful, but we knew then that we were in a tough match, with two totally different cultures fighting for supremacy. Quite out of character, John lofted one to long-on, and the initiative swung back to the green team. I couldn't wait to get out there, so I grabbed my bat, helmet and gloves and raced off down the stairs adjusting my equipment as I went. By the time I reached the ground, surrounded by a loud din, I was swinging the bat in my customary fashion, one swing with one arm, one with the other.

As always, I looked directly up into the sun, took three or four blinks and thus adjusted my sight. Now my breathing. As I drew deep, slow breaths my pace slowed and when I approached the middle I was starting to lift my shoulders and walk tall, letting the opposition know that I'd arrived.

I was facing Mushtaq first ball so I took my time getting ready, knowing he had a short, quick run-up. I delayed him a bit longer than usual, just to let him think about who he was bowling to. He was young and inexperienced and I was gambling on his immaturity.

Sure enough, second ball was just what I was looking for, slightly full of length, so I moved quickly and hit it on the full through mid-wicket for four. As it beat the fielder I looked at Mushtaq. His head sank. He was mine if I wanted him, and I wanted him! But I needed to work on each ball, concentrating on simple thoughts, watching the ball leave the hand. Letting my instincts take over, I began to work the ball around, into the gaps. Before long I had 25 at a run a ball. Andrew Jones at the other end was steady but not punishing, but we managed to add 48 in good time, taking the total up to 87 off 25 overs.

Andrew was then beaten by a beauty from Mushtaq. Changing ends, he bowled a shade quicker and hustled a top-spinner into Jones' pads. Plumb lbw. Now the game was poised, and Ken Rutherford took an age to find his feet. I could see from his body language that the occasion was getting to him. He couldn't score for 25 balls and for seven overs I took a single off the first or second delivery only to see him block out the over. Instead of ones or twos down the ground he was playing little cuts and sweeps, bringing him only 10 runs from 40 balls.

We met in the middle. 'Rudder, back yourself, man. Let go and play some shots.' I had raised my voice.

'Okay, okay, I'm coming,' he replied, geeing himself on.

As if the switch had flicked on, he danced down the wicket to Iqbal and smashed him back over his head for four. 'Yes,' I yelled, 'next time into the stand.' Ken was away. He had performed superbly during the cup, particularly in the opening week when he opened up with back-to-back 50s and led us to our first victories. He had become invaluable, just as Wally and I hoped he would. He had earned respect and recognition; he was a man in control. So, from scoring only 10 from 40 balls, he raced to 50 in 65 — 40 runs off 25 deliveries. The man was on fire. I sat back and fed him the strike, and he turned the game completely in five overs. The greenies were scattered, arguing among themselves while Ken carved them up. I've never been so pumped up as when batting with Ken that day. We were slapping each other ecstatically over every four or six.

Then he played a hook that wasn't on: it travelled straight up and Moin took the catch. As I ran through I felt my left hamstring twang. At first I hoped it would be cramp, but I soon knew that the hammy had shut down. With Ken we had put on 107 in 113 balls, and we had the game in hand. We were 200 for four with eight overs to go. But my hamstring became worse as I limped a two, and I had to ask Imran if I could have a runner. As Mark Plummer ran out I slumped to the ground, saying to umpire Steve Bucknor, 'This could be the end of my World Cup.' Mark arrived and spent three minutes strapping me tight. Then Paddy emerged from the pavilion as my runner. Great, I thought, Paddy's the quickest. My score was 81.

Chris Harris scored a quick 13 and then Ian Smith strode out ready to add the final barrage. I hooked a six off Imran, faking to leg and then stepping to the off, hitting high and hard. Next I pushed a possible two to deep extra cover. As Ian approached my end I yelled in excitement, 'Go, Stockley, go.' As he touched he put his head down and took off for the other end. I looked up to see Paddy yelling, 'No!' It was too late; Ian was going so fast no one could stop him. With that hesitation I was run out by a metre. The crowd hushed, and Paddy looked absolutely remorseful. Never mind, there was still plenty of batting left, so as I trudged off the park I turned to Paddy trailing behind me, 'It's okay, it was my fault.'

I watched the rest of the innings on the dressing room TV as Ian, Dipak Patel and then Gavin Larsen all hit out brilliantly to take the final total to a staggering 262. The boys came downstairs and the atmosphere was euphoric. We had done so well. 'We're in the game!' Concern came over a few faces as they saw I was in trouble. Wally, hoping I could recover, couldn't look as Mark iced the leg. 'It's no good,' was Mark's verdict. 'He can't go out there. He wouldn't make the final.' I looked up towards Wally and Ian and quietly added: 'It's all right, Wrighty can do it. He's been there before.'

NEW ZEALAND

M.J. Greatbatch b Aaqib Javed	17
J.G. Wright c Rameez Raja b Mushtaq Ahmed	13
A.H. Jones lbw b Mushtaq Ahmed	21
* M.D. Crowe run out	91
K.R. Rutherford c Moin Khan b Wasim Akram	50
C.Z. Harris st Moin Khan b Iqbal Sikander	13
† I.D.S. Smith not out	18
D.N. Patel lbw b Wasim Akram	8
G.R. Larsen not out	8
Extras (b 4, l-b 7, w 8, n-b 4)	23

7 wkts, 50 overs   262

1/35, 2/39, 3/87, 4/194, 5/214, 6/221, 7/244
D.K. Morrison and W. Watson did not bat.

Bowling: Wasim Akram 10-0-40-2; Aaqib Javed 10-2-45-1;
    Mushtaq Ahmed 10-0-40-2; Imran Khan 10-0-59-0;
    Iqbal Sikander 9-0-56-1; Aamir Sohail 1-0-11-0.

CHAPTER 4

Brothers in Arms

Through these fields of destruction,
Baptism of fire,
I witnessed your suffering
As the battle raised higher.
You did not desert me
My brothers in arms.
— DIRE STRAITS

'Sorry Wrighty, it's no good. It's all yours. You can take us to Melbourne.' John Wright had come over to the physio table where I lay on my back. 'Give them short spells, mix them up a bit. Save Dipak for three overs in the middle, and Jonesy as well for a couple — that'll give you cover later. Keep plenty of options, mix 'em up, you know what I mean. Good luck, mate, you'll be great,' I finished.

At the meeting the night before we had gone through our plan. Danny Morrison was to open from the broadcasting end in a spell of no more than five overs, mainly because he tires quickly. Then Willie Watson for five exactly, as he would swap to the other end later. After Willie would come Chris Harris, about the 21st over or earlier, and he would bowl three or four overs, maybe less. Then we would try Danny again with two, Andrew's off-spin for two, possibly three, and then Harry for another two or three. So by this stage we would be about the 43rd over, if all went well, with Danny ready to finish off. Chris Harris would be in reserve with about four left, and Andrew if need be. At the other end Dipak would open the bowling.

Dipak had bowled outstandingly for the whole month. Incredibly, he was the most economical bowler of the entire World Cup, which for a spinner was a triumph. He had thoroughly deserved his success. He had not played much one-day cricket for New Zealand as a spinner, so his improvement and overall performance were without question key factors in our campaign. He bamboozled every opening batsman. When he bowled at a steady spinner's pace on our slow wickets, the batsmen couldn't hit him. Many tried but usually saw their poles

44

knocked over, or our waiting fielders gratefully swallow each catch. It was inspirational to watch and the disbelief shown by the experts after the Aussie match was pure joy to us.

So Dipak would open the bowling from the terraces end, with a maximum of seven overs, or less, depending on how he was going. After him, Gavin Larsen would bowl, preferably in the 16th over, again if all was well. This way he could start with sweepers out if need be, but certainly with no close catchers. After a while we would drop back mid-on and mid-off, making the batsmen hit across the line if they wanted boundaries. There would be a leg-side sweeper but none on the off-side. We would have three in the ring, fielding close together in a straight line from extra cover to point. Paddy at extra, Harry at cover, Ken at point. Nothing to get through. Third man and long-off completed the long straight line of defence.

Gavin would try to bowl seven overs in a row and then back would come Dip to finish his last three. I especially like Dipak bowling to Javed at this time, or any new batsman who had just come in. This way Dipak would finish his 10 overs economically, spared the later slog. After Dipak would come Willie, who had bowled five from the other end, to bowl two more, then Gavin for his final three, leaving Willie to finish off, also with three overs.

So in the last 12 overs we would use at least four bowlers, with Chris Harris and Andrew Jones still spare for either end if we needed a drastic change. The key was bowling Andrew, as it took pressure off the others even if only for two or three overs. It specially helped Chris, who in turn wouldn't need to bowl out, but could cover for the others. Having cover and plenty of options was crucial.

In all, we should make a minimum of 13 bowling changes, and sometimes 16 or 17 if Andrew or Chris bowled in one- or two-over spells. All fielders knew where they were to field for each bowler: Paddy at slip and extra cover, I would take mid-wicket, Ken gully and then point, Chris Harris cover for one over and leg-side sweeper the next, Dipak third man, then mid-on. Everyone knew.

But, for me, one of the most important rules of the plan was to have everyone facing the wicket at all times, and each player must look at me after every ball. This would help our focus, and certainly help me if I needed to make a change. No one was to sign an autograph or take their eyes off me, or they were dead meat!

I was now upstairs in the players' dressing room. I'd hobbled the stairs and positioned myself at the far side of the room almost behind the sightscreen at the West Stand end. My feet were up, the left leg strapped in ice, and I also had a view of the TV monitor, up and to my right. I could hear chat in the corridors behind us; everyone was excited, already packing their bags for Melbourne.

The Pakistanis were next door, pretty quiet, ready to give it their all. The boys ran out and the crowd lifted the stadium two metres off the ground. This was really showtime, but now, sadly, I was watching, helpless, from the stand. As I looked out I saw that Dipak, not Danny, would open the first over. This surprised me, as Danny had dismissed Sohail at Christchurch first ball, three days ago. Then I remembered that John Wright hadn't played that match.

Anyway, the first over goes safely, Dipak full of bustle and chat. Danny then starts bowling from the West Stand end, which is the correct end for him, but he's got a very attacking field with two slips and a gully. I'm conscious that we mustn't overattack, but an early wicket would be perfect.

Sohail and Rameez play solidly, with Rameez looking the better of the two. Then, in the ninth over, Sohail sweeps at Dipak and is well caught by Andrew Jones. The score is 30 for one. What I don't like about Dipak bowling the very first over is that he will have to keep going for eight overs to allow Gavin to operate after the first 15, when the field can retreat outside the ring.

After 10 overs the score is approaching 35 and Danny has done his job well. Then Wrighty throws him the ball again. I can see that Danny is tiring, and as he runs in to bowl his sixth over I turn to Chris Cairns and Murphy Su'a and say, 'I hope he's not having one too many.' The over costs 14. It's just that Danny hasn't bowled such a lengthy spell for a long time. Wrighty is trying desperately to get another wicket, but patience is crucial as well. Three cracking fours from Rameez, and the Pakistanis next door are beginning to murmur.

As it turned out, Dipak bowled eight overs in a row, to give Gavin his protection. You would expect one bad over in eight but unfortunately the last over was the costly one — hit for 12. Imran had promoted himself to number three and begun very, very cautiously. In fact, when Willie started to hit a good line and length, Imran was letting a lot of balls go straight through to the keeper.

46

He was obviously keeping wickets intact, but the scoring was slowing, particularly when Rameez sliced one to Danny off a deserving Willie Watson. Willie bowled superbly, but with Danny bowling out six, and then Willie having six, I began to worry about when Chris Harris would bowl. This also left only eight overs between our top two quickies in the final quarter, and Dipak with just two left. Three bowlers all but done and Chris hadn't even bowled yet. Andrew, too, had to bowl soon.

Meanwhile Gavin was moving through a great spell, as he had been match in, match out. The pitches suited him perfectly, and the length he bowled was immaculate. Imran and Javed were playing as if it were a test match. Suddenly, just to jolt me again, Imran hopped down the wicket and hit Gavin for a massive six. The fifth bowler, or bowlers, now had to come on and bowl a number of overs consecutively or they would be exposed at the death. So Chris Harris began.

Javed pushed and deflected while Imran, now receiving most of the strike, realised that he had a train to catch. He went after Chris and succeeded, until he skyed a catch to Gavin on the fence. Chris was on for too long, though, conceding more than six an over as Javed picked him off, toying with him. Andrew should be sharing the load.

Then I remembered — the weather! Where was the rain, the thunderstorms? It was now 4.25 pm and there was no sign of any disturbance overhead. With Pakistan behind the run rate and more than 25 overs gone, I prayed for rain. Where was it?

With Imran gone the game centred on Salim Malik to make the real charge. The required run rate was rising all the time and Malik had to move. We knew that early in his innings he tended to drive in the air through the off-side, inside out, feet nowhere.

He settled in quietly, but he knew he would have to launch a huge assault, very soon, to be in the hunt. After 34 overs the greens were 139 for three and the game in the balance. I was still concerned that Chris had five overs left, with no sign of Andrew bowling, and that Dipak hadn't bowled out either, meaning he would have two overs left when the slog was on. I wondered what Wrighty was thinking, as eight an over meant nothing unless we had cover. I limped slowly down to the dressing room to grab a drink and see what Wally thought. He was sitting behind the door, chewing his fingernails, feeling the same concern as me. 'How do you see it, Wal?' I asked. He didn't respond.

Gavin was preparing to bowl his 10th and final over. He'd bowled magnificently but soon he would be gone. 'What's the plan?' I asked myself. Javed had taken a single early in the over so now Gavin was bowling to Salim Malik. Our tight-lined wall on the off-side was ready as he drove at a ball on the up and Rod Latham, substituting for me, reached forward and swallowed the catch. Eden Park erupted.

Relief! Thank God for that, I thought, as I exchanged a wink with Wal. The game now looked ours, or so the scoreboard suggested. Pakistan 140 for four off nearly 35 overs, with a required run rate of 8.2. We had scored 80 odd off our last 10 overs so the critical period had arrived, with five overs until the 40th when the death would begin.

I start to relax, seeing Malik return to a silent visitors' dressing room. With Inzamam-ul-Haq taking strike I hope we bring on Andrew and Dipak straightaway before he settles in. Facing the slow bowlers isn't easy first thing, and we can rush through three or four overs before they've realised where they've gone. Gavin comes in for his last delivery and Inzamam flicks through square leg. A single to keep him on strike could work well if a new bowler comes on, but ... As I follow the ball out towards square leg I notice there's no one there — no sweeper.

It doesn't make sense. Here we are in the 35th over defending a score to make the World Cup final and there are only two men on the boundary! The ball dribbles over the line for four and Inzamam is on his way. Even though the score is still only 144 for four, the young Pakistani is oozing confidence as Javed approaches him with a huge smile. We've taken the pressure right off him, we haven't made him struggle for his first boundary or two as the run rate mounts, especially with the spinners coming on, if the spinners are coming on. No, Chris starts another over — his sixth in a row. I can't believe we haven't brought on a new bowler to the new batsman. Javed takes another single and Inzamam, on strike, easily works up to 10 off 10 balls as the drinks break arrives after 37 overs. Pakistan, 158 for four, need 104 to win off 13 overs at exactly eight per over with both batsmen looking good.

I decide to have a proper chat with Wally. I'm getting anxious and I need to talk with someone. 'What's he going to do with his bowlers now, Wally?' I plead.

'I'll never forgive Wrighty if he loses this,' is all he can say. Then, incredibly, as if on cue, Wrighty bursts in the door. As he races to the toilet he yells, 'Who's to bowl next?'

'What?' I'm amazed.

'Can you write down a plan of who to bowl next?' He disappears into the toilet.

'You're kidding! You mean you've ... Jeez, Wrighty ... Plumley, give me some paper, quick!' I'm nearly hysterical as Wrighty runs back out, his face etched with worry, saying, 'Send somebody out with it.'

'I can't believe this, what's he doing?' I ask nobody in particular.

Wally is speechless, nearly in tears. I grab the paper but I need to calm down, take a few deep breaths and think about a revised plan. I calculate that Wrighty has made only four bowling changes, with Willie coming on for Gavin, as the last. I draw a circle for a cricket field with two sets of stumps in the centre. I then write out this list of bowling changes:

Terraces End

Willie 2 (to finish)
Chris 2
Dipak 2 (now)

III
III

Andrew 2 (now)
Willie 1
Danny 4 (to finish)
(Chris in reserve with 2)

West Stand End

I check it over and confirm to myself it can work. But Wrighty has to bowl Andrew now, so I call Chris Cairns to come down and get ready to take the note out. It's too late. Chris Harris bowls another over and Wrighty is forced to take him off because Inzamam hits it to all parts, 14 off the over.

By the time Chris Cairns reaches the middle, Willie is ready to start another over. Wrighty takes one look at the note and stuffs it deep into his pocket. Javed, seeing his young charge ablaze now, just keeps feeding him the strike. After drinks, Inzamam goes from 10 to 50 in 21 balls. Willie is kept on but, try as he may, even he can't stem the flow of runs. In 10 overs together the two right-handers have added 87 runs before Inzamam is finally out for an amazing 60 off only 37 balls. What an innings and what a time to do it! Now Willie has bowled out and Chris is forced to bowl at the very end, with only 36 runs to win off the final five overs, Dipak conceding 22 in his last two overs. In all New Zealand has made only seven bowling changes in the entire innings.

By this stage I had walked out of the tunnel and stood 10 metres from the boundary line, leaning against the wall of the stand. Wally was on the line, surrounded by some of the players' wives and girlfriends. The lads were gone. No one was looking to the middle, no one was talking, no one was fielding in their correct place.

People all around me were cursing. 'What's going on? Why does he bowl that rubbish? They're gonna lose this!' This was awful. Standing there, watching from a distance, there was absolutely nothing I could do. I looked over and saw Don Neely to my right. Hands in pockets, he knew we had gone. So did Wally. So did I.

Then the final overs. The simple efficiency of Javed, one of the world's greatest players, still working the strike, and Moin Khan, who launched into Harry's last over with a huge six and then the match-winning four. The Pakistanis ran everywhere. From the tunnel they swarmed onto the ground to meet their heroes. Javed kissed the turf, and the rest just danced and shouted, shouted and danced. Imran walked around coolly as if he knew it would always happen. I went over to him and shook his hand, then retreated out of sight for a few minutes. I was stunned. The Pakistanis finally jigged their way back into their dressing room and closed their door on the world. They were off to Melbourne.

PAKISTAN

Aamir Sohail c Jones b Patel	14
Rameez Raja c Morrison b Watson	44
* Imran Khan c Larsen b Harris	44
Javed Miandad not out	57
Salim Malik c sub (R.T. Latham) b Larsen	1

Inzamam-ul-Haq   run out   60
Wasim Akram   b   Watson   9
† Moin Khan   not out   20
Extras (b 4, l-b 10, w 1)   15

                                    6 wkts, 49 overs   264

1/30, 2/84, 3/134, 4/140, 5/227, 6/238
Iqbal Sikander, Mushtaq Ahmed and Aaqib Javed did not bat.

Bowling: Patel 10-1-50-1; Morrison 9-0-55-0; Watson 10-2-39-2;
    Larsen 10-1-34-1; Harris 10-0-72-1.

Umpires: S.A. Bucknor and D.R. Shepherd.

Pakistan won by 4 wickets.

The spectators were in shock. 'What happened? How did we lose? Oh, no!' Then I saw Ian Taylor. He was crying, and so was Wally, but it hadn't hit me yet. Ian wanted us to gather together and walk a lap of honour around the ground. We slowly converged, reluctantly agreeing. This was so difficult, but we had only taken a few steps when the crowd suddenly rose again and cheered, thanking us. I looked the full circle, and no one, not a single soul, had gone home. Everyone was looking at us. They were thanking us. We had lost, but they were still saying, 'We're so proud. Well done.' I felt numb.

Then I saw Rod Latham, who was bawling his eyes out. He hadn't even played this game but he was hurting. The tears began to well in my eyes. Gavin Larsen, the tough Wellingtonian who had bowled us back into the game, couldn't hold back. Paddy grabbed me around the neck and said, 'Sorry.' He could barely speak. Neither could I. I hugged him and then broke away to start waving back to the cheering thousands. Dipak was expressionless, Andrew the same, Ken looked calm but sad, Chris Harris was in shock, Danny and Chris Cairns were hugging each other, trying to smile, to hang in there. Willie looked tired, really tired — there were no big smiles now — and Wrighty just grimaced.

I felt for him. He had come in cold to take over, hardly having played during the World Cup. He wasn't to know the plan as I knew it, or as the others knew it. He did it his way, the only way he knew how. He had made a huge effort, but tactically he didn't give the team what they had become used to. It was a hard thing to get exactly right, unless you had played all the time. Throughout the entire World Cup, Wrighty had been our inspiration off the field. He'd sit us down and tell us how good we were, how much it meant to play for New Zealand. He'd pump us up, care for us, make us laugh. He was outstanding.

During practices on our warm-up lap we'd stop halfway — just the players, no coach or manager — and I'd have a quick word and pass over to Wrighty. That's when he was in his element. Leaning into the circle, looking the guys squarely in the eyes, giving it to us straight. He helped us immeasurably, so I felt for him because I'd always loved Wrighty and now he felt responsible.

Finally I saw Ian Smith running past with his gloves high in the air. He was saying goodbye, he was retiring. I choked once more. The little man had given so much, had done all the hard work behind the stumps. Often unnoticed, he was much more than just the drummer in the band.

When we reached the tunnel again it was starting to hit me. No World Cup final, no Melbourne. Reaching the dressing room, I shook Ian's hand and thanked him, but then I went into my corner near the shower door, put my head in my hands and broke down. I couldn't look up. Finally, when I did, I realised everyone else was doing the same. There was a stony silence. This was hurting. Ian Taylor plucked up the courage to come and tell me that I was required for the media.

I washed my face, strode out blindly and turned left to face the television cameras. I didn't know what to say except that Pakistan had played well in the last hour, and that maybe we'd panicked. I didn't mention any names or John Wright's tactics, just said that I thought we had panicked a little. Should I have said nothing? I was upset.

After the media conference I went back to the dressing room and began to go around each team-mate, shaking hands and thanking them for a great effort. I really meant it. They'd all performed beyond belief. They had excelled and extended themselves as never before. They had fulfilled their potential as sportsmen, and you couldn't ask for more than that. I felt enormous pride in seeing these New Zealanders display such courage.

Suddenly the door burst open, and all the wives and girlfriends poured in, each searching for her companion, each at emotional breaking-point. The tears flowed unashamedly now, with everyone in the middle of the room together, consoling, comforting.

We then turned to see Bryan Waddle, the radio commentator who had been on so many tours with us, walk in, full of emotion. He'd lived every minute of that World Cup, enjoying each ball as he called it, bringing us closer to the final. He knew there was nothing in it at the end, except that we'd missed. It was great to see him showing so much passion, so much feeling for our plight. I thanked him again for a terrific job.

Then the DB boys arrived. At last, I thought — Dave Christiansen and Peter Wills, the greatest sponsors in the world. The DB cans snapped open and the spirits in the room climbed a thousand notches as the beer flowed and the smiles flooded back. Dave and Peter were picking us up again. They had stood by us through thick and thin, they'd always been there for us, encouraging beyond the call of duty. The atmosphere changed and the laughter and relief came loud and clear. The women had calmed and the joy was back in their eyes. Their men had finished and now they could go home.

Chris Cairns grabbed his boots and, in a dramatic ceremony, cut them up and burned them. We all cracked up. 'Throw your gloves in, Stockley', shouted Cairnsy to Ian Smith, but the great little man was content to suck quietly on a beer and reflect. Wrighty, too, was subdued. I handed him a can and said, 'Drink up, mate', but he couldn't speak. I sensed he was upset that I had mentioned on TV that we had panicked.

This wasn't going to be an easy night. I had a couple more beers and packed my coffin, throwing away old gloves and shoes I didn't ever want to see again. I noticed they were all snaffled up by the time I had closed the lid. Back in the hotel with Simone, I just dived for the bed and cursed the world. Lying there, I couldn't believe it, and Simmy said, 'I knew you should have gone out onto the field, I just knew it. I said at lunchtime that I should have come down and told you to get out there.'

I felt worse now, and I slammed the pillow. 'Damn it!' I didn't move for 40 minutes. After a while I picked myself up, had a shower and we went out to dinner with Simone's family. All they kept saying, all night, was that I should have gone out onto the field. I guess I should have, one leg and all. If I had, I would have risked the leg and probably have missed the final, assuming we had won with 262 on the board. I didn't risk it, and I saved the leg to try and be ready for Melbourne. Now I think I should have gone out. Losing, watching helpless in the stand, was my worst nightmare. To rub it in, the rain continued to thunder down throughout the evening.

South Africa were then beaten, more by the rules for rain-affected matches than by England, leaving two teams in the competition. England would meet Pakistan in the World Cup final at Melbourne on 25 March.

I didn't watch much of the final, just the last two hours when Wasim Akram turned the game Pakistan's way with a magnificent performance. It was Imran who had the final say when, on lifting the superb crystal trophy, he said, 'I'm so glad I have finally won my World Cup.' Imran seemed to think he was Pakistan.

Pakistan had certainly timed their run to win, but there was no doubt in everyone's mind that New Zealand had surprised and delighted the cricketing world. We had played above ourselves, we weren't as talented as the eventual winners but we *were* prepared to try anything to confuse and defeat our opponents.

My personal triumph was in playing to a standard I had only touched in the past, and to score consistently against the world's best on cricket's biggest stage, and at home. It's hard to describe the feeling of satisfaction in knowing that for one day — or in this case one month — you have played as never before. I had fulfilled my personal motto, 'to be the best you can be'. For the record, I scored more runs than anyone else, totalling 456 runs from nine innings, five undefeated. To average 114, with a strike rate of over 90 runs per 100 balls faced, was way beyond my expectations.

It was also gratifying that, over 18 months, we had built up a strong motivation and the will to play well. I honestly believe we were capable of winning the World Cup had we not lost our way in the last 15 overs of the semi-final. I had relished the challenge of captaincy, of being in charge and able to take control. Given time, and the patience, I was able to bring out the best in my players, from a tactical point of view. I also knew that sometimes I had become intolerant and frustrated when players misunderstood their roles and failed to perform. This was where Wally showed his skill, teaching me to treat everyone as an individual. I had needed time to work it through with them, to get them to relax under my leadership and have faith in themselves and their own contribution. I needed to encourage those who were struggling so that everyone would share in the team's common goal of playing at their peak. During the World Cup they achieved that. They were all my heroes.

Having tasted the joy of winning, the satisfaction of success, I longed for the team to hold onto it for as long as possible. For that whole month of the World Cup the nation came alive in helping us to try and achieve the greatest triumph. It was the best feeling I'd had since picking up a bat for the first time in the backyard of our Titirangi home many years before.

Part Two

Beginning the Quest

CHAPTER 5

Runs in the Family

> I realised that if I was going to achieve anything in life I had to
> be aggressive. I had to get out there and go for it.
> — MICHAEL JORDAN

My father, Dave, collected Wisdens, those small, thick, yellow books
that hold every historic cricket fact and statistic ever recorded. Even
though I was very young I knew what a statistic was, a world record, the
names of the legends in the game. I studied those Wisdens inside out. If
I was eight when I said to Dad how much I wanted a test century at
Lords, then I must have been about seven and a half when I knew every
great who had graced the sport: Jack Hobbs, Don Bradman, Walter
Hammond, Garfield Sobers, Fred Trueman, Keith Miller. I wanted so
much to be recognised and respected, adored and admired, as those
men were. My desire, my dream, was to become a great player, so I
buried myself in those Wisdens throughout my youth, hoping one day
to join those immortals of the game.

So, intentionally or not, Dad had created around me an environment that was to have a huge influence throughout my life. But he never
pressured me into anything. I was transfixed by these cricket bibles;
from an early age, I knew that this game was to be my religion.

My father was born in Blenheim on 18 October 1933, the second
son of Jack and Lois Crowe. Jack was an entrepreneur, travelling a lot,
trading, inventing — a character if ever there was one. Dad had three
brothers, Peter, Alex and Charles, but Charles was tragically drowned in
a diving accident at the young age of 17. Dad went to Christ's College
and it was there that he fell in love with the game of cricket.

He quickly developed a reputation as an effective left-hand opening
batsman who could hit hard, and also as a crafty leg-spinner. He managed to work his way through the grades to playing Brabin (under 20)
representative cricket, and then, after a few successful club seasons, he
made his debut for Wellington in first-class cricket. He played only one
match before being called up for military service, later playing briefly
for Canterbury before finishing his competitive cricketing days in the

Auckland premier grades. He played first for Suburbs and then for Cornwall, where he coached youngsters before turning out in the President's grade for a team he helped recruit from his old mates and their sons. As the boys progressed to senior levels the oldies continued, renaming their side 'Dad's Army'. Several of them had played first-class cricket.

My older brother Jeff had started playing when he was eight, quickly showing a talent for the game. One day in 1967 I went along with Dad to watch a school match in which Jeff was the captain. It soon became apparent that only 10 players had arrived so, without hesitation, Dad told me to get out there and complete the team.

So there I was, at the tender age of five, starting my cricket career! Naturally I batted at number 11 and before long I was walking out to the middle. I had borrowed some gear, only to find the pads were so big so it was very difficult to walk, let alone run. All I can remember now is that I hit the ball with a cross-bat shot through mid-wicket and began to run. I fell over, but managed to regain my crease and play out the over. Very next ball number 10 was bowled so I waddled off, reasonably proudly, nought not out. Incredibly, the next morning the local paper ran a story about the five-year-old named Martin Crowe, who had scored 0 not out. I proudly cut it out and kept it.

After that I was at Dad and Jeff constantly wanting them to bowl to me, or at least play on the home lawn. When I asked if I could have my own pads, Dad cut some down so that they were small enough to run in. I then registered at Cornwall Park for Saturday morning cricket, where both Jeff and I could be seen racing around One Tree Hill in our super little white shorts with our socks pulled up to the knees. It was the biggest day of the week for us.

Audrey, my mother, would have everything ready for us around 8 am and then we would leave 36 Grendon Road, Titirangi, for the half-hour drive to Cornwall Park. I loved it there — so beautiful, such a privilege to play in those glorious surroundings. We would all line up in front of the pavilion and wait to be put into teams. Out-of-towners like me had to join a composite side. One year I joined the Hogan's Heroes composite team, was named captain and have kept the nickname Hogan ever since. We played teams like the Baa-baas or sometimes the local schools. A great Cornwall stalwart, Arch Maclean, would parade the top steps, keeping everyone in line before announcing who would play who and on which pitch. I always hoped it would be No. 3 because it had a short leg-side boundary. I'm sure this is where I developed my penchant for the pull shot! Looking after us during the games was usually Dad or Harold Whitcombe. Although Harold had a number of talented sons playing, it soon became clear that he felt he could help my game technically. For years he encouraged and coached me, and I've never forgotten that. Almost every year throughout my career I've asked Harold to look at my batting and keep it on track. He's been a great influence.

Mum was excellent at sport in her own right. After we had gone to cricket she would be off to pennant tennis or golf. In 1966 she won the Auckland hard court tennis championship and I became convinced that she was keen for her children to play tennis as well as cricket. Because we could play only one sport on a Saturday, tennis was kept for holidays or sometimes a Sunday. Dad would pack his car with every conceivable kind of ball and off we would all go to the Remuera Rackets Club, where Dad played his competitive squash.

My sister Debbie, the eldest, would constantly keep us boys in check, making sure we contributed to other aspects of family life. Debbie was good at badminton, but she was determined not to let sport dominate her life as it did ours. As time went by she repeatedly revealed her strengths, her ability to care and support and always be there. She became an outstanding nurse and, as she raised her daughter Sherry, a loving mother. It was Debbie who always kept the family together, communicating and listening to all our problems, wanting to see us happy and content. Although she worried about sport dominating our lives, she became proud and respectful of our cricketing careers.

It was Audrey, though, who was my closest companion. When Dad went to Brisbane to help the family business for six months, and Deb and Jeff were living in Australia, Mum and I were alone together a lot. She is a strong, determined, capable woman, an achiever whether in sport, work or the job of raising three fairly active kids. Having been brought up by rather Victorian parents, Mum became slightly rebellious, wanting to be her own person, yet respecting everything that her family stood for. She always stressed the need for me to be thankful and always to keep my head up. She noticed that I had a habit of walking with my head down. I assured her that I just liked to watch where I was going but, in all honesty, it was a sign of shyness, and still is. Being in the public eye isn't something with which I'm naturally comfortable.

I had always enjoyed the down to earth nature of our household. We lived well, but not extravagantly, and being in Titirangi meant we could enjoy the native bush, or the beaches close by. We were like any other New Zealand family, particularly in our love of the outdoors — and in our passion for sport. We were a competitive rather than an openly affectionate family, which also, I believe, made us similar to a lot of New Zealand families.

There was no question, though, that I'd go over the top when competing; sometimes even a friendly contest became a do or die situation. I hate to lose and as a child I was a terrible loser. My battles with Jeff were fierce, unhealthily so. I'm sure this constant sparring got in the way of our proper emotional development. Dad would always try and teach us to be humble but the competition was so intense that too often it would bubble over and someone would get hurt. I'm ashamed to say that I once lashed out at Jeff with the nearest object I could reach, a cheese slicer, and cut his hand open. That was a huge lesson for me and I've avoided physical confrontation with anyone since.

Being four years Jeff's junior, I always had to work hard to stay in touch, whether in sport or any other pursuit. Jeff was my yardstick. If he did something unsuccessfully, then I vowed I would learn from his mistakes. I loved it when Dad's father visited us. Jack would offer me a dollar if I caught 50 catches in a row, as he threw them down to me from the top balcony. Jack would challenge me, always with pocket money, and so I began accepting any little challenge that was put in front of me. I would add up Jeff's runs and try and beat them. Audrey was always finding bits of paper with targets written all over them, and she would check secretly from time to time to see if I was successful.

I loved my sport, but even more I loved being taken to the next adventure, the next match or the next club, so I could learn and play some more. It was great, too, playing against Mum and Dad, trying to get a set off them in tennis or squash. Playing Dad at squash was my hardest assignment. He was an A grader at Remuera, had represented Auckland and had become an international referee. I loathed playing him as he would toy with me, teasing me, and he always won. For years I would try and 'beat the old boy'.

As I got fitter and he became older, nursing some dodgy cartilages, I found I was drawing closer. Finally, one day, I struck gold. Two-nil down, I reached up for a backhand volley only to catch Dad square on the nose. It split in two, blood gushed everywhere and we raced him to the dressing room. After 10 minutes the bleeding stopped and I applied a bandage to the wound. Then I said, 'Okay, let's continue.' Try as he could, he was unable to stop me taking out the final three games comfortably, while his nose ached and ached. I had defeated him, unfairly you could say, and upon doing so I announced my retirement from playing him ever again.

Dad was our great mate. He treated us like his best friend, and in that way we were able to learn so much and share so much with him. He was a great host, too, and had a charming style when looking after his guests. I adored Dad and all he stood for. Like Jack, his father, he just wanted to be happy, to smile and laugh, to celebrate a job well done with good red wine and Mum's famous cooking. Sometimes I felt he was too kind, too trusting, and we'd talk about the virtues of winning, even at all costs. To him this wasn't on; the aim was to achieve success with dignity and skill.

I couldn't help but crave success, to win, to achieve. Before long I was entering Auckland Grammar School and I was determined to be the best. Jeff was already there, in his final year, when I started as a 13-year-old in 1976. I was lucky to be allowed to attend Grammar as we lived out of zone, but Jeff had been accepted by headmaster Henry Cooper, a cricket fanatic, in 1972.

Jeff had enjoyed great success as a cricketer, captaining the Grammar First XI in his final two years. He was also skipper of the school squash team but, unbelievably, he had failed to become a prefect. He must have been the only first team captain in the school's history not to do so, but he had put sport ahead of his studies and didn't pass all his exams. So it became my goal to achieve all the necessary academic qualifications and, in time, to become a prefect. Whatever Jeff didn't achieve, I would attempt to.

So on my first day at Auckland Grammar I waited nervously, as every third former did, for direction from the masters. What class, which teachers, would we get? What cricket team? As I sat through the enrolment formalities, I turned to my right to see who was sitting next to me. His name was Grant Fox. He was a promising rugby player, a first five-eight from Putaruru. The form master read out the names of those who would be in 3C. We were both in the class, and we became instant mates.

The friendship lasted and for the next five years we enjoyed a fantastic respect and comradeship. We were inseparable. We soon discovered, too, that we were right up there at our chosen sports. By the end of our second year, Grant was on the verge of making the First XV while I had settled into the First XI. We were chatting one day about how many Grammar pupils had represented New Zealand at rugby or cricket, and we decided to make a bet: 'Whoever plays more tests for New Zealand, wins'. We were both 15 years old. The next year Grant went on to play superbly at first five, and I watched in awe as he stood up against opposition twice his size. He won so many matches with his boot and tactical awareness that Grammar remained unbeatable, as it had been since the days of the late Nicky Allen. Grant always talked about Nicky and how brilliant he was. It was interesting because Jeff and Nick had been great mates at Grammar.

By 1980 Grant had taken up cricket seriously, and I'd resumed my rugby career from primary school. We each made the other's teams, and I enjoyed the most marvellous six months of teamwork, camaraderie and excitement in the First XV rugby team. I'd tried First XI soccer the year before but soon became bored. Grant talked me into a trial and it was there that coach Graham Henry slotted me in on the right wing, and suggested I get serious about rugby. I gave it a go and managed to combine well with Grant and Ian Wood, the future North Harbour centre. I scored 24 tries, only four off the school record, but then, with four games remaining in the season, prop forward Kevin Thomas decided, as a prank, to flip me over his shoulder, smashing my right knee into the hard gym floor. I never played rugby again.

Grant and I both passed School Certificate and University Entrance comfortably and then were made prefects in the final term of our sixth form year. Of the half dozen or so selected that year, one would be named head prefect the following year. It seemed certain that Grant would be made head of Tibbs House, the boarding house, which would exclude him from the race, so it came down to Dave Morris, an academic, and me. Just before the last term break-up, the headmaster, John Graham, rang to ask if I would be the new deputy head prefect. To this day I can't remember what I said but John insists that I replied, 'You mean I'm not the head?'

'No, Dave Morris will be.'

'Then of course I accept.' It was a proud moment.

Even though I'd got second best it turned out to be a great decision. I came to respect and admire John Graham, the former All Black captain. He was so tough, but so fair. He'd listen and he'd understand. Relating to John was like going to finishing school. Grammar had provided the perfect foundation, and John was ruthless in polishing you up. I loved the school and it was a wonderful experience, too, to work with Dave Morris, who was the perfect leader — caring, diplomatic, disciplined and highly skilful. We had a great partnership, so much so that Dave asked the boss if I could assume a new title of associate head prefect. John looked at me as if he thought that it was my idea all along. Maybe it was!

Grant and I left Grammar at the end of 1980 and embarked on our new lives, knowing we wouldn't see as much of each other over the next few years because of different playing seasons. I insisted to Grant that our greatest achievement over the years at Grammar wasn't in rugby or cricket, but that we just failed to win the senior tennis doubles final!

For me, another achievement at school had been to represent New Zealand at secondary school level. Every year for three years I travelled to Australia with the team to play in the Kookaburra Shield with all the Australian state sides. It was such a different level from what we were used to. It was on these trips that I developed a liking for Australian conditions — the hot sun, and the faster wickets. I captained New Zealand in my last year, heading a team that included top players like Trevor Franklin and Rod Latham. I received the great honour of player of the tournament for breaking the most runs record held by Dirk Wellham: I became the first player to score 400 (407) runs in the week. A week later, in January 1980, I scored 51 in my first-class debut for Auckland, against Canterbury at Eden Park. I was 17 years old.

By this time Jeff had settled in Adelaide, playing for South Australia in the Sheffield Shield inter-state competition. I didn't see him much for five years, but Dad kept a close eye on him, believing that one day he might play for Australia. I'd always had mixed feelings over Jeff leaving New Zealand. I'd felt lost initially, wondering how I would fare without

The Crowe family at Grendon Road, Titirangi, in 1963.
Left to right: Debbie, Jeff, Dave, Martin (aged 1) and Audrey.

Above: My father Dave at 18. He was a fine cricketer in his time.

Left: Eight years old. I had already been playing cricket for three years.

The 'Bird Brothers'. Here Jeff is in aggressive mood as I take the gloves off after being beamed by Indian pace bowler Manoj Prabhakar. Nothing like brotherly support in a tense situation.

Raising the bat to a standing ovation after completing a gutsy 100 at Lancaster Park in 1986. Earlier, on 51, I had been struck in the face and taken to hospital for ten stitches. Jerry Coney offers congratulations on my fourth test century.

Hooking Malcolm Marshall for four during my innings of 119 in the first test against the West Indies at the Basin Reserve in 1987.

Turning to leg on my favourite New Zealand test ground, the Basin Reserve.

Gordon Chadwick looked after me when I returned to England, a shattered young man, following my first test series. At his home in Alwoodley, Leeds, I was treated like a seventh son. Tim, the second youngest, is in the background.

his inspiration. I'd always been known as 'Jeff's younger brother'; now I could forge my own identity. What I didn't realise was how quickly — much sooner than I expected — that identity would take on a new and exciting look.

CHAPTER 6

Way Too Soon!

What a day it had been so far! Playing against Central Districts for Auckland at Pukekura Park I achieved the first real milestone in my career. Batting at number four in our first innings, I reeled off my maiden first-class 100 before lunch. Everything I swung at hit the middle of the bat. With only one over remaining in the morning session, I stood at the striker's end 90 not out. Roger Pierce, a part-time medium slow bowler, was given the last over to try his luck. Most times, with only an over to go, a batsman will see out the last six balls quite carefully, making sure his team will make it through till lunch. This is what I would normally do as well — except for one thing. Only two weeks before I had been dismissed for 99 against Northern Districts at Eden Park, one short of what would have been my maiden 100. I was devastated, and vowed not to be so negative when nearing the century mark again. So when I smashed Roger Pierce's first warm-up ball for four, and then the third for four, to move to 98, I remembered my vow and set my sights on completing the 100 in the same over. From the very last ball I played an agricultural heave and sent the ball over square leg for four to raise my first ever first-class century.

After lunch I continued until caught and bowled by Denis Aberhart for 150. It was a special feeling to play so well, to hit the ball so cleanly. After the day's play we were sitting around in the dressing room when, over the radio, came the announcement of the New Zealand team to play Australia in the one-day series in February: 'The New Zealand team to play Australia is Geoff Howarth, Northern Districts, captain; Lance Cairns, Northern Districts; Jeremy Coney, Wellington; Martin Crowe, Auckland; Bruce Edgar, Wellington …'

On 31 January 1982, at the tender age of 19, I had been selected to represent my country. This was, as the cliché goes, a dream come true. It was an extraordinary feeling, for everywhere I went that night people were looking at me and congratulating me on my selection. I had felt nothing like this before — to play for New Zealand. Wow!

It was great, too, that Aud and Dave were there to see the maiden 100 and embrace me when the announcement was made. There were tears of joy in our eyes as the three of us huddled together, cherishing the moment. It would be an understatement to say they were both over the moon.

So my international career was about to begin, and I was shocked at my selection. I had played only 18 first-class games to date, had just the one century score earlier that day, and was very inexperienced and naive. I hadn't yet established myself fully in the Auckland side, a team loaded with senior pros. I always wondered whether I had the respect of the senior guys — John McIntyre, John Cushen, John Wiltshire, John Reid, Austin Parsons, Peter Webb, Warren Stott, Gary Troup and Martin Snedden. These guys were all figures I looked up to, players I admired and from whom I had enjoyed learning my craft. It was a marvellous environment to play in, especially with such characters as 'Tube' McIntyre and Austin Parsons. The Auckland side wasn't necessarily studded with internationals, but was a team keen to win trophies in the Shell Series. Batting alongside John Reid and Peter Webb was the perfect introduction to first-class cricket, as they had enormous skill and expertise. Watching John Reid, in particular, was a great education — keeping so still, playing the ball so late. He was a great player of spin bowling.

I loved playing for this Auckland team along with my good mates Trevor Franklin and Phil Horne. The three of us were only in our second or third year in the team, but we all felt welcome and part of the set-up. A lot of this had to do with the superb man management and leadership skills of John Wiltshire, our captain. He wasn't a great player or a brilliant tactician, but more a facilitator, who encouraged communication, openness and honesty. Well liked for his wonderfully calm approach to everything, John became a close mentor for me, to such an extent that, when he left Auckland a year later, I followed him, another year on, to join Central Districts in the 1983–84 season.

This wasn't the only reason, mind you, for leaving my home town. One thing annoyed me so much that I had no hesitation in moving south. The arrival, for the 1982–83 season, of one John Bracewell from Otago made all those fun times playing in my first few years seem a distant memory. Although we all welcomed the skill and determination John brought to the team, I couldn't stomach the way he carried on in the field. During the final match I played for Auckland at Carisbrook, he upset Trevor Franklin so much that Trevor threatened to take him out if he continued to criticise his efforts at short leg. Poor Trevor had enough worries fielding there anyway, since he stood 2 metres (6 foot 7)! Fists were drawn and the team split with the younger guys such as Paddy and me supporting Trevor. I'll never, though, forget those happy early days playing for Auckland, all part of my progress towards being the player I had always dreamed of becoming.

So it all seemed a little strange and unsettling to say goodbye to my Auckland team on this unforgettable day of my national selection, and move off to prepare in a team that was filled with players from whom I'd sought autographs only three or four years before. To be quite honest, I was terrified. Up to this point my progress had been constant and steady, my confidence at first-class level healthy and growing. The next month, however, changed all that when I was asked to do something I was not ready for: play against the mighty Australians.

I don't think the selectors really thought it through, weighed up all the options, visualised the possible outcome of selecting someone so young. They didn't realise it, but my whole personality took a negative turn, my positive mind became for the first time cluttered with anxieties and doubts. It felt as though my confidence had been undermined.

In my first one-day international at Eden Park on 13 February, in front of a record 43,000-strong New Zealand crowd, I ended up at number eight in the batting order. Richard Hadlee and Lance Cairns had been promoted so I wasn't required to bat. Although I managed to enjoy a productive day in the field, even capturing two late wickets, I felt alone in a dressing room full of battle-hardened men.

Just 20 minutes away from start of play at the next international at Carisbrook, I was ordered by the captain, Geoff Howarth, to bat three after John Reid had suddenly pulled out with a back injury. Number three! I hadn't even batted number three for Auckland, so was stunned by this amazing promotion. I scored a very nervous three runs against Dennis Lillee and Jeff Thomson before edging Terry Alderman to slip.

The final decider at Wellington began with John Wright edging the first ball of the match to slip. Instead of dropping into my more familiar number in the order, I was again forced to bat three. I couldn't believe what was happening as I again failed against the new ball. We were bowled out for 74 and lost easily. By now my confidence and belief in myself was gone. I knew I was out of my depth, particularly where

Howarth had put me. Still, I hoped I could improve on my poor start in the test match starting in a few days' time. The selectors relieved me of the possibility of being subjected to number three again, and duly restored John Morrison to the line-up. I dropped, thankfully, to number six. Even so, facing Lillee and Thomson, at the time the greatest fast-bowling duo in the world, was an assignment well beyond a 19-year-old starting out in the game. Wouldn't it have made more sense to introduce a new young player against Sri Lanka a year later?

I duly made my test debut at the Basin Reserve on 26 February 1982. It was an extraordinary match. It rained for all but five hours of the first four days, enough time for Lillee and Thomson to show their pace, giving John Morrison in particular an awful battering. I finally walked out in a test for the first time just before lunch on day five. What debutant ever had to wait so long to get on the field!

In my first over I scored my first single off Bruce Yardley, a tickle to short fine leg, then a four through square leg off Greg Chappell before he decided enough was enough for the young lad. He ordered Lillee and Thomson to take the new ball. Twice in the opening overs from Jeff Thomson, bowling from the R.A. Vance Stand end, I walked out to square leg to retrieve my helmet after jerking my head away from another thunderbolt. Once I was struck on the back of the head, my ears ringing from the impact. 'Jeez, those things make a helluva noise, mate,' said Rod Marsh, wandering past.

The problem was I just couldn't pick up Thomson's delivery. His javelin style action made it impossible to see the ball leave his hand, especially out of the dark pavilion background. The new sightscreens at the Basin weren't (and still aren't) sufficiently high, especially if the day is gloomy, as this one was.

I survived five overs, once jabbing down on an attempted yorker, making contact and then watching in amazement as the ball sped off down the ground for four, such was the speed Thomson was bowling. There was only one man in front of the wicket as 'Thommo' bowled his spell — tiny Bruce Laird at short leg. Graeme Wood was at point, the rest behind the wicket, obviously enjoying the demolition. Then I was run out, for nine, pushing the ball to a vacant mid-on, and racing three-quarters of the way down the pitch, only to be sent back by Geoff Howarth. I felt that if he had backed up the normal metre or so, so I could get down the other end, the run could have been on. Instead, I took a mauling from the fastest bowler in the world. There was no way that I was prepared for anything of this magnitude.

Nevertheless I got the feeling, in the dressing room, that this was test cricket and that if you wanted to make it, you had better get used to it smartly. Talk about a baptism of fire. But that's what it was like in this New Zealand team. These were experienced, successful, self-sufficient individuals in a professional, hard-working but ruthless set-up. If you were good enough to be selected, said Howarth, you were good enough to look after yourself. At 19 I didn't even know what looking after yourself meant. When I sat next to Jerry Coney on the plane to the next venue he simply turned to me and said, 'You're a threat to me!' It wasn't surprising that I felt in awe of everyone, both the Australians and my own team-mates.

Of the experienced players (and that was most of the team), John Wright and Stephen Boock went most out of their way to help. John was great. He would talk to you, advise you, tell you that you were a great player. Stephen was different, a more humorous character, but he too, wanted you to succeed. I'll never forget his support on the 1985 tour to the West Indies when, like most of the batters, I struggled to score runs. After I'd failed twice in the first test, 'Boocky' gave me heaps of encouragement going into the second test.

While I was compiling my painstaking 188 at Guyana, Stephen kept sending out notes of praise and reminders that he would be all fired up when he came out to bat with me at number 10. At each interval he would be practising his technique, stating that he would be the one to see me through to a double century. When he finally came out to bat, the anticipation was unbearable. Before facing up to the extreme pace of Michael Holding, Stephen spent ages surveying the field, taking guard and then at last gave me the thumbs up as he settled into his stance. In came Holding off 40 paces as Stephen, and all of us, waited with bated breath. He didn't have to wait too long as the first ball, all of 145 kilometres an hour, cannoned into his middle stump before he had even lifted his bat — bowled for a golden duck! I cracked up, falling to the ground as I held my sides in laughter. Poor Boocky surveyed the damage, then turned to me and just shrugged his shoulders, holding back the laughter. But I appreciated his support throughout.

Later he was to bowl over 70 overs in an innings to the Pakistanis at Eden Park in 1988–89 and, upon conceding his 200th run on the flat, bare, barren pitch, he knelt down, kissed the dirt and then yelled to Ewen Chatfield that he had now given him the perfect wet spot to aim for! Stephen was not only a great character but a fine left-arm spinner. Personally I thought he should have bowled a lot more for New Zealand; I regarded him as the best spinner we produced.

Geoff Howarth was pretty tough on me during my early years in the side. Sometimes, to try and jolt me, he would say from his corner of the dressing room, or at the hotel bar, 'Hey, pretty boy!', or 'You're just a show pony, Crowie.' He said it was his way of motivating me, of keeping me on my toes so I wouldn't waste my talent as he felt he had done, but I hated it. I didn't need motivating — I was as hungry as hell — but I was young and scared and feared failure. I needed more of what Wright or Boock could give me. After I'd been in the side for a while, Lance Cairns said to me, in reference to Geoff's tactics, 'I don't know why you didn't piss off and go surfing ages ago rather than take that stuff.' I don't think Geoff and Lance got on too well!

So, although I respected him, I never really developed a warm regard for my captain. He was a superb tactician on the field, quick to think on his feet, seemingly cool under pressure. He called the right moves many times and New Zealand prospered under his leadership. He also, I might add, had an excellent team to work with; bowlers like Richard Hadlee were a captain's dream.

The New Zealand team of the early 1980s, and in particular the senior pros within it, took the game to a new level. The building up of players, and a professional attitude throughout the 1970s, created the success for the 1980s. For example, the development of Jerry Coney, Lance Cairns, Bruce Edgar, Ewen Chatfield, Warren Lees and Stephen Boock as the non-county pros was critical in working alongside the full-time pros such as Howarth, Wright, Hadlee, John Parker and Glenn Turner (when he played). The success achieved by this band of men gave the next generation the direction to carry on the good work. Young players such as Ian Smith, John Reid, John Bracewell, Martin Snedden, Jeff and myself all came into a side where the recipe for success was already well tried and established. This quickly gave us the taste for winning, although the invitation into the side was far from welcoming or pleasant. But then that's what test cricket can be like.

My first test series was a total disaster. Having registered scores of three and seven in the one-dayers, then nine in the first test, my whole psyche was crushed. Fronting up to the Aussies was unrelenting. They had come to New Zealand to wipe us off the park and the rivalry between the two cricket nations was at fever pitch. No quarter would be given. Ever since New Zealand beat Ian Chappell's 1974 Australians at Christchurch, finally killing off that awful arrogant 'you can't play' attitude, the Aussies have grown to respect our ability to compete.

This Australian side, led by Greg Chappell, had no inclination to start a trend of losing to a bunch of Kiwis. They were highly motivated to keep us pinned down in the lower ranks of world cricket for as long as possible. But when we beat them off the park at Auckland in the second test I witnessed at first hand what trans-Tasman rivalry was all about. I didn't get sledged at all, because I was never around long enough, but the language that one or two used, notably 'Thommo' on Bruce Edgar during his outstanding 161, was mind boggling. When they came back to level the series one all at Lancaster Park, the Australians really showed what a great side they were. Of course a great side needs great players and this team had a who's who list — players such as Laird, Wood, John Dyson, Chappell, Allan Border, Kim Hughes, Marsh, Yardley, Alderman, Lillee, Thomson and Len Pascoe, legends in the world of cricket. Two players, apart from Lillee and Thomson, left a huge impression on me: Greg Chappell, that masterful stylist, and Allan Border, the pugnacious Aussie battler.

In Greg Chappell I saw the kind of player that I aspired to be. He was tall, elegant, confident (or nicely arrogant), very determined and he loved to win. His mental approach to the task in hand was worth noting. First, he knew the importance of preparation. His ability to focus inwardly and to visualise precisely the performance he desired far outweighed his skill of leaning into an on-drive. Mind you, that was one hell of a shot! I couldn't get over how mentally tough he was. Very little expression on his face, always holding a positive and confident body position, always ready to offer his opposition an insight into what he really thought of them on a cricket field. Totally and utterly professional. Add to that his style at the crease, which was simply magnificent. His poise, composure, footwork and serene swing of the bat all combined to create a classic cricket stroke. I marvelled at his presence while he was scoring runs. His innings of 176 in the third test (100 before lunch when resuming 76 not out) was a display of technique and stroke play, of placement and dominance, that I'll never forget. Watching him bat was the highlight of my test series and he left an impression on me that was to last for a long time. He was to me like the perfect textbook; whenever I needed help I always thought about what Greg Chappell would do and I began to copy this master batsman from Australia.

Allan Border, on the other hand, wasn't a player who caught my eye as he batted. But what did make me respect and admire this man was that he was out to make the most of every single bit of talent he had. In many ways 'AB' was limited, but with his dogged, unrelenting attitude, he opened doors that very few have done before or since. Just as obvious was his fierce determination to help Australia beat its opponent. It wasn't just a contest to him, but a declaration of war between two proud nations and there was to be only one winner. For him, playing alongside Chappell, Lillee and Marsh must have been a priceless experience. And all those who ended up playing alongside Allan Border would have thought the same of him.

In my first six innings for New Zealand, I scored three, seven, nine, two, nought, nine. During the two at Eden Park, I was dismissed in unusual circumstances. Dennis Lillee was the man bowling to me and soon I was caught bat-pad by Graeme Wood. As Lillee charged down the pitch signalling the end for me, Steve Woodward the umpire called not out. I stood for a second taking in this lucky break, and then decided to walk off all the same. Lillee stopped celebrating and stared at me as I walked by. The next day when he was batting, a break in play gave him the opportunity to walk up to me at short leg and say, 'Thanks for walking yesterday, mate, it was real gentlemanly. Don't fucking do it again.' Then he walked away. He was right. I'd succumbed to being overawed, and had forgotten that the umpires are there to make the decisions, whether they get them wrong or right. The theory is that it all evens out over time, good and bad decisions. Unless it was obvious, I never walked again.

During the third test, I was in my tracksuit, watching in the stand as John Wright and John Morrison began a partnership. We were one down. Then Morrison was lbw to make us two down. As he left the field I wandered down to the dressing room to get ready to bat at number six (four down). As I reached my gear a roar went up and Wrighty was caught behind. I was in next. I quickly threw my tracksuit off, grabbed a shirt and pulled on some trousers. As I laced up my boots, another roar

73

went up and Jerry Coney was bowled second ball for a duck. I was in! Now, I was in a real panic. Within seconds I had my pads half on, my thigh pad and box in, and was in stuffing my shirt, grabbing my sweater. Next Jerry walked into the room while the game was waiting for me to walk out to bat. Would I be timed out? Two minutes had well passed as I searched for and found my bat and gloves. As I reached up for my helmet and turned to walk (run!) out, I tripped on something and fell flat on my face.

By now everyone was worried. I wouldn't make it. I ran through the tunnel and out onto the ground, sleeves flapping, struggling to get my gloves on, let alone my helmet. Luckily, it was the end of the over and everyone on the ground was slowly moving into position, so I was able to strap up properly and get organised while Geoff Howarth faced up to Jeff Thomson. We ran a single. I took strike and then received a bouncer that flew over my head, over Rod Marsh's head and, after one bounce, into the fence for four byes.

Next I got down to Lillee's end, still on nought, and first ball sparred at one that moved away and edged behind. Crowe, caught Marsh, bowled Lillee, nought. I was now in very distinguished company. But what a performance! It showed my immaturity for that level and certainly taught me a lesson that I'd never forget. I managed to hit out in the second innings, determined to be positive, but I lifted my head to an ugly slog and was bowled for nine. That was it for me for a while — and quite rightly, too. I was picked to go on an emerging tour of Australia later that year but didn't score well enough to be in contention for New Zealand when we resumed domestic cricket at home. One spectator who witnessed my second test performance was brother Jeff. He heard of my selection in Adelaide, and returned home to see me play. He decided then and there to come home for good and attempt to play for New Zealand.

After one first-class match for Auckland in which he failed (and I scored 119), Jeff was picked for the first time to represent his country. This time the announcement came over a loudspeaker while we were fielding against Otago on the outer oval at Eden Park. The only 'Crowe' read out had 'J.J.' in front of it. Jeff had taken my place! It felt bizarre — and it was also embarrassing to be dropped while fielding in front of thousands of people. I didn't know how to react. Not long after, when the ball came out to me on the boundary where I was fielding, I picked it up and hurled it in so hard and so angrily that it cleared the keeper and was quickly backed up, by Jeff himself. Soon a wicket fell and I was able to run in and shake Jeff's hand. I was very proud for him but deep down I was devastated for myself.

Frankly, though, it was the best thing the selectors could have done. Later that day Frank Cameron, chairman of selectors, came up to me and said, 'We feel you need to work on bowling an out-swinger instead of those in-swingers.' I laughed. I knew what he meant but it seemed a funny thing to say when I had really been dropped for Jeff because my batting wasn't ready yet. Anyway, I knuckled down that season, scored a record number of runs for Auckland, including three centuries, and completely regained my confidence. I was a year older, with more runs under my belt, but, hard as I tried, I couldn't bowl that out-swinger!

The New Zealand team arrived home from Australia after a fairly successful campaign. They made the finals through some inspiring performances, especially against England; particularly exciting was the win at Adelaide where they knocked off 296 in extreme heat. Everyone watching at home was beginning to catch the bug of one-day cricket with close games like this. In fact, since the under-arm incident at Melbourne a year earlier (just before my first series), the New Zealand public had got behind the fortunes of the national team. That delivery really united everyone and interest was growing. Jeff scored some good 50s, including one at Adelaide in that great run chase, to confirm that he was a player for the future. Now I needed to be given another chance and, I hoped, to join him.

Fortunately, that chance came quite soon as New Zealand and Australia were to play each other in a charity match at the Sydney Cricket Ground in aid of the bushfire victims around Australia. Jeff was rested to allow me in at number four. On a sporting pitch, but played in a series manner, I felt this was a good test to check my development a year on. After some very nervous early moments I loosened up and began to play the innings of my life up till that point. In one sequence I managed to score off 18 consecutive balls and finished with a match-winning 66 out of 134. Buoyed up by that, I also captured two wickets in a tidy spell and was a very happy man to receive the Man of the Match award. It was the turning point I wanted. I can't remember much of the innings except how badly I wanted this to be a positive result. It helped to bury the memory of my first disappointing performances. I could, I felt, expect to be given more chances in the home series against Sri Lanka.

Jeff made his test debut in that series, the first time the Sri Lankans had visited New Zealand. He, too, was run out in his first test innings while I watched as 12th man. We did, however, manage to bat together for the first time at Napier in a one-dayer, seeing the side through to a win and scoring 40-odd not out each. We now felt that we had every chance of making the touring side to go to England in a month's time to play in the 1983 World Cup and a four-test match series against the Poms.

A week later came the announcement that we'd dreamed about as a family: Jeff and I had both been selected to represent our country. Aud and Dave were delighted and immediately booked tickets to follow the whole tour. This, I felt, was the proper start to my career: an opportunity to enjoy a three- to four-months tour, learning every step of the way. I was determined to make steady progress rather than try to atone for my test average of five in one big suicidal attempt. The selectors hadn't helped me with that premature selection but I knew it was in my hands to determine my own destiny and fashion a record I had desired ever since burying myself in those Wisdens.

Just before the domestic season finished the New Zealand team decided to employ a commercial business manager in order to capitalise on the growing interest being shown in the fortunes of national cricket. As a team, we interviewed a number of candidates about what they could do for us in the seasons ahead. In Auckland, we gathered at the Waipuna Lodge to listen to the final two candidates who believed they could make a few extra bucks for the team kitty.

First up was a rather interesting-looking character called Darryl Sambell. He described himself as a rock concert promoter — his experience previous included managing Australian pop singer John Farnham for nearly 10 years with great success — and he had since promoted concerts in Australia and New Zealand. Now, after meeting John Wright through their love for horses, he was keen to get involved in sport management. He was very nervous in his presentation, but quickly spelled out his intentions to make the cricket team $100,000 a year in endorsements.

The second interview was with someone we all knew, Lindsay

Singleton, who at the time advised Geoff Howarth and Lance Cairns. He had been around cricket circles for a while and knew the board members and the set-up, so it was no surprise that he was chosen over Sambell, who received only three votes. Those votes, incidentally, came from Jerry Coney, brother Jeff and myself, voting purely on the proposed income that Darryl projected for us. No one else we had interviewed had named a figure like his. A couple of days later I decided to approach Darryl personally and see if he was interested in managing individuals such as Jeff and myself. He jumped at the idea and promised to put me on the front cover of more publications than Richard Hadlee. At the tender age of 20 I had my own personal business manager.

At quite an early stage in our association Darryl told me he was gay. His social life was no concern of mine; I was just interested in seeing that he did a good job in managing my business. He loved his new challenge and looked after Jeff and me so keenly and enthusiastically that, within a couple of years, he had established so many contracts and endorsements for us both that our profiles, but especially mine, were indeed right up there with Hadlee's. We were making money, and with it an image of success and good living. Darryl sang our praises from the rooftops to such an extent that people began to get brassed off. Before long the rumours started that I was one of Darryl's 'boys'. The more success I had on the cricket field, the more Darryl wanted to run my life. In the end it all got out of hand. I couldn't shake off the rumours about my sexuality, and there were more and more objections to my high profile. I'd been turned into something Kiwis loved to hate — a fast-growing, opinionated, tall poppy from Auckland.

I arrived in Britain before the rest of the team and drove to Leeds to put in some serious training and practice while staying with my great friends, Gordon and Shirley Chadwick, who had looked after me the year before when I played for Bradford during the season. We had had a great time, winning the Yorkshire League, and I hit a record total, opening with Bob Chadwick, the third of their six sons. I loved the Chadwicks and the life in Yorkshire. They took me in and treated me like another son. Gordon, who was Bradford's captain and keeper, became a real mentor. We went for long walks around Eccup, near where they lived, discussing cricket and the tactics of the game. He made sure I aimed high, encouraging me to increase my tally of 100s. Shirley was forever filling me up with Yorkshire puds and then it was off to the pub to wash them down with a few pints of Tetleys. There's no better education for a youngster than playing a season or two in Yorkshire.

The England tour itself was a wonderful experience. I played well in the county games but failed to post the big score in any of the four tests. Still, I was making progress. It was hard to put out of my mind the shame of scoring so poorly the year before; I had a feeling this would take a bit of time and a lot more cricket.

The highlight of the tour was undoubtedly the first win over England at Leeds. Despite the fact that Richard Hadlee failed to take a wicket, everyone contributed superbly to secure an excellent victory. The celebrations after the match were so emotional that it took us weeks to come down from our high. John Wright had led us through some great sing-songs, reciting an amazing piece of poetry himself. He had all the supporters and players in stitches for hours, especially as he did his act wearing only a cricket shirt and his pale blue holey Y-fronts! Later, in the bus, he kept pleading with us all to 'believe in ourselves, 'cause we're better than they are!' Jerry and Lance stood next to him, screaming, 'I believe, I believe in the Rigit.' Hence Wrighty earned a new nickname, Rigit.

We lost the test series three-one, because we never knuckled down again after the great heights of Headingley. I was pleased to top the tour batting averages and, in doing so, began to feel more welcome and established within the team. Then came another lucky break in my career. During the fourth test at Trent Bridge, I suffered a nasty blow to my left middle finger, which all but put me out of the test. While I was off the field for the first three days I did an interview on the BBC's *Test Match Special*. I talked about how great it would be one day to play county cricket to gain more experience. The chairman of Somerset County, Michael Hill, happened to be driving towards Nottingham to watch the test, and heard my comments on his car radio. As soon as he arrived at the ground he asked to see me and suggested that Somerset were looking for a replacement next year, 1984, for Viv Richards and Joel Garner. I indicated that I would sign then and there if necessary, that I would be absolutely thrilled to play.

A month later I got the shock of my life when Michael Hill rang to confirm that I would be Somerset's overseas professional. It was hard to work out. I was only 20, had scored only 183 runs at 15.25 and taken only two wickets at test level. I was hardly a proven international. Was this to be another premature selection? Was I ready to provide the sort of performances that Somerset supporters had expected over the years? All I knew was that my dream of playing county cricket had come true. I wanted the whole experience to have the same kind of impact on me that it had had on Richard Hadlee, John Wright and Glenn Turner. What I didn't quite realise was just what huge shoes I would be filling. Soon I was to be the stand-in for the great West Indian, Vivian Richards.

CHAPTER 7

Help from 'God'

Since 1976, when he hit 1710 test runs in that calendar year, Isaac Vivian Alexander Richards has been the greatest batsman the world has seen. He dominated bowling attacks so brutally and fearlessly that he stood alone at the top during the next 10 years. He was the king of Somerset, of Antigua and of the Caribbean. He is the proudest man I have ever met — proud of his ancestors, proud of his country, his creed and his colour, his people, and naturally, very proud of his family name.

I saw this pride one day at Taunton in 1984 when, in a benefit match for Ian Botham, Viv was named Man of the Match. After the game the adjudicator announced over a microphone, 'the Man of the Match ... the greatest batsman in the world'. Viv just stood, with the rest of us, waiting for the name to be called. Everyone knew it must be Viv, but he stood firm, waiting for his name, refusing to walk forward until it was called.

After a minute's embarrassed silence everyone gestured to Viv to step forward. The announcer spoke again: 'Here he is, the greatest batsman in the world, Viv!' Reluctantly, Viv stepped forward, looking angry and offended. He took the award hurriedly and stormed back into the dressing room. I stood there as he threw the award, a bottle of brandy, hard into the wall where it smashed violently. 'My name is Vivian Richards, not "the greatest batsman", you understand! Why won't he call me by my fucking name!'

To me, he was 'God'. When I looked at him it was with awesome respect. I would watch his every move, every expression, so as not to miss a single action or word. He had everything that I wanted. A player like Greg Chappell influenced my thinking and approach to batting, particularly from a technical point of view, but Viv fuelled my competitive spirit and inspired me to attempt to be the best.

I remember watching him on TV during the 1979 World Cup final when he scored the most outrageous 138 not out to set the West Indies up for their consecutive victory. His body language towards the bowlers was so arrogant and commanding; he was boss and everyone knew it.

He could step onto the front foot and hit the ball in any direction, especially through mid-wicket, or he would swivel off the same foot and play a kind of front foot pull or hook, totally demoralising any bowler.

Off the field, Viv was most approachable and liked to chat about anything, particularly if it was funny — he had a great sense of humour. On the field he meant business. No mucking around, it was all-out attack. I felt, though, that people liked to watch Viv and find flaws in his game, in his personality. I considered this to be very unfair; he didn't have to measure up to anybody or anything, he just wanted to be himself, and to be a proud West Indian. He had certainly been loved in Somerset ever since he arrived there in 1974, along with Ian Botham.

It wasn't until three years later, starting in 1977, that Somerset enjoyed the best years in its history, mainly through the leadership of Brian Rose, and through the talent of those growing stars, Richards, Garner and Botham. Now in 1984, under Ian Botham, they were looking forward to continuing that success. With the West Indies touring throughout the summer of 1984, which took Richards and Garner away from Somerset, the county decided to invest in a youngster who could bat and bowl and who was keen and fit to play every match. So there I was.

During our summer at home I had notched up my first test century, against England at the Basin Reserve in Wellington. This gave me extra confidence to take to Somerset. Before the county's pre-season training in April, however, we embarked on a short test tour of Sri Lanka. Having beaten England in a test series at home one-nil, we were favourites to beat Sri Lanka, even under their unfamiliar and difficult conditions. This we duly delivered, taking out the series comfortably two-nil.

Comfort was not the world I would use, though, for my own experiences during the tour. First I suffered a broken thumb, and then a bout of food poisoning from eating a couple of mussels at what seemed to be a reliable local restaurant. I became really ill only hours afterwards, with the most hideous vomiting, diarrhoea and dysentery. I vomited myself to sleep in the end, only to be woken not long after by a searing pain in my mouth. It felt as though I had swallowed a bee, and been stung inside the lower lip. I raced to the bathroom again to see what the hell was going on this time. As I curled back my lower lip I saw this sore begin to grow and expand, twitching and stinging until it was the size of a grape. In a panic, I banged on the doctor's door and pleaded for some relief. He applied some ointment and put me to sleep.

I stayed in bed for two days until I was required to bat at number nine in our first innings of the second test, the mussel incident having occurred on the night of the first day's play, after that broken thumb. I scored nought and went back to bed. You think at these times that you really are going to die, such is the debilitating nature of the illness. On the final day of the test Geoff Howarth insisted I bat at number five with orders to play for a draw. So there I was, all covered up in handkerchiefs to soak up the feverish perspiration, while I defended with one hand.

History shows that I became the slowest scorer ever of double figures in a test innings, 210 minutes for 10 runs, finishing on 19 not out. I recovered sufficiently to be picked for the final test but my energy levels were low and something didn't seem quite right. It was a relief when the tour ended as it meant I could get off to the more congenial environment of Taunton.

As soon as I arrived I was welcomed by Ian Botham and taken straight to his flat, where he offered to put me up for the season. Ian's flat wasn't quite what I expected. It was a small pad, with little furniture or atmosphere, characterised by the number of boxes scattered around. For Ian, it was a place to sleep for a few hours here and there, maybe to watch a video if he had a night to kill. Unfortunately for me, staying there only encouraged loneliness.

Ian had a huge schedule since this was his benefit year, and he was also captaining Somerset and playing for England. I hardly saw him and was very much on my own at first. When we were together he was great company. He loved to get outdoors and enjoy himself, whether playing a round of golf, or fishing in the rivers. 'Beefy' was warm and good-natured, although he liked to be in charge, playing out the gang leader role. He seemed always to need someone around him, someone to party with, to share his adventures. Being such a legend (and he was probably the biggest thing the British had had since Winston Churchill) must have made him lonely and isolated at times. Everywhere he went people wanted a piece of him. Refusing to accept this, he was determined to be himself and that was that; he wasn't going to change for anybody. I admired that, but he was a daring fellow and, when he was on a mission, you needed plenty of stamina and guts to keep up with him.

I could never last the distance, especially early on at Somerset.

While I would be beginning to wake to a new day, Ian would be getting a lift home via the milk truck doing its morning deliveries around 6 am. His approach to matches could be interesting, as he would sometimes arrive at the ground in what could only be described as bad shape — not a pretty sight, particularly considering that he was the captain; once or twice he never even ventured out to look at the wicket! At Bristol in our match against Gloucester, turning up completely hung over, he ordered his minder, Andy Withers, to get him two pork pies, one cup of black coffee and a large Alka Seltzer. He then lay on his back and snoozed until it was time for the toss, which he proceeded to win from a horizontal position, chose to bat and went back to sleep. What he didn't realise was that he had chosen to bat on the greenest result wicket you've ever seen. We lost two quick wickets for 11 before Nigel Popplewell and I managed to graft out a long, painstaking but effective partnership of 132, which saw us into safer waters. We both departed before tea just as Ian was waking from his slumber. He then proceeded to march out to the wicket and smash the most brilliant 69 in under an hour, sending the ball to all parts of the ground in a sensational hitting display. We were all out half an hour before stumps with the excellent score of 390. Ian then ran in, bowling rather rapidly, captured a wicket and couldn't wait to get into his first pint of the evening.

Naturally, the next morning Ian grabbed the headlines with his whirlwind innings even though I had battled long and hard in tough circumstances for a 108. Naturally, too, he turned up for the second day plastered, and again ordered the secret potion of pork pies, coffee and that Alka Seltzer. Unfortunately for Ian, though, this time he had to go out and field instead of sleeping it off as he had the day before. The wicket had retained its greenness and moisture, and was therefore ideal for someone of Ian's ability. So what did he do? He threw the ball to me! I was rather bemused by this style of leadership and shared my difference of opinion with the captain, but to no avail. So I decided to play Ian's game and proceeded to dish up the biggest load of rubbish ever bowled in Somerset colours; I bowled five overs and conceded 36 easy runs.

It worked beautifully. Ian grabbed the ball off me and told me to get off to slip while he marked out his run-up. Over the next two sessions he spearheaded our attack so inspirationally that we wrapped up the match just before stumps, winning by an innings and 83 runs. Ian bowled almost throughout the day in both innings, capturing seven for 123 off 45 overs, and rewarded himself with a free third day, so that he could have a really big session on the turps. He told me later, when he decided to have a chat over a pint about my bowling performance, that his sole motivation for the day was to ensure that he could visit a few mates back in Taunton and not have to drive back to Bristol the next day. The amazing thing was that his form never seemed to suffer and that he consistently produced match-winning performances. Ian, like Viv, had an impregnable belief in himself, setting him apart from most of his peers.

In my first weeks with Somerset the food poisoning I had suffered in Colombo continued to have a bad effect. The diarrhoea dragged on and my energy level was still low. I went for tests at the local hospital and saw specialists, but they couldn't tell me anything. So I just carried on.

Not surprisingly, my form suffered. I couldn't get a run, and I always seemed to be doing lots of bowling to make up for it. My spirits sunk as I wasn't meeting expectations. I was very lucky, though, to be surrounded by a superb bunch of team-mates. By and large it was an experienced side, with one or two youngsters like myself added to balance things up. Of those who had been around for a while I particularly enjoyed the company of Somerset's famous established local heroes, Brian Rose and Peter Denning.

Brian had handed over the captaincy to Botham and was enjoying playing purely as the classy batsman that he was. He had represented England on a number of occasions as a top-order batsman, scoring a couple of elegant test 50s. He was a gentle, kind person, someone who would listen and then encourage, calmly keeping things in perspective. Peter Denning was a different character, who called a spade a spade. He would walk past you in the dressing room or come up to you in the middle and say, 'Come on, Crowie, *fight!*' 'Dasher', as he was known, was a real street fighter, not pretty to watch but highly effective. He held the bat like an axe and literally cut everything that was bowled short enough. He got players going, encouraged them to compete and to make the most of their talent. He taught me to grind away day after day. '*Fight*, Crowie.'

Another duo of renown was the educated pair from Oxford, Peter Roebuck and Vic Marks. They had joined Somerset together, around the same year as Botham and Richards, and were very much a part of the successful reign of the 1970s and early 1980s. Peter was an opening batsman, technically correct, determined and prepared to bat long hours in support of the stroke-makers gracing the batting line-up. He was a quiet, introverted character, very intelligent, really interesting.

I didn't really get to know Pete at first, probably because we changed in opposite corners of the dressing room. But one day, playing Leicestershire at Taunton, we were set 340 to win in just over two sessions. At lunch we were two wickets down for nought as Pete and I resumed the innings. As he strode ahead of me to the middle he turned and muttered in my direction, 'Come on, let's show some bloody Somerset pride.' 'You bet!' I replied as I caught up with him. We put on 319 together, setting an all-time third-wicket record which took us to a wonderful win.

It was a sweet victory too, as during the first innings I had experienced the most heated confrontation of my life, with West Indian great Andy Roberts. He was moving through a very effective spell of fast-medium away-swing bowling to knock the top off our first innings. I had been in great form in the previous two matches so my confidence was high as I prepared to re-establish our innings. Roberts concentrated mainly on moving the ball away from me, looking for an edge. My judgement on off-stump was good, however, and I began to frustrate him by constantly leaving the ball until he bowled straighter, which gave me a chance to work for runs. Roberts shelved the away-swinger and instead slipped into top gear and used a different approach — body-line bowling. By lunch I had four large bruises on my upper body. Employing a lighter bat and a more offensive reply, I began to counter-attack his intimidatory bowling. At one point Roberts gave me two fast bouncers, which I avoided. Thinking he'd pitch the next one up, I took off down the pitch and smashed him high over his head into the stand. Peter Willey, fielding in the gully, said, 'Oh lad, you shouldn't have done that!'

The next two deliveries Roberts overstepped the line, wide of the crease, and let go the fastest deliveries I've ever faced. Fortunately Willey's remark gave me an insight into what was coming, so I had retreated well outside leg stump as he bowled, to watch the missiles fly by. I looked back at Roberts and saw the meanest, angriest eyes I'd encountered on a cricket field.

Overs later, Roberts cleaned up the tail to finish with seven for 74 and I walked off shaken and pale with 70 not out. It was one hell of a confrontation.

Peter Roebuck noted that I played better when I was a little angry! He was right. From that point we began to relate a lot more, and I enjoyed tapping into his vast knowledge of cricket and many other topics. Vic Marks was also great company, naturally warm and approachable, very shy and humble, but a truly committed and determined allrounder. He enjoyed success with England, mainly as a one-day bowler, and was invaluable for Somerset with both bat and ball. 'Skid' was a delightful man, one of those team-mates about whom you never had a bad thought.

After six weeks of struggling to find form and make an impression, and of living in Ian's flat, I decided I would move out. I told Ian I needed my own comfort, thanked him for his help and moved in with another friend, Nigel Felton. Ian was really disappointed, unable to understand why anyone wouldn't feel relaxed within his environment. But his lifestyle was simply too fast and furious for me, so I went looking for my own piece of mind. Ian's attitude towards me soured somewhat because he felt a lot of people thought I had left because of his supposed sex, drugs and rock 'n' roll behaviour. This was quite untrue. I just wanted to do my own thing and, apart from the pace of Ian's life, I saw nothing that raised my eyebrows. Ian also felt that my leaving started a campaign within the club to undermine him, and Viv Richards and Joel Garner, but I never noticed this. All I wanted was to start performing in my capacity as the overseas professional, and moving out of Ian's flat was part of that commitment to succeed.

It was a good move. Nigel Felton was fighting for his place in the First XI, so we both worked hard together on our respective games, sharing a lot of common interests. Suddenly, with a rush, my form came in during festival week in the beautiful, sleepy, romantic little town of Bath. The surroundings had a nice calming effect on me as I started to hit top gear. Within four weeks of changing abodes I had rattled up over 700 first-class runs, including four centuries in successive matches. I was away, and from there I never looked back.

I levelled off a bit early in August but managed to finish well as I attempted to be the first rookie ever to score 2000 first-class runs and take 50 wickets in the same season. I finished just short, notching up 1870 runs and 44 wickets, but it was a summer of wonderful experiences, especially that magical week in Bath where I rediscovered my belief in myself. The game against Leicestershire was a great education for me, as was the opportunity of opening the bowling in a number of games. I scored six centuries and eleven 50s during the summer and took just one five-wicket haul (five for 67) versus Leicestershire away. The club finished seventh in the championship and made the quarter-finals in both knockout one-day competitions.

Most important, though, were the friendships I made within the club and the marvellous support and rapport I had with the Somerset supporters and public. I absorbed and appreciated so much that I hoped I could one day go back again. In particular, I learned so much from Ian Botham on the field that I couldn't help but be influenced by his command over all aspects of the game. But the man who continued to have the biggest influence, as he looked down at me from his portrait on the club's dining room wall, was Vivian Richards. Even when he wasn't around I could feel his presence in the dressing room. It was as though he were reminding me that I was only keeping his seat warm until he returned. As he told Simone one day, with a glint in his eye, 'Ah, Richards and Crowe, yes, the man and the boy.' I couldn't help but agree, but I was prepared to take him on.

CHAPTER 8

Stoking the Fire

The BBC news came on. Somerset had sacked Viv Richards and Joel Garner. The cricketing world was absolutely stunned. Two of the world's best had been dumped for the relative newcomer from New Zealand. Martin Crowe to replace Richards and Garner? Don't be stupid. I couldn't believe it. It was Saturday, 23 August 1986, the third day of the third test at the Oval, when Somerset announced their decision. It took a while to realise that the world's number one batsman had been dropped for little old me. I had never believed they would do it.

I realised the responsibility when the outcry split the county and led to a bitter debate that raged throughout the winter months. Caught in the crossfire, I honestly didn't know what to think. Viv Richards was my idol, but I was also ambitious, single and eager to stake my claim to being regarded as the world's best batsman. This was my big chance. After the Oval test I returned home to New Zealand and began training hard for the coming domestic season and then the ultimate challenge: a test series against the West Indies with Viv as their captain and Joel leading the pace attack.

I was highly motivated for this confrontation, but to be completely prepared I needed to be very fit and technically ready to succeed against the best bowling attack in the world. So while I worked on my fitness, I also continued to fine tune my batting technique. Ever since my first test series against Australia in 1982, when I failed badly against their fast bowling, I knew I had a lot of work ahead of me to develop a technique that would stand up to the very best bowling. With my batting coach Harold Whitcombe, I began creating a back-foot defensive technique to help me bat for long periods against short-pitched bowling. We would work away for hour after hour in the Auckland Cricket Association indoor nets against the bowling machine, practising a back-foot defence over and over. Harold got me opening my hips so the ball could come onto the bat close to the body, with my head over the ball. My back foot needed to stay square to the crease, giving me a firm foundation to defend, no matter what the bounce. Then I would practise avoiding the bouncer by dropping my back knee to the ground; this allowed me to keep my head looking at the ball while I dropped under the bounce. If the ball failed to bounce enough I was still in position to sway in either direction because of the way I was holding my head. For two years Harold and I worked during pre-season time, trying to perfect a strong defence. By the time I had had two seasons at Central Districts on harder pitches and a season at Somerset, I was ready to begin applying the graft in the middle to the search for big scores.

As it turned out, the tour to the West Indies in 1985 was going to give me a very clear indication of how my defensive technique would stand up. After failing in the first test at Port of Spain because of over-complicating my footwork, I settled back into what I had learnt with Harold Whitcombe and concentrated on one simple technique.

The first thing that I had to overcome, facing these quicks, was the belief that I could not move into position quickly enough. Before that first test I didn't believe this and therefore moved my feet too much and suffered as a result. For the second test in Guyana I decided to keep still, open my hips and back myself to move into position once I'd seen the ball leave the bowler's hand. Once I'd got over some initial nerves and a bouncer from Michael Holding to the side of the head, I settled in for a big score. I batted and batted, working on that simple back-foot technique and growing in confidence as the innings progressed. I scored 188, batting for more than nine hours, and enjoyed some excellent partnerships as we chased the mammoth West Indies total of over 500.

The partnership I enjoyed the most was with my room-mate Ian Smith. Ian, with his penchant to cut anything short, was a master at upsetting the opposition quicks with his deft back-foot offence. Actually it got to a stage in our record partnership of 143 for the seventh wicket, that Malcolm Marshall went completely off his rocket and began yelling at Ian, 'Smith, Smith, I'm going to kill you at Barbados! Wait till I get you in the next test, Smith!' Ian was beside himself, totally and utterly petrified.

As soon as Ian walked out to bat in the Barbados test, Marshall went around the wicket and proceeded to try and hit him with short-pitched bowling. It didn't take long. A nasty bouncer reared up and struck Ian's left forearm as he protected his face. The sound of the blow gave the impression that his arm was broken, so he immediately left the field and was rushed to hospital. He sat in pain inside the waiting room while an

X-ray was organised. While he waited a little boy came up to Ian handed him an autograph book and said, 'Man, please sign'.

Ian flicked through the book looking for a clean page and, in doing so, noticed that a number of fine cricketers had already signed the book.

'Gee mate,' Ian said, 'you must go to the test matches a lot to get these autographs?'

'No man, I just come straight here to the hospital!'

That to me summed up what it was like playing in the West Indies. Three times I went for X-rays to see if a finger or a rib was broken! There was no question that having a good back defensive technique was crucial. Even though I struggled for the next two tests I still retained the confidence from batting at Georgetown to know I was on the right track.

What I needed next, though, was consistency so I could produce the big scores regularly. To achieve this I had to learn how to apply my mind and keep it focused for long periods in the middle, let alone match after match. This I learned from our coach on the 1985 Australian tour and one of our country's greatest batsmen, Glenn Turner. Glenn taught me to concentrate better, by turning off after each ball, conserving energy between balls and then switching onto the next ball. As a result I was staying fresh for each delivery, providing better focus when it came to watching the ball leave the bowler's hand. Before that I used to keep keyed up the whole time, which was energy-sapping, but on that Australian tour I began to feel fresh at the end of each day's play. I started that tour with 242 not out against South Australia and then followed with 188 again, in the first test at the Gabba. It was a marvellous technique, one I never forgot.

It was at this point, too, that I began reading about sports psychology and mental techniques such as visualisation and goal setting. In Australia I came across a brilliant book written by Rudi Webster called *Winning Ways*, which talked about improving one's performance by applying mental skills. It quoted many great sportspeople, including top cricketers such as Greg Chappell, and helped me to understand the essential need to train the mind as well as the body. A couple of years later, when I started my own sports consultancy company, I named it Winning Ways; it is still in operation today.

So by the time I began leading Central Districts for the first time in the Shell Trophy at the start of this important 1986–87 season, I had become highly pumped up to perform in every match I played. I felt I had acquired the right mental approach, the necessary batting technique, and was fit and raring to go as never before. I was ready to start stoking the fire in my attempt to be the world's best.

Our season started at Christmas with a one-day competition of which I played only the last match, owing to a fielding injury, but I was ready early in January to lead the side for the first of eight games to decide the Shell Trophy. Our talented team was of similar age to me, around 25, when we took on Northern Districts in the first game and won by 15 runs. I had promised positive cricket and results to the team, so we started as we meant to go on. Then, from the second match, came a run of scores I had never even dreamed about. After 160 versus Wellington, I proceeded to break the record for runs in the trophy and for a New Zealand cricket season, before the tests had even begun. Six centuries with five scores over 150 meant I was able to lead the side from the front and take us to a huge win in the Shell Trophy competition. Every ball I faced was a challenge, a force to be confronted. I batted with such concentration and determination that only one bowler, Stephen Boock, had the measure of me and kept me guessing.

I felt unstoppable and, by the time of our last game, against Canterbury, I believed that we would score whatever we needed to win. Canterbury, led by John Wright, batted first and amassed over 400, batting, I felt, too long into the second morning. We had no choice but to get past the follow-on mark, about 260, and declare. I scored 144 before holing out and now we waited for the final run chase to determine whether we or Otago would become champions. Canterbury batted on and on, however, eventually setting us the difficult target of 380 in 75 overs. It seemed a tough call, but at Pukekura Park anything was possible. With the championship at stake we really had no choice but to go all out and hope for the best.

Fortunately, Wrighty applied no pressure on us and soon Paddy and I were into one of our huge partnerships, batting at three and four respectively. Even with Richard Hadlee operating for much of the time, nothing could stop us. We cruised to a five-wicket win with five overs to spare and, in so doing, won the Shell Trophy. I had added 151 to my first innings century, producing the best first-class match of my career to that point. The tests were only two weeks away and I knew that, with a

little rest and some solid practice, I would be ready to take on the West
Indies.

It was six months since the Somerset committee's decision, but only
weeks since a large meeting of members was held to discuss the large
split throughout the county. I had seen Joel Garner on TV, standing at
the back of the room listening intently to the whole drama. I liked Joel
and felt for him at this time. He and Viv had given Somerset 10 great
years and they were being dumped unceremoniously. Would there be
any animosity towards me from Viv and Joel? I had been badly mis-
quoted by an English tabloid in reference to their sacking. I figured the
animosity would only be revealed in the weeks ahead, especially when
we met for the first test in Wellington. In a strange way I was looking
forward to it.

We were in trouble immediately after the Windies won the toss and sent
us in. We were still persevering with Ken Rutherford as an opener and
he suffered the same fate as he had in his first tests in the Caribbean,
hardly troubling the scorers. I was in early but didn't last long as Court-
ney Walsh angled one into my pad to have me lbw for three. We struggled to 228 all out on the first day and then, in reply, Haynes and
Greenidge wiped off 150 of it on their own. They had a lead of 117
when we batted again, with over two days to save the test.

Once more we were two for zip when I joined John Wright, who
was playing well after a dogged 75 in the first innings. I was feeling positive after the initial nerves had gone, getting in behind the ball comfortably and picking off the odd loose delivery. After being 28 not out at
stumps, I went to 119 the next day by wearing down the Windies pacemen first and then pouncing on their weariness later. Viv bowled many
overs into a stiff northerly wind, so I was able to gauge his feelings at
close range. He was quite calm, concentrating on the job, trying to
break through our partnership. But as frustration set in I noticed his
glare becoming more obvious and finally he outlasted me when I hit a
tired shot to short mid-wicket. By this time the game was saved and I
had proved that my mental and technical skills worked well.

Having scored seven centuries already that season, I felt in total
control. My game plan of playing each ball on its merits, wearing down
the bowlers, showing patience, then jumping on the loose ball, was
working. There was no reason to change tack. We travelled to the sec-

ond test at Auckland and found a really green grassy strip on which to tackle the big boys. The feeling was that our strength lay with Hadlee and Chatfield and that, to win, we required a pitch on which they could excel. We needed to win the toss, sure enough, but in an inexplicably bad fielding display we let the West Indies off eight times as they mounted 418.

Gordon Greenidge played one of the three best test knocks I have ever seen first hand, the others being Greg Chappell's 176 at Christchurch in 1982 and brother Jeff's 112 at Kingston in 1985. Gordon's technique during this innings was outstanding and the power he showed in playing his shots was awesome. He made 213 on a pitch that seamed sideways.

We followed on after failing to come to terms with the pitch, but this time we had to survive only a day and a session as rain had interfered with play. This period was still difficult as the pitch continued to seam around, as it had on the first day, and we lost early wickets until Jeff and I settled through to stumps.

The final day was testing and it wasn't until John Bracewell joined me with five down that we could counter-attack in some way to ease the constant pressure from their bowlers. Then they tired and I was able to capitalise by racing from 60 to my eighth century of the season in the hour before tea. After tea I batted another hour for only four runs more as the Windies took the second new ball and came in for the kill. We failed to hold out and Haynes and Greenidge had four overs to score the necessary 10 runs to win.

Again I had batted with control and paced myself well but this time it wasn't enough. Viv Richards approached me after the game and congratulated me on my form, which I appreciated, but he stepped up the intensity of our battle when we met for the third and final test.

Between tests Richard Hadlee, in his newspaper column, had criticised our lack of professionalism in the second test, something I agreed with, particularly our lateness in arriving at morning warm-ups. But coming out and speaking through the media instead of discussing it among the team members left captain Jerry Coney and coach Glenn Turner visibly angry. Jerry cornered Richard and demanded an apology from him for going public. Richard, hurt and isolated just before the third test, felt inclined to pull out.

So, with this huge falling out between our captain and the great fast bowler, the test against the Windies at Christchurch proved a fascinating match in which to be involved. There was to be no communication between them for the entire match, which made for an interesting first day. We decided to bowl on a fresh, fast pitch and immediately 'Paddles' got Desmond Haynes. But we sensed that he was still upset and struggling for his rhythm. After five overs he just walked to gully and stood there. John Wright had to come in from mid-on to tell Jerry that Richard was not bowling until he felt ready again. A stunned Jerry quickly had to summon Martin Snedden from fine leg to bowl without any warning. Meanwhile Ewen Chatfield had ripped the heart from the Windies by taking out Greenidge, Gomes and Richards in quick succession. Richard came back and, in a hostile spell, took the last five wickets to finish with six for 50. Ironically, Jerry took three super catches off his bowling yet not once did they acknowledge each other.

With the Windies bowled out for exactly 100 we set about building a lead that would help us to square the series. Two early wickets fell again and then Jeff and I amassed our highest test partnership together with 156, before I departed for an aggressive 83. I had taken the attack to the Windies this time and now Viv was breathing down my neck. He'd had enough and after a few well-chosen words along the same lines as he gave to Fred Goodall, the umpire in the second test, I came back with some of my own, but did my talking with the bat. I was stunned by Viv's vicious abuse of Fred Goodall. It was extraordinary. Despite my enormous respect for Viv, I couldn't condone or forgive him for that kind of psychological warfare. As it was the first time I'd seen him react to this extent, I assumed he was under the strain after the previous year's sacking and the ensuing controversy.

I got carried away with overattacking and played a diabolical shot to a straight ball from Marshall. Expecting it to be short, I stepped inside ready to hook and ended up leaving my middle stump exposed to a wild swish. It was about the first pre-determined shot I had played in 20 innings and over 1600 runs. I missed out on three 100s in consecutive tests and in scoring New Zealand's 100th test century.

Nevertheless we reached a good total and had a sizeable lead. The Windies started out badly and never recovered. We required only 33 to win when the Windies came out smoking for the last time, bowling so quickly and angrily that in no time our score read 30 for five. John Bracewell and I scrambled some singles and, with one run to win, I ran through and grabbed a stump, leaping past Viv and yelling, 'You bloody beauty.' His face was furious.

We'd squared the series and I had finally played three consecutive tests in a mature and commanding manner. I felt I was on the way up. It had been an incredible 11 matches through the season and I had set a record that would take some matching. Although a little concerned about my reception, I was ready to go to Somerset with my head high.

First, though, we had to go to Sri Lanka, a tour hastily arranged by the New Zealand Cricket Council, considering the increasing friction resulting from the conflict with the Tamils. I was disappointed that the tour would interfere with my fresh start at Somerset and even more upset when John Wright was allowed to withdraw and take up his position at Derby as that county's beneficiary. This, however, enabled Jeff to take up the captaincy, while I was entrusted with the vice-captaincy. I looked forward to this, particularly with Jeff in charge as he was tactically excellent and highly respected by his team-mates. We took a new coach, Gren Alabaster, and together knew that, although the tour would be difficult, we would cope.

This tour was to last only 10 days, a three-day match at Galle and then the first test in Colombo. The test was a slow boring draw with time for only one and a half innings; Sri Lanka, scoring 397 for nine, declared and then New Zealand just passed that total, with both Richard Hadlee and Jeff on unbeaten centuries. On the way back from the ground the bus took a different route to drop Phil Horne off at the physio before we arrived at the hotel.

There we learned that, five minutes before, a huge bomb had exploded only 400 yards away, killing 150 people at a bus shelter on the very road that we normally travelled every day of the test. It was 21 April 1987 and everyone was in shock. The Tamils had laid the bomb and the devastation was all too evident. Civil unrest was at fever pitch. A curfew was imposed on the city of Colombo and no one moved for two days. Next day a busload of 30 civilians was stopped on the road to Kandy, the venue for the second test, and butchered.

The team held a meeting and it was clear immediately that everyone wanted to go home. The locals set up another meeting with security experts and the high commissioners from the embassies; they couldn't guarantee our safety and even the Sri Lankan players felt there was danger in remaining. Later that night we took a secret ballot. I sensed that some had changed their minds out of sympathy for the local board, but when the tally was announced locked at seven all I couldn't believe it. I knew Jeff was keen to stay because this was his first tour as captain and he'd just scored a ton in the test. I felt for him, but the situation was too serious to mess around.

Sanity prevailed and a 10–7 vote was finally counted, which meant we could at last pack our bags. I had very little time to spare before Somerset's season opened at Taunton against Lancashire, so I checked out and boarded the next plane for Heathrow.

Viv Richards off the field, a warm and loyal person, seen here with baby daughter and other aspiring youngsters.

Richard Hadlee, the finest cricket professional I've known. Richard is a very serious operator and a good friend.

Ian Botham: enormous belief, huge spirit, the ultimate competitor.

Greg Chappell, my batting role model. I prefer to watch Greg batting more than anyone else.
Classical and elegant, he was a tough opponent.

PHOTOSPORT

Above: Grant Fox made himself into the greatest first five-eighth and goalkicker ever. A lifelong friend and a great New Zealander.

Right: Michael Jordan. More than any other athlete I've seen, this man excites and entertains. His attitude inspired me to aim to become the best I could be.

PHOTOSPORT/ALLSPORT

Above: Parachuting from 10,000 feet over the Remarkables at Queenstown. Never again! After this I received a stern letter from NZ Cricket for putting my career at risk.

Left: Walking the Milford Track.

CHAPTER 9

A Summer Set to Conquer

I really loved Taunton and the surrounding Somerset villages. The people were so kind, so supportive and really knowledgeable about cricket. They knew when you were trying, giving your best, and when you weren't. You could hear them murmur and whisper if things weren't right, and cheer and encourage when life was good. I couldn't thank the club enough for their faith in me, and for the opportunity to learn so much about the top level. The period in 1984 had been critical in my development and now in 1987 I had the chance to repay their faith.

In 1985 and 1986 I had come back to Somerset for short periods to play in the Second XI and continue the work and camaraderie I had struck up with the other guys of my age, the young pros. We had set up our own club, the Young Nags, who met often at the Nag's Head pub, for fines meetings and chats about becoming better cricketers. It was all good fun and I got the impression that many people at Somerset saw something different happening to the youngsters now that they had someone to relate to. In other words, these players saw me struggle early on and then transform my fortunes through dedication and hard work. It was an example they could follow more easily than the genius of a Richards or a Botham. Also, I was their age, wanting to do the things they did.

In 1986, before our New Zealand tour of England, I spent a few weeks at Taunton getting in some practice. During that short time I sensed some problems arising, especially as a result of the performances of the First XI. They had come last in the championship in 1985 and were near bottom again. Still I was grateful just to be part of such a great club, and felt loyal to them at all times. I hoped to play for Somerset officially again, but as Viv and Joel obviously had many years left, I sensed it might only be every four years or so when the Windies were touring. Then, while on tour, I received a call from Doug Insole, the Essex chairman.

He told me that Allan Border was not returning to Essex — would I consider a two-year contract? This was a fantastic offer, but I needed to be released as a registered player from Somerset. I would never get another opportunity to play two years of county cricket now, while I badly wanted it, even though my loyalties were with Somerset. They had two of the best players in the world and so, rightly, I wouldn't have the chance to play for them. I spoke to Michael Hill, who was disappointed but understood that I had to say yes to Essex. So it was all on — I would play for Essex in 1987 and 1988.

There was, however, more going on at Somerset during that 1986 season than met the eye, and it wasn't until I read Peter Roebuck's 1991 history of the Somerset County Cricket Club, *From Sammy to Jimmy*, that I realised the problems that had existed. In Chapter 34 of this book, 'Through Fire', I read Roebuck's account of the events leading up to the sacking of Viv Richards and Joel Garner:

Once more Somerset was distracted by scandal. Nor was that all. Other newspapers were threatening to print further and grimmer allegations, and desisted from doing so only because saturation point had been reached on Botham stories. Distracted by these affairs, spirits slowly declined in Somerset's cricket team ... things fell apart within the team. Men screamed their anger and frustration in the dressing room and sometimes in the opposition room too ... the divisions were great, especially between playing staff and administration. Men felt they were due much and owed little. For far too long heads had been buried in the sand, as if the nastiness would go away, as if it were some minor fault rather than a terrible divide ... Somerset's cricket team had become a patch and woe betide those who would invade it.

Much of this was hidden from outsiders [me, for instance], hidden within a dressing room which leaked only to umpires and opponents, who could scarcely miss the arguments ... Ever more Richards and Botham were living in a world apart, scarcely hiding their contempt for officials and some colleagues.

In Botham's case the reasons for his conduct were apparent, for he was seemingly led a merry dance by his own fantasies ... Richards was a more complicated case, for here was a man who had been, and could be again, an inspiration and a joy. And yet now to be near him was to be near a volcano, and those who had not risen with him were dismayed.

> Upon reflection it is plain that two things were gnawing away at Richards' temper. First he was unused to playing in a poor team, unused to finding himself surrounded by such mediocrity ... Richards lost all faith in Somerset; he suspected plots to remove him. And yet no such notions existed, until the end of July anyhow ... Maybe Somerset needed to start afresh. Membership began tumbling, for it was a view widely held. A showdown was inevitable. And then suddenly Somerset were presented with a dilemma. Towards the end of July Essex asked for permission to approach Martin Crowe ...

Had I known of the extreme difficulties and bad feeling existing within the walls of the Somerset CCC at the time, it is entirely fair to say that I might have signed for Essex instead. Basically I was walking into a minefield, if not a war zone. I thought I was re-entering a club that needed a fresh start, for sure, but with the brief of bringing on the youngsters and supporting the senior team management. And I never actually believed they would give me the job until that fateful August Saturday morning.

Roebuck recalled the events leading up to the final announcement:

> At once an impromptu meeting was called. Was Somerset prepared to release Crowe? Somerset had hoped that Crowe might return with Richards and Garner in 1987 in preparation for their absences in 1988. Plainly this was not feasible for it had gone beyond compromise.
>
> Michael Hill, club chairman since 1983, was the leading advocate of change ... No doubt the revelations about Botham's private life, and the failure of Viv Richards to take a random drug test in Bristol in July, had hardened his opinions. From this meeting onward it was plain that Somerset was intent on crying enough. Their duty, they decided, lay with the present and the future, not the past, however glorious.

Still, that, of course, was only one side of the story, and the man to provide the defence for Viv and Joel was obviously Ian Botham. In his own autobiography, published in 1994, Ian set out his version: 'To my mind, the man who deserved all the blame for what happened was the captain,

Peter Roebuck ... There had been trouble and unrest simmering away beneath the surface ... and it was, looking back, just a matter of time before events came to a head. The catalyst for the impending developments was Martin Crowe, who had been with us in 1985 when he played a few second team games in which he showed a huge amount of promise, enough to make Essex interested ...'

A few second team games — thanks very much, Ian! He actually thought that I had taken my offer from Essex back to Somerset and set up a kind of a Dutch auction. In fact, I had told Michael Hill that I was going to Essex, instead of waiting for the two West Indians either to tour England or retire. It wasn't until I was speaking to club secretary Tony Brown that I sensed there was going to be a problem about getting released to sign for Essex. Tony had indicated that Somerset weren't letting me go just yet and that he wanted to see both me and my manager, Darryl Sambell. Tony spoke with Darryl in New Zealand and it was then that I realised that there was something brewing. Darryl flew to England within the week and met up with me before the Lords test. He told me that there was a move afoot by the Somerset committee to try and get me signed up for the next three years. I couldn't believe it. During the rest day of the test, I spoke with Tony Brown again and he confirmed that a deal was in place if the committee could be influenced once and for all.

My first reaction was to want to speak to Ian Botham and see how he felt about all this. I was quickly shut up as that would only have let the cat out of the bag, such was the secrecy involved. I didn't think they would go through with it and so convinced myself that I would be playing for Essex next season; I even told Graham Gooch, the Essex captain that I was looking forward to playing with him next year. Darryl kept assuring me that the deal was on but I heard nothing from anyone at Somerset for the next month or so, until that BBC announcement in late August. The chairman, Brian Langsford, did ring me that morning to confirm their decision but I was so dumbstruck I couldn't remember anything else he said.

Next thing I knew, Ian Botham had announced he was leaving as well. This made life very uncomfortable since I was playing against Ian in a test match at the Oval. Once the test was drawn I did the usual thing of wandering down to the England dressing room to thank them for the game and the series, and then confronted Ian. He could barely look at me and his reluctant acceptance of a handshake left me under no illusions that he was as bitter towards me as anyone. When I saw his face, I realised properly for the first time how dramatic this whole situation had become, bearing in mind that I had never before thought it would happen. Unfortunately Ian and I never communicated much again until 1992 when Simmy and I invited him, Allan Lamb and Robin Smith for dinner one evening and put the whole episode behind us.

The 'Somerset mutiny' became a bizarre and strange event in a usually sleepy county. My feeling, in the end, was that Somerset had become a powerful side through the services of the big three — Botham, Richards and Garner — but hadn't put a future development plan in place and got those players to encourage it, to lead the team from their era to the next. Ian Botham and Viv Richards needed to be encouraged to lead the county into the future, or move on. Lack of communication caused a lack of forward planning. So, finally, once things became worse, Peter Roebuck probably took the bull by the horns and called for changes, and anyone who called for changes involving three such great players would have been branded and criticised as Peter was. The Somerset committee should have taken the winter to discuss the situation with everyone involved, and I should have gone to Essex. If they had determined that their future lay with a new captain or overseas player, they should have given Viv and Joel the best possible send-off, then searched for the most suitable replacements. No one person should ever be asked to carry the kind of responsibility or influence that was required of me. I felt I could definitely help to improve the existing situation, but this shouldn't have been at such a high cost to so many people. In the final analysis, what Somerset had was a huge personality clash between Peter Roebuck and Ian Botham.

It seemed incredible that, with all the drama surrounding my place in the Somerset team, I wasn't even going to be able to start on time owing to the Sri Lankan tour, and then a bomb explosion allowed me to arrive just 16 hours before the opening match of the season. It was, without question, a scary time. The atmosphere at the club was tense, with everyone showing obvious anxiety. Would the protesters who had argued so strongly against the sacking of Viv and Joel turn up at the game to cause further problems?

For the start of the new season we had recruited some new players from other counties. Fast bowler Neil Mallender came from Northants and another quick, Adrian Jones, from Sussex. Graham Rose was an all-rounder from Middlesex seconds, Jon Hardy a batsman from Hampshire, and Neil Burns the Essex seconds wicketkeeper. Burns, in fact, signed only once it was confirmed that I was the overseas player. He wanted to join a stable, hard-working staff and have a chance to succeed in a new environment. That was a compliment to me, so I looked forward to working with this conscientious newcomer. Ian Botham had walked out, as he had threatened, and was now lining up for Worcester.

The first game, against Lancashire, started quietly enough. No protesters, no problems. I settled into my innings of 65, knowing that the pressure and the spotlight were mainly on me. The match went reasonably well for the team but we gambled on the last-day declaration, eager for a result, and Lancashire cruised to a comfortable win. Still, we were underway and free to get on with the job of posting some improved performances with this new-look, relatively inexperienced team. Only Roebuck, Vic Marks, Colin Dredge and I were regulars from 1984. Many had fallen by the wayside during those last two turbulent years, and so now we had the brief to rebuild for the future. The scars would take time to heal but the boys were keen, even if we looked, on paper, to be understrength, especially in batting.

I felt a huge responsibility to lead the way, but, having been in top form since New Year, I began setting some additional goals to push myself to the limit. First, I decided I wanted to be the first batsman to 1000 runs at county level that season and that meant taking every opportunity to score. Second, I wanted to be top of the first-class averages at season's end. Third, I aimed to be, some day, the best batsman in the world, to replace Viv Richards as the number one.

The second match at Taunton was against the feared Surrey side, with the lethal West Indian fast bowler Sylvester Clarke. Sly had a reputation for hitting batsman, usually on the head, so it was nice to join the select group early on when he smacked me flush on the side of the helmet, spraying paint flakes everywhere. I saw him off, however, and scored a solid 148 to set up the season.

I felt good, really sharp. My fitness was at its peak and I was confident of achieving my goals. The team, on the other hand, weren't quite firing, as you'd perhaps expect, and we just had to remain patient. We qualified comfortably for the quarter-finals of the Benson & Hedges

Cup, a 55-overs competition, by defeating everyone with some excellent one-day displays. In fact, our one-day cricket looked really promising, for we could rely on key players to win us games, as opposed to being less confident all round in the three-day matches for the English county championship.

In the quarter-final against Northants at home, acting captain Vic Marks threw me the ball, desperate for 11 tight overs. I had bowled a little during the season but certainly not as much as in 1984. We bowled first and went all out to knock Northants over. I bowled my 11 on the trot, dismissing Allan Lamb for nought, so by the break I was spent and feeling very sore. It seemed I'd done something to my back as it stiffened so quickly and so painfully that I could hardly walk, let alone play a big innings. I survived three balls and headed straight for the physio's table. We lost narrowly by 25 runs and I reflected that, had I not bowled so much, I could have been in a better position to win us this crucial game.

Next day Brian Rose, our coach, drove me to Abergavenny in Wales where I had a scan on my lower back. It revealed a stress fracture of the fifth lumbar, a condition known as spondilythesis. The surgeon told me I shouldn't bowl again, and that I should begin a rehabilitation programme to build up all the surrounding muscle groups, otherwise I'd face ongoing problems. It wasn't the news I wanted to hear. I'd always had some back pain but this was major, so I advised Somerset of the news and officially retired from bowling. Well, fast-medium bowling anyway!

I worked on the back programme daily and concerned myself totally with my goals. The team soon plummeted to an all-time low with an embarrassing first-round loss in the NatWest Trophy to minor county Buckinghamshire at High Wycombe. The pitch was a disgrace, designed to reduce our effectiveness; it was so low and slow that their keeper stood up to every bowler. This loss hurt the team's confidence severely and I noticed the heads drop quickly with a resigned 'someone else will do the job' expression. This was the type of problem which had manifested itself in previous years; by late July we had developed that wretched hang-dog look.

I tried to plough on to the 1000, so that when we arrived at Edgbaston I required 173. I realised it had to be this match as Wilf Slack of Middlesex was only 90 away. It was a greenish pitch but with good bounce, so once in and playing well, I could aim high, really high. Early on I had to combat the extra pace of Allan Donald, the South African. So I dug in, determined to make this opportunity the one to take me past 1000. With newcomer Nick Pringle I laid the foundations for the big assault. I worked really hard up until the century. After my 100 the runs really flowed and then finally a push for two and I was there. It was immensely satisfying. By scoring 206 not out, I'd pushed out Wilf Slack by just one day. One down, two to go!

I attempted to play every innings as if it were my last, to work on that average — and on goal number two. At one stage I had a few days off and drove to London and Lords where I had three days' practice with Don Wilson and the MCC young professional staff. I had been lucky enough to win a scholarship to Lords in 1981 after finishing at Auckland Grammar and enjoyed the most wonderful cricketing education for six months. Every day of the week we would arrive at Lords in jacket and tie and then practise and learn all there was to know about becoming a cricket professional. My stay in London, though, had begun in very inauspicious circumstances. On only my second night after arriving Western Australian Tim Zoehrer, later to represent his country, had invited me to go to the West End of London and see the night life. I had been encouraged to try a Carlsberg Special Brew, only to discover later that it was the most potent beer you could drink. I ended up in very bad shape! I had watched what I drank from that moment on, especially as I was now under the watchful eye of our coach, Don Wilson.

I had found him hard but very helpful, as he taught the virtues of discipline and a professional attitude. He had pushed me all the time and, as a good left-arm spinner who had played for Yorkshire and England, he had taught me how to play spin bowling. He had also introduced me to numerous famous players of the past and I would spend hours picking their brains. Lords in 1981 had been so special, with a 100 on debut there and many enjoyable outings for the MCC as well. I would go back there, and to Don, at every opportunity, to pay my respects and, on this occasion, to get in some valuable practice before going on to Trent Bridge to face Notts, with Hadlee and co.

A week before I had been selected for the MCC bicentenary team to play the Rest of the World at Lords in a five-day test, starting in two weeks' time. This was a great honour and a huge thrill, the perfect stage on which, perhaps, to achieve my third goal of becoming the world's best batsman.

I trained for three days, staying with Don, and then travelled to Notts for our important county clash. For many years I had come up against Richard Hadlee in Shell Trophy matches and now in county cricket. I had faced him on about eight occasions and he had never dismissed me in a first-class match. At New Plymouth the previous year I had taken twin centuries off him, as well as 175 not out at Lancaster Park on a doctored green pitch, so I felt the urge to deny him one of his 1000 first-class wickets. This, too, became a goal and I reminded him of it constantly. I think after a while it began to annoy him.

So this match at Trent Bridge was his best chance to take my scalp as the pitch there was always green and fast. I had a challenge to survive the great man on a juicy strip and my plan was always to get well forward, cover movement, try not to play at anything outside the off-stump and force him to bowl short, maybe bouncers, or full on middle where I could work him away for runs. He always fancied getting top-order batsmen to nick the ball and therefore never bowled many short.

In this match the plan began to work immediately. On a few occasions he would pitch middle and off and move away, beating me all ends up. There he claimed a moral victory but he still couldn't claim my wicket. Paddles would bowl only in six-over spells and I would see him off, looking for singles to rotate the strike, sensing what he would bowl next. Having watched him bowl thousands of deliveries as I stood at slip for New Zealand, I felt I had the right idea.

Again I kept frustrating him and when I began to pick off the bowlers at the other end I could feel another big score in my grasp. Perhaps four 100s in four innings against R.J. Hadlee? Clive Rice, Paddles' best mate, was bowling now and began to whack the ball into the pitch, extracting more bounce and venom than Hadlee. All of a sudden a ball kicked off a length and struck very hard on my right thumb. The pain was excruciating and I jumped in agony. The thumb looked bent and I feared it was broken, but I decided to continue, hoping it was just a bruise, and went for every shot. I raced to 93 before holing out and then raced to hospital for the dreaded news. It was broken.

I was out of action now for four weeks and would miss the bicentenary match at Lords. I was devastated. I cursed that my form and my best chance to prove something were gone. Ironically, Clive Rice, the very man who broke my thumb, was to replace me at Lords in the MCC side. I watched the game from the Lords balcony as acting 13th man and found it a sobering experience to see the world's best compete on that hallowed ground. I decided to spend a lot of my time picking the brains of one of the all-time greats, South African Graeme Pollock. I was interested to hear him talk about how to play spin bowling. He felt that the best way was to keep as still as possible until you had figured out what length the ball would pitch. More often, he said, you could dominate the spinner off the back foot. He rarely looked to go down the wicket unless the ball was lobbed up, thereby making it easy to skip down the pitch and hit the ball on the full or half volley. He also never used his pads, preferring to lean on the ball with his bat only. I took this valuable information with me and began practising this new technique.

I actually left after three days of the match, unable to take any more, and returned to Crowcombe, my little village just out of Taunton. That big goal would just have to wait. All I could now do was train and get fitter, while the thumb mended, keeping in mind that the 1987 World Cup would start soon in Asia. I managed to come back for a handful of matches at the end of the season, keeping in mind goal number two, and I achieved it by finishing on top of the English first-class averages for 1987 with 1627 runs at 67.79.

The last month of cricket for Somerset was a struggle. Too many players relied on me or other key performers to carry the side, and failed to deliver themselves. This was going to be a long, patient haul for Peter Roebuck, the club captain, and the rest of the staff. We had to start changing attitudes and encouraging players to become more responsible and self-sufficient. The opportunities were there but too often lost through mediocrity.

I became frustrated as I couldn't see Somerset being good enough to push for trophies, at least not in the next year or two. We were always going to be a middle of the table team, unlike Essex, who cleaned up one or two titles every year. I was mentally drained from the season's exploits, particularly from pursuing my own goals but also from having to carry the load. I clearly began to change in character, becoming very intolerant and unable to respect my colleagues, not unlike the Vivian Richards Roebuck had described. In fact, Peter commented to me late in the season that, once too often, he had seen a darkness in my eyes.

I was simply annoyed with coming second and showed my temper far too often. Batting recently at four for New Zealand had also had an effect on me, especially since the retirement of Jeremy Coney, Bruce Edgar, John Reid and Geoff Howarth. The more I succeeded, the more expectation and pressure I felt, and the more intolerant I became towards some of my batting partners. It wasn't the right attitude, as I began distancing myself more from players around me. So, by the end of the county season, I asked myself whether I had been right to accept Somerset's offer, instead of going to Essex. My loyalty and appreciation of Somerset had kept me with the club, but it was going to be hard, playing cricket all year round while both the county and New Zealand teams were rebuilding. The trouble was, it wasn't going to get any easier.

CHAPTER 10

Climbing to 4000 Feet — and Crashing

After a break of three weeks I felt fresh and recharged as I joined John Wright on board for the flight from England to India. We were heading off to the fourth World Cup to be held in India and Pakistan. The next month would certainly be a change from the first-class and test-match cricket I had mostly played during the year. Now it would be only one-day cricket.

For most of my career I had never really enjoyed one-day cricket, especially the English version of 40-over games on Sundays as opposed to the longer games. I had found them so restricting and limiting on the individual, putting incredible pressure on key players to do most of the work in a short time span. New Zealand had started to play well in the 1980s but in recent years we had faded. I felt that if our team were to produce winning cricket we had to understand that everyone must play their specialist role well. In other words, you couldn't afford to have your opening batsmen taking an eternity over their runs since this could ultimately lose you the match. Too often, in the past, I had found myself continually having to repair the run rate after the openers had cut it to pieces.

In this World Cup I had visions of seeing my brother Jeff, as captain, holding aloft the cup as David Kirk had done in the inaugural Rugby World Cup only months before. John Wright came back as vice-captain but Richard Hadlee failed to make the trip, badly affecting our chances. Playing in India for the preliminaries was never easy, but we had a good draw facing Australia, who were not fancied, India and Zimbabwe. India would be tough at home but I felt we could beat the other two sides.

So, after defeating Zimbabwe by just three runs in a classic one-day match, we went to Indore for our first battle with the Aussies. Chasing 199 in an innings reduced to 30 overs because of rain, we responded brilliantly through John Wright and Ken Rutherford, and then I began to play out of my skin as well, as we got to within seven runs with one over remaining, and four wickets left.

At this point I was in charge, choosing my shots and executing them successfully. I needed to play one more big shot and we would be home, on our way towards a semi-final berth. Steve Waugh was to bowl the last over and I looked around at my options. I could go over square leg, long-on or extra cover to hit a boundary, or I could aim to accumulate twos and even a single and give Ian Smith a whack. Seven runs, six balls. The game should be ours.

Stupidly, as Steve ran in to bowl, I got caught in two minds — was it long-on or extra cover? As the ball was delivered, I choked on which option to take, sending the ball up over cover and into the incoming sweeper's hands. What had I done? The Aussies were jubilant as the game appeared even. As I neared the dressing room I realised that I had committed the very act that all top sportsmen fear the most — choking. I turned and looked out to see Ian's poles go everywhere. Then Martin Snedden got run out and we had lost by four runs. I put my head in my hands and sulked.

After that I berated myself for missing such a big chance and never really played well for the rest of the tournament. I watched the Australians cruise through to the semis, into the final, and then walk away as world champions. I couldn't forget my mistake but tried to tell myself that it was an experience, that my turn would come again and that next time I would triumph.

Returning from India in late October didn't give me much time to rest and then build up for the next tour, across the Tasman to meet the Aussies once again. We'd had the measure of them recently in test cricket, and it seemed clear they were beginning to rebuild under Allan Border. We had defeated them convincingly in 1985, two tests to one, but that should have been three wins to us. We had a great side in 1985. Led by Jerry Coney, and spearheaded by Richard Hadlee, it was full of experience and skill. The Brisbane test, the first of that series, was the perfect example of how well we could play. Of course it will, and should, go down in history as Hadlee's match, for he took 15 superb wickets during the game. But many others chipped in as well, John Reid and I scoring excellent centuries, backed up by Jeff Crowe, Coney and Hadlee himself in the batting, and great support from Chatfield and Snedden with the ball. Allied to that was our slick fielding and overall professionalism. We had given Australia their worst nightmare — an innings defeat by the Kiwis!

We lost in Sydney owing to some very negative instructions by Glenn Turner about how to play against the turning ball. We were told not to sweep, yet when John Bracewell arrived at the last minute from New Zealand to take his place in the side, having missed the team meeting, he proceeded to sweep everything in sight and keep us in the game. We resurrected our approach by Perth, the third test venue, and secured the series with a comfortable win. Richard Hadlee dominated throughout, taking a staggering 33 wickets, while I managed 309 runs to make up for my dismal first series against the 'Okkers'.

Watching Richard bowl during that series was out of this world; I've never seen a bowler sustain such amazing rhythm over a series. He must have felt in the greatest form of his life as, day in, day out, he went through the Australian line-up like a knife through butter. I really liked Paddles, finding him to be a genuine, warm, highly motivated New Zealander. He never had a nasty word to say about anyone, demanding only high standards and total professionalism.

In this regard he was a great role model for someone like me. I often would ask him about ways to find extra motivation and he was always approachable. During the home series against Pakistan in 1984–85 I had gone to him in desperate need of some direction. After spending a good hour with him, I was ready to inscribe his nickname, PADDLES, on my bat before the second test began, because he had turned it into an inspirational acronym: show Pride, Application, Desire, Determination, (be one of the) Lads, and Enjoy myself in order to achieve Success. I repeated the word before every ball, which helped me to focus, and I was delighted with the result: scoring 84, 57 and 84 in the last two tests to help us to consecutive victories. Once I knew that Richard was only too willing to help if you asked him, I understood and totally respected who he was, and what he was trying to achieve. I regard Richard as a lasting friend, who has always helped and supported me during my career.

Then we had the return visit from the Australians during the summer of 1986. This was the series where I played what was arguably my most courageous innings. It was at Lancaster Park on a pacy pitch when, in reply to Australia's healthy first innings, we were soon in trouble and facing a follow-on. Jerry Coney began a partnership with me until I attempted a hook off Bruce Reid, the 2 metre plus (6 foot 10) left-armer, and copped a nasty blow to the jaw. I was rushed to hospital and required 10 stitches to my open wound. I dozed in the dressing room for an hour or so until Wrighty and Glenn Turner encouraged me to go back out at the fall of the next wicket and face the music. I was still a little groggy but decided I had nothing to lose. So, resuming on 51 not out, I threw the bat at everything and raced to my fourth test century. It was an emotional ovation I received from the Canterbury crowd when I returned, last out, for 137.

What stuck in my mind, though, was the ruthless attitude of the Australians. As soon as I faced up upon my return to the crease, Allan Border called in Bruce Reid to give me a full barrage of bouncers straightaway. It was pretty heavy artillery, too, but I managed to see it out, regaining my confidence at the same time. But it showed how uncompromising the Aussies were, in particular that tough little man, Allan Border. He was a real fighter. He carried that Australian side for a number of years, following Kim Hughes' resignation in 1984. 'AB' never sought the job, but in time showed what a fine leader he could be. By winning the World Cup he proved that, with patience and the right approach, anything was possible. Playing against a fired-up Australian team was about as hard as it could get.

Before the 1987 Australian tour I began thinking about the goals I would set. It occurred to me, with help from Dad, that I required only another 670 runs during the tour to become the seventh batsman in cricket history to score 4000 runs in a calendar year. I had five matches, including three tests, to reach it. It was the goal I needed.

In the short time available I began training really hard. I lifted my fitness a good notch and couldn't wait to hit the crease, first at the WACA against Western Australia. We batted first and scored well. Dipak Patel joined me and together we put on 164 before I holed to the second new ball. I was annoyed with myself as 119 wasn't quite enough, after having got in for a big score. Still, it was a good start.

Next stop Adelaide. When Jeff had returned from five years in South Australia he told me how much I would love the Adelaide Oval. I adored the place and having scored 242 not out last tour I wanted another century or two now. I also enjoyed playing against the local hero, David Hookes, that brilliant left-hander who turned the 1977

111

Centenary Test by hitting Tony Grieg for five successive fours in one over. Jeff and David were good mates from Jeff's Sheffield Shield days. Hookesy was a fine leader too and I always enjoyed his theories on playing the game. As a true Aussie, he felt that the camaraderie created in the dressing room after play was vital. So, when he said once in public that the problem with Australian cricket was that there weren't enough beers drunk after play each day, somehow the message was missed. He used to crack me up when I'd come in after batting and he'd say, 'That's the worst 242 not out I've ever seen!' Once when he batted in a state match and his partner Wayne Phillips hit four fours in a row, he walked down the wicket at over's end and said simply, 'Anyone can hit fours', then proceeded to hit the next four balls for six!

It was great to be back at the beautiful oval, especially after a minor hiccup following my innings in Perth when, suffering from tonsillitis, I missed the up-country game at Renmark. I staggered out of bed for the South Australian encounter and immediately felt better on the hard pitch under a bright sun. Before long I was away. After reaching 100 I cut loose and shot up to 144, before falling to a good boundary catch off Tim May. The target was reducing all the time and I knew, after scoring 56 not out in the second innings, that the test series would have to provide the rest of my goal. The tests were to be played in Brisbane, Adelaide and Melbourne, and I needed 351 to reach the magical 4000.

Because of the usual state of the pitch at the Gabba, you always hope to win the toss so that you can send in the opposition. We lost it and straightaway Ken Rutherford was gone. Andrew Jones, in only his second test match, played in the most ungainly, unorthodox manner you can imagine and was ridiculed by the commentators. After an hour he lost his leg stump and I strode out to get into my work.

At that stage I was very nervous, scarcely able to watch at times, so I was relieved when Craig McDermott overpitched and I was off the mark with a three through mid-off. I worked hard, relying on a straight defence, but we were losing wickets and I sensed that I must take control. Merv Hughes thundered in and I smashed a rank long hop through point only to see Steve Waugh jump, from nowhere, and pull in the catch. Ouch! Gone for 67 and we collapsed to 186 all out.

The game disappeared as Australia amassed 305, with David Boon playing superbly for 142. In our second turn we again started badly, although Andrew produced more unusual technique for 45, setting the commentators off again. I was unable to keep down a full-blooded hook off Hughes and the innings went into decline. Only Dipak offered any resistance, although we made enough to set Australia 94 to win, which they achieved for the loss of only one wicket. With only 92 runs to my name in the match, I brought out my new favourite saying about the three certainties in life: death, taxes and a 100 at Adelaide!

Before the second test it was so good to get back to those magnificent Adelaide Oval practice pitches, the best in the world. I started to feel in control again after some solid workouts and a quick calculation showed that I needed 261 with a possible four knocks left.

Jeff won the toss and decided to bat. This time Ken was dropped from the side and Jeff himself opened. I worried about that as he had no form and was getting depressed. He was out third ball and I really felt for him. Again the nerves were racing and I was up and down like a yo-yo, watching one minute, dozing the next.

Andrew began to play positively while John Wright held firm as ever. In fact Andrew started batting furiously, obviously stung by the criticism at Brisbane. He unleashed some huge shots through the off-side so by lunch I had relaxed as our score mounted toward the 100 mark for only Jeff's wicket. Halfway through the middle session Wrighty got a dodgy bat-pad decision so I was on my way down the steps and out into the hot, blazing sun.

Australia had selected two spinners for this match, both from Adelaide, so I had no problem about what to expect. I was so pumped up that I raced to 30 in 20 minutes, clean hitting Peter Sleep over the Vic Richardson gates. Tea arrived and our score looked good. I couldn't wait for tea to end, so that Andrew and I could continue to dominate the tiring bowlers on a pitch which was flattening out by the minute.

Andrew reached his maiden test century and I was proud of him for showing up his critics. He was pretty rapt himself. In the last half-hour we negotiated the second new ball and at the end of the day were able to sit back and enjoy a long, cold beer, knowing we were in control of this match. We were 268 for two, with Jones on 128 and I was sitting on 88. I need 12 more to overtake Congdon and Turner as New Zealand's most prolific test century-maker. I slept well and decided to be ultra-positive in the morning.

Tim May opened up and I hit him for four, one bounce, second ball. At short leg David Boon gave a deep groan as the ball sailed past him to the fence. He seemed to sense that I was extra keen that morning. Next May over, third of the day, I lofted him again over long-on down to where Dad was sitting, for my eighth ton. As always it's a special moment to look up and see those three figures on the famous old scoreboard. Then I went berserk. Knowing we had to score quickly to make the most of the match, I started climbing into Craig McDermott and Peter Sleep. By drinks we had added 60 odd and I was sitting on 137, contemplating the really big 100 to take me to the 4000 with a game in hand. Too soon! First ball after drinks I tried my hand once too often and skyed a ball from Sleep out to Hughes at long-off.

I was disappointed as I had wasted the opportunity to take charge of both my team and personal concerns. I sat tight-lipped as the rest of our innings plodded on laboriously. The game dwindled to a boring draw as Allan Border achieved what I should have, stroking his way to a majestic 205. We had most of the last day to bat out but I couldn't get myself motivated and succumbed to Sleep for eight.

Afterwards I realised how stupid I had been to waste such an innings — 40 or 50 runs would have gone a long way toward the target. I left the game frustrated and annoyed that I had still to score 116 at Melbourne. It was hard, but at least I knew I couldn't rest on my laurels and I was dead keen to play at the MCG. I had always dreamed of scoring 200 there after seeing Viv Richards do just that in 1984. The Boxing Day test was always a great event and I wanted to make my mark alongside the great Viv, presumptuous though that might seem.

Once in Melbourne, I spent a lot of time at the ground, walking around it, roaming the museum, sitting on the roller at one end of the pitch, looking down the famous strip, visualising the Aussie bowlers, going over the game plan, the runs to be scored. I even wandered down one afternoon after practice and found some Asians mucking around so I asked them to bowl to me in the nets on the main oval. I loved the MCG, I felt that I belonged there, in the vastness of that stadium and on that perfectly grassed outfield. I was hoping like hell that Jeff would win the toss so I could bat in front of the Boxing Day crowd. I also hoped the sun would shine.

We enjoyed Christmas with the whole family at a large banquet at the Hilton and I started to believe that Melbourne would be the stage where I could score my first double and smash the 4000 barrier. Waking on Boxing Day to sun blazing through the windows, I jumped out of bed to prepare for the big event. Down at the ground I watched Jeff toss and then inform Border that we would bat.

No nerves this time, just dead keen to get out there. Phil Horne went in with Wright to open but he, too, could not get a real start in the number one slot. Wrighty, however, was on his way, solid in defence and more positive in attack. He had always been a good shot-maker but at test time had often batted more conservatively to give New Zealand the solidity it needed. In many ways he was the gutsiest player I had played with, prepared to dig deep and bat for days. He never gave his wicket away and without him New Zealand would have crumbled much more frequently, exposing the middle order to the new ball. If Hadlee won games for New Zealand, Wright saved them and gave Hadlee the platform from which to strike. I hoped he would go on and reward himself with a 100 at the MCG.

Andrew Jones was out in controversial circumstances. He glanced a ball fine down the leg-side and the Aussie keeper Greg Dyer dived to his left but came up with the ball in his right hand. He claimed the catch but obviously didn't realise that 10 cameras around the ground could show the ball rolling along the ground before he scooped it up. Dyer was crucified in the media and only a year later disappeared from first-class cricket. The contrast was all the more marked because, in Adelaide, Jeff had disclaimed a catch off Border (when on 66) although all at the ground, including the commentators, thought it was out.

I strode out, head high, blinking at the sun, swinging my bat once or twice. There were 60,000 people at the MCG on this momentous Boxing Day and I felt honoured to be able to walk out and play in front of them. The ball found the middle of my bat. I started to find the gaps, then the boundary. At one stage I stroked Steve Waugh three times through the covers for four. This was paradise. A hard, fast pitch to bat on, a huge crowd, a very significant goal.

Wrighty moved onto 99 and I backed up that little bit further. But instead of attacking he doubted himself and edged a half-hearted push off McDermott to fall one short. I felt for him. He deserved his ton, but he would continue to stumble later in his career when close to 100. At Lords in 1990, on the other hallowed turf, he would fall for 98, and then in 1992, at Christchurch, for 99 again.

I carried on, thriving in the atmosphere, and when McDermott took the new ball I had great pleasure in leaning on an on-drive and see-ing it whizz across the out-field like a billiard ball. At stumps I looked up at the scoreboard to see 'M.D. Crowe 76 not out'. I felt on top of the world. I slept well that night, playing the innings over in my mind, really enjoying the experience.

Next morning the sky was overcast and a breeze had come up. I went to the ground early to have a good net and noticed the ball swinging a lot. Then I padded up and walked out with John Bracewell to resume the innings. Mike Whitney was bowling fast, running in quite aggressively while I struggled to move my feet. McDermott continued from the previous night and immediately bent the ball towards the slips. As he pitched one ball on middle and leg, I aimed to drive it through mid-on but the ball swung late and away, off the back of the bat for a smart catch at third slip.

'Hold on a minute, I haven't begun yet,' I thought. Then I realised that I hadn't looked like beginning. My whole approach had been nar-row — thinking about the sun, the crowd, the large score — and now the conditions had changed. Had I adjusted? No chance. 'What an idiot,' I said, as I climbed out of my dry kit. 'Adjust, you fool! Nothing comes on a plate, you have to earn it. Respect the situation, graft a little, wear them down.' I didn't even get to one 100, let alone attempt two. I cursed myself. I was throwing away a royal opportunity to join six others, six greats, and still I needed 34.

The whole match seesawed with neither side gaining much of an advantage, so by the time I went out to bat on the fourth day we had to build up a lead for something to bowl to. We also had to score quickly enough to give ourselves time to bowl Australia out and level the series. We had contained them well in the first innings and in particular had continued the horror run of the Aussie number three, Dean Jones. At the start of the series we had read that Dean thought Hadlee was just another bowler whom he would hit around the park. This was just the sort of ammunition we wanted to put under Paddles' nose to get him completely fired up. Next I approached Dean, whom I knew well from schoolboy tournaments, and suggested that we have a simple little $10 bet for the one who scored the most runs in each innings of each test, $10 a time. As you would expect, Dean was dead keen, his confidence nicely pricked. I informed the media and Hadlee of the bet and away we went.

Hadlee got Dean for two at Brisbane, nought at Adelaide and, in the first innings at the MCG, he was out for four. So when Richard had him caught behind for the latest failure he suggested to Dean as he departed that perhaps he should take on Ewen Chatfield for $10 in the second innings! Deano, the legend, was finished as far as this series was concerned. In future encounters Dean refused to talk to me or anyone else because he said he had been ordered by Bobby Simpson, the Australian coach, not to acknowledge the Kiwis again. As a result, Dean was seen to be the most arrogant Okker you could meet. I was disappointed with this attitude as I liked him, especially his willingness to have a side bet. This, however, was an attitude that the whole Australian side adopted in the late 1980s and early 1990s. Dean didn't loosen up until 1993 when his place wasn't so secure and he had seemingly fallen out with Simpson. I thought him one the finest players I'd seen, especially, of course, as a one-day batsman. Hence our huge desire to see the back of him on this 1987 tour.

With the match evenly poised and a final chance to reach 4000, I desperately needed to get in, build a foundation and ready myself for a possible onslaught later. So I played myself in gradually, picking up the odd loose ball from Peter Sleep and accumulating singles as the score mounted steadily. Then Sleep started to lose his length and I fastened onto a short ball, pulling it hard and straight to the fence. Then another, and suddenly I was on 33 and facing Whitney. As he charged in, I moved across to the off-stump ready to get in line, and there it was, a flick off the hip and the magical 4000th run to fine leg.

No one at the ground, and there weren't many on this working day, knew the significance of the occasion. The Aussie players had no idea, but then over the loudspeaker came the announcement and I was relieved and delighted.

The moment passed quickly and soon I was settling into another long knock. As the day wore on I shifted into a higher gear so by the time the tea interval was close I was thinking of a 100 by the break. Border changed his bowlers and Tony Dodemaide, on his test debut, came back for a spell. I felt I could really get after him as he was the right pace to stand and deliver — but I forgot to have a look at him first.

His first delivery called for a big shot over the off-side when I realised the ball wasn't quite there so I stabbed at it to knock it dead. It caught the outside edge and flew between the keeper and first slip where

Border, who had just moved there, flung out his left hand and the ball stuck. Smack. Out for 79. Again I'd wasted another ton. I was beside myself as I walked off. To blow two innings like that was plain stupidity and I couldn't forgive myself. Suddenly I'd forgotten the significance of reaching the 4000.

At stumps I sulked in a corner and refused to speak with the media. That was stupid as well. I relented to do a press conference when I was back at the hotel, explaining how disappointed I was at missing two chances of tons and not realising my dream of a double century. 'How could you aim to score 200 in any given match?' asked a reporter. It wasn't a bad question. How indeed could one aim to score 200 at a certain ground in a certain match? When I felt like it? It wasn't sound goal setting and I'd merely depressed myself by not achieving such a tough and unrealistic goal.

The goal can be achieved, but through a specific process of completing lots of small goals step by step first, as I had done with achieving the magical 4000. I was thrilled with reaching this unique milestone, deeply satisfied that I had climbed to that figure through perseverance and belief. I felt I had accomplished something special, something no other New Zealander had done. Later I was to be disappointed not even to be nominated for New Zealand sportsperson of the year for my 1987 work.

So the year was over for me personally, but not before we had embarked on one of the great fightbacks in cricket history. We captured six wickets, mostly to Hadlee, in the last session to reduce Australia to nine down, well short of the target of 247. The last pair, Craig McDermott and Michael Whitney, had 30 balls to survive the test, 18 of them from Hadlee. Paddles had bowled 13 overs in a row and was exhausted, but he was hungry for Whitney as he needed only one more wicket to go past Ian Botham's world record of 373 for the greatest number of test wickets. He had planned to achieve this milestone at his home ground of Lancaster Park in a few months' time. In other words, he hadn't expected to take so many wickets in the Aussie series, especially in this final session when we seemed to be in dire straits. So Mike Whitney stood between Richard and the world record. The number 11 kept lunging forward, keeping the great man out, while at the other end Danny bowled to McDermott. He finally trapped him plumb lbw, back leg, middle stump, the test all over, the series squared, the trans-Tasman trophy ours. Except for the umpire, who blandly declared McDermott not out! We were devastated. 'Not out? You're bloody joking!' Whitney saw out the last over from Hadlee and Australia had won the series.

The World Series began after New Year's Day 1988, with our engagement with Australia and Sri Lanka. I was feeling flat following the heights of reaching 4000, struggling for motivation, lacking a new goal. The prospect of another month of one-day cricket didn't inspire me and I began to wane mentally while my body started to ache. I had been on the road for over a year now, non-stop, had played in over 65 tests, one-day and first-class matches and scored more than 5000 runs at this level. I was burnt out. I needed a break but there was no chance of this as we still faced a series at home with England before the next county season. My energy levels seemed to drop and the problems with my back, which had begun in Somerset in 1984, were returning.

I was also becoming despondent and concerned about Jeff, who couldn't buy a run. He became consumed with wanting to know what the papers (especially those in New Zealand) were saying about his form. He was trapped in his own self-doubt and I feared that there was nothing anyone could do. Sooner or later it would have to reach the stage where he was questioning his own form. I tried to talk him through it, to get him to start again, to forget the media and play the way he did back in 1984–85. As captain, he had everyone else to look after and would never put himself first. I felt he made a big mistake not taking the number three spot, his favourite position; in giving it to Andrew Jones he launched his career but killed his own. He was totally unselfish. The players admired and loved him and, as captain, he had everyone's respect. We just wanted him to perform, for himself.

The bottom line was that he could really play. When he was positive and focused, he was a hell of a batsman to watch. His years in Adelaide had turned him into a dynamic back-foot player, superb at the hook or pull. Since his return he had, at times, struggled with his footwork on our lower New Zealand pitches and became susceptible to lbw dismissals. But on overseas tours, such as Pakistan, the Windies and Sri Lanka, he was more often than not our most consistent and versatile performer. I'll never forget his batting in the Caribbean, where he took on Marshall, Garner and Holding in the most courageous and daring manner. His 112 at Sabina Park, Jamaica was one of the best knocks I've seen. He had the ability, but he didn't always have the belief in himself.

Confidence ebbed and flowed with Jeff and a lot of that had to do with indecision about where he would bat. Within 10 weeks he lost his job, sacked by the selectors after the second test against England at home, and he never played much for New Zealand after that.

All this was hurting me, and during the England series it was clear that I was struggling. I had an average series and then returned to Somerset. This time, though, I didn't want to be there. I was exhausted. I lacked motivation and energy and the responsibility of carrying the team again was too much. When I arrived I went down with a horrible virus and took two weeks to get out of bed. I battled my way back, and in my last two matches managed two 100s to lead us to successive wins, before jumping into a car in Manchester after the game at 7 pm. When I reached Southampton at 12.30 am I couldn't move. My back had gone. It had seized up completely and the pain was hideous. I pulled out of the match, let Steve Waugh take my place and went back to the club doctor. We decided I should return to New Zealand to try and fix the problem.

By June I was home and by late July Dr Gerald Gibb had diagnosed that I'd had salmonella poisoning living in my system for the four years since I had fallen sick in Colombo in 1984. He confirmed that this had affected my back, that chronic stiffness would occur after exercise, that I would perspire incredibly and be unable to control it, would suffer from diarrhoea, and worst of all, would lack energy. I couldn't believe it.

For years GPs had thrown antibiotics at me to clear up the latest illness or virus. Now I knew. Salmonella. I pulled out of cricket of any kind for six months and went on a course of homeopathic treatment to draw the toxin out of my system. It took eight months. My biological score, the strength of the toxin, was extremely high. From a scale of 0–20 I registered between 17 and 18. While I was on the medicine a dramatic change came over me. The colour of my skin turned to pale grey, I lost 7 kilograms as I began to train religiously and some idiots in Auckland started a rumour that I had Aids. The knocking machine was now in full swing.

In October I pulled out of the tour to India for obvious reasons and, in doing so, missed my first matches for New Zealand through injury or illness. I concentrated on gaining peak fitness under the brilliant guidance of Jim Blair, already renowned for his success with the All Blacks and America's Cup squad. I went to the gym every day, and also did a lot of yoga to help fix my back problem. It wasn't long before I was in great shape. The salmonella was disappearing and all my energy returned.

I spent a lot of my time training with rising tennis star Brett Steven. He was also undergoing rehabilitation for an elbow injury and so we knuckled down together to re-establish our careers. One evening we both decided to go to a motivational lecture being given by a Canadian called John Kehoe, in the country introducing his mind power discoveries and putting people through a course called 'Thought Dynamics', a four-week workshop on how the mind works. Brett and I went along to listen to his introduction evening, and found him inspirational. We both enrolled in the course and, by the end of it, I had found a new motivation, and a new set of brilliant techniques to help me in my quest once again to be the best I could be.

I learned to observe my thoughts on a regular basis, and came to see how negatively I thought at times. I was taught to remove the negatives that drift in and out of the mind and, by using affirmations and visualisation, to replace those with new and creative thoughts. Using these techniques helped me to picture clearly in my mind the sort of goals I wished to achieve — such as scoring a double century in a test match. I began visualising the sort of scenarios I would encounter in trying to reach this milestone, the feelings I would go through, the effort required, the concentration I would need, the opposition that I would face. I wrote down all the thoughts and feelings I associated with scoring a double century and assembled them in a huge cluster on a big page. Then I would visualise this cluster of thoughts in a real-life situation of a test match. I visualised often, but only when I was relaxed.

My first games back were captaining Central Districts in the Shell Series, and it was here that I took some time to find form. The time off had taken its toll and I felt a bit rusty and out of tune. I knew, though, that I had to be patient and work progressively towards winning a place in the New Zealand side to take on Pakistan.

After a few failures I finally hit the big score I needed, just a week away from test selection. Not surprisingly, it came at Pukekura Park. This marvellous ground in New Plymouth had brought me nothing but joy every time I walked onto it. From the time I scored my maiden 100 there and in the same day gained New Zealand selection, I'd relished the journey to Taranaki — the marvellous amphitheatre setting, with the

121

crowd looking down on you from grass banks and the glorious natural forest in the background. With the region's good weather they always produced a fine cricket pitch. Every time I marched onto Pukekura Park my confidence rose, I felt in command, as though I were on my own personal stage. And my batting was helped by the huge white sightscreens, the fast out-field and the usually excellent light. In eight first-class matches on the park during my career I managed seven centuries and a 97. So, with the test only a week away, it was a relief to score 141 off Wellington and assure my return to the national team.

Unfortunately the Pakistan tests became the most uneventful series I could recall. The first test was washed out, and the remaining two were played on the flattest, most lifeless pitches that had almost a Karachi look about them. Javed Miandad and Shoaib scored freely, with big centuries in both matches. Meanwhile I began concentrating on feeling comfortable playing in a test match again. By the end of the first day back I had played well to be 89 not out. The next day I continued, visualising the big innings, working towards 200. Alas, I stuttered on 174, the ball coming so slowly off the sluggish pitch that I mistimed a hook and was caught off the back of the bat at first slip. I had tried to pick up the pace after reaching the 100 but it was a difficult wicket on which to play shots, so I stuck to my plan of focusing and simply playing, to see how far I could go. I nearly made it. The techniques I had learnt had really helped me to get back into the mode of performing well at test level. By the end of the series, though, I felt that, owing to the horribly slow pitches, I couldn't free up and let go. Instead I just accumulated runs in a calculated, machine-like way. I was keen now to rediscover my aggressive instincts.

I decided to go to England again during our 1989 winter to play in a series of exhibition matches, involving international players. My intention was to re-establish my flair, to re-ignite the natural instincts. The plan worked well. The exhibitions were the perfect place to let go and enjoy the freedom of instinctive shot-making. It was fun.

I came home to join the New Zealand team on a brief tour to Australia involving just one test, in Perth. Immediately I reached the middle I found some anxieties returning, especially the fear of getting out in case it exposed our batting line-up. Man, it was frustrating; I couldn't let go in the big games. Our cricket had fallen into a 'we-must-not-lose' style, and we found ourselves always batting out for draws. The Perth test was of course the 'Greatbatch match'. The big fellow batted for near-ly 15 hours in the test and 11 hours in the second innings to score 146 not out and save the match. It was extraordinarily defiant batting.

What was so amazing was that Paddy had come into the side at number three in place of the injured Andrew Jones. He didn't have a lot of form, and on the bouncy Perth wicket it was felt that his front-foot play wouldn't help him. But he proved, ball after ball, that courage can make up for a limited technique. By the second innings he was showing superb back-foot defence and had no problem avoiding the short ball, while counter-attacking with exquisite driving when the Aussies pitched up. Paddy inspired all those around him; Jeff, Chris Cairns and Martin Snedden were playing above themselves. It was a performance that totally captured the nation. I watched in awe. Through this display, Paddy was picking me up too.

Heading back to our domestic season I pleaded with myself to free up. For Central Districts I enjoyed some thrilling moments, including 242 versus Otago in under a day at Pukekura Park. We then took on India and it was in this series that John Wright also broke loose and played the best cricket of his career. His captaincy began to flow like his shots, and in 1990 New Zealand enjoyed a golden summer, beating India and Australia. Wrighty was absolutely outstanding. I played the innings I was looking for, a fast 113 against India at Eden Park in our second turn at bat, to prove, finally, that I was back where I wanted.

I continued to go for my shots when we arrived in England for 'the big tour'. I felt a million dollars as I began chalking up a few quick 50s, but the tour turned out to be a real disaster. We had come to the crossroads as a team, with many players talking of retirement. The first was Richard Hadlee. He had secured the world record, gone past 400 wick-ets and was creating a benchmark that should remain unchallenged for a long time. But he was nearing 40 and felt that his body was telling him his time was nearly up. He decided that the England tour would be the perfect swansong. A test at Trent Bridge, his Nottinghamshire home, and one more at Lords, would see New Zealand's greatest cricketer go out on top.

Ever since I had joined the team in 1982 Paddles had been in peak form, dominating world cricket. I watched in awe as the great man went about his business, his preparation, his planning and goal setting, his mental training, his masterly execution. He was a big hero to me. He could bat, he could catch and, man, he could bowl. He had cricketing genius. To be knighted while still playing was something no other cricketer had achieved, and was testimony to his standing all around the world. He deserved it. Fancy having 'Sir' up on the board next to your name as you walked out to bat!

The team, on the other hand, became disjointed during the tour. Others were also going to announce their retirements. John Bracewell aimed to do the double, 1000 runs and 100 wickets, and call it a day purely because he never wanted to play if I became captain. Earlier in the year I had written him a letter *after* he had said in his *Sunday News* column that if New Zealand was to be captained by Martin Crowe, then God help us, or words to that effect. I told him that I was sick of his attitude towards Richard Hadlee and me, which arose from envy of our ability to get the best out of ourselves, and be rewarded for it. If he didn't like my leadership, then he knew what to do — it was no skin off my nose. The fact is, if he had wanted to play, he would have been a certainty for selection.

Then, unbelievably, John showed the letter to most of the Auckland team, in order to gain personal support, I suppose, while also attempting to show me in a negative light. Apparently John used the letter to help motivate the Auckland side when they played against me. Instead of sending him a personal letter, I should have just pinned it up on the Auckland dressing room door. Coach Bob Cunis got us both together before the India series was due to start, to try and sort things out, but there was no chance.

Martin Snedden had decided to spend more time with his family and he had a law practice to go back to, so he retired also. Ironically, he went almost straight onto the New Zealand Cricket Board, which was a welcome appointment as he proved to be instrumental in ensuring that the players' needs were listened to. Sadly, Jeff, too, had come to the end, unable to reach the heights of the mid-1980s.

Then came the bombshell. John Wright and Andrew Jones announced that they did not want to tour Pakistan later that year. Six players, all vastly experienced, seasoned performers, gone. The tour lacked conviction; the unity and steel a team needs to succeed, had gone. We finished the series badly and lost to a team we should have beaten.

One of the few positives to come out of the tour was the emergence of 19-year-old Adam Parore, a young wicketkeeper who had become a protégé of the master, Ian Smith. It was felt that, within three years, Adam would assume Ian's mantle and serve New Zealand for a long time. I spent hours with Adam in the nets working on his batting technique which, at this point, was not too good. By the end of the tour we were known as 'Batman and Robin', but no prizes for guessing who was who!

I was pleased to see Adam learn so fast that I predicted he would become a more than useful batsman at the top level. I thought, in fact, that he would turn out to be a better batsman than a keeper, if not a full-time top-order player. He certainly proved later in 1994–95 that he could be an outstanding number three if he chose to. His keeping, on the other hand, was also classy, but he seemed to make too many fundamental mistakes to be as great as Ian Smith was. I felt he stood too far back and sometimes caused problems for his first slip when half-going for balls just wide of him. I discovered this in the match at Chelmsford when he half stuck out a hand from an under-edge that flew very fast between him and me, and deflected the ball straight between my eyes. I raced to hospital to receive six stitches and one hell of a headache. But, beside that hiccup, I really admired his attitude and ambition.

Another incident, though, which stuck in my mind, showed the sort of confidence Adam possessed — and to which many people didn't warm. This was when he borrowed Sir Richard Hadlee's car at the end of the tour. After spending a superb week watching the British Open at St Andrew's, a group of us, including Adam and Paddy, drove towards Newcastle to catch a flight for a week's fun in Paris. Adam was driving the great man's sponsored car to the airport about 7 am to get his flight, which was an hour before ours. So by 8 am the rest of the group were driving through some farm lanes when we saw Richard's car in a crumpled heap down a ditch on the side of the road. The car was a write-off. We stopped and checked the scene but there was no sign of Adam — only, lying all over the back seat, the cricket cases we would need for a few festival games after Paris. So we contacted a few people to inform them of the accident, and assumed that Adam had continued on to Paris. Arriving in the city we noticed Adam nicely situated in a side street cafe, feet up, sipping on a quiet beer. 'Adam,' I said, 'have you seen the mess you left in Newcastle?' 'Yeah,' he replied, 'I thought I'd tidy it up when I got back!'

I had played poorly overall on the tour. My desire to attack and free up left me batting only a couple of hours at the most in a county innings, which was bad preparation for the tests. The county games had become sponsored and big money was available for results. It cost me ultimately. I scored a fast 59 in the first test but failed thereafter. With this tour dying on its feet, I began to think of the Pakistan tour, setting new goals. And I was to be the next New Zealand captain.

Part Three
The Captaincy

CHAPTER 11

Mission Impossible

> I think a leader is someone who has a certain vision, almost an ability to look ahead or to anticipate what's coming. But along the way you have to stand up for what you believe and hold onto your convictions.
> — MICHAEL JORDAN

Ian Smith made a magnificent gesture I will never forget. As a senior member of the team, he had every reason to feel that he was a strong candidate for the captaincy — basically, it was either him or me — but during the tour to England, Ian pushed my name forward to lead the team. He informed the selectors that he thought I was the right man to do the job, with him as vice-captain, but that I would need alongside me a coach who would complement and support the sort of style I displayed. Ian knew that my main weakness was my man management skills and that the team would require someone to care for the players' day-to-day personal and emotional needs. He saw my strengths as being those of a tactician, a planner and a player who could single-mindedly lead from the front.

Because we had lost so many experienced players, it would be vital to appoint a management team who could cover every possible area a New Zealand side would need. New Zealand Cricket began interviewing a number of candidates for the coaching position, but it seemed a mere formality, once the job description was defined, that Otago coach Warren (Wally) Lees would be the man.

I had initially questioned the need for a coach at all, but that was more a reaction to the performance of the last coach on the England tour. Ian was quick to point out that we would need someone like Warren Lees to complete our management team and give us that strong variety of skills and personality we must have to execute our task well — in other words, to cover for what we couldn't do.

Wally had established a fine reputation for leading a seemingly weak Otago side to many successes as a player, a captain and a coach. He had that ability to mould a bunch of triers into winners. He knew people

John Wright, a wonderful team mate who gave 110 percent to his batting, motivated those around him and served his country with great honour.

Jeff Crowe. On his day, he delighted crowds with his silky strokeplay and sometimes daring aggression. A true team man, and a great support to me.

The world record partnership of 467 with Andrew Jones, set during the 1991 series against Sri Lanka, still stands. Here Andrew and I walk out onto the Basin Reserve after tea on the final day, requiring just one run to beat the record.

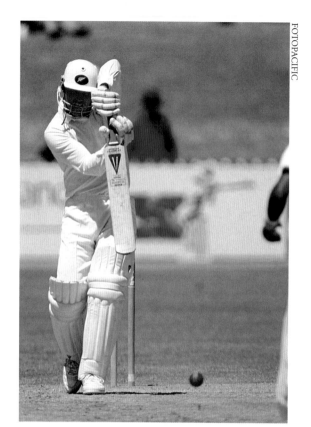

Showing a straight bat, whether in attack or defence, has been crucial in my quest to make big scores. I played this shot often during my 10-hour innings of 299.

Celebrations afterwards wouldn't be complete without loved ones there to share it.
Left to right: Simone, me, Andrew, his wife Amanda and daughter Madeleine.

Above: Simone and I walk down the aisle on 19 April 1991, Baradene College chapel, Auckland.

Left: Celebrating with sister Debbie and niece Sherry.

Contesting the Italian cricket team spaghetti-eating competition in Cortina, Italy, 1992. Great food, great wine, great guys, bad cricket. I'm in good form, third from the left. Actually, Italian cricket has improved out of sight since then.

Together with Simone on the Amalfi coast in 1993, sailing the Mediterranean on Don and Maureen Robertson's yacht, *Miro*. I wrote most of my book during this trip — I've even got my writing glasses on.

and he cared for them deeply, and had experienced enough heartache himself to understand the feelings of those who might struggle. He was perfect for me and Ian, and so we joined together and began planning for the future. The latter was mainly my area: finding a long-term vision, setting goals accordingly and planing the execution of the mission ahead.

At the top of the list of goals was to play in the 1992 World Cup, reaching the semi-finals, and then, we hoped, winning the cup. We also aimed, by the end of the tournament, to be the best fielding side on show. From there the list worked back through the 18 months, highlighting the kind of success we needed and the process for achieving it. We worked on creating new ideas for our training sessions, placing the priority on fielding skills. We set new standards for fitness and conditioning through the thoughts and ideas of Jim Blair and embarked on raising the whole level of physical preparation.

We held our first camp in October 1990, before leaving for Pakistan, staying in the barracks at the Devonport Naval Base for four days. We laid out the plans for all the players to see, the long-term goals, the aims for the coming tour. We spent a superb few days creating an atmosphere where the players could speak their mind and thoughts, sometimes emotionally, in an endeavour to build the trust that would become so valuable.

I took time out to meet the media in both Wellington and Auckland, highlighting our intentions and keeping them well informed. They were casual gatherings sponsored by Dominion Breweries, in which much relaxed banter was evident. I felt I had a good relationship with the media at this time and looked forward to continuing the rapport. The very next day in Wellington, however, I read in the *Dominion*, a statement that Peter Bidwell, the sports editor, had credited to me regarding the proposed use of independent umpires in the forthcoming series in Pakistan. As though quoting me, he wrote: 'Any umpire, whether Indian or Sri Lankan, would be better than a Pakistani umpire.' No way did I say that as New Zealand captain.

The New Zealand Press Association sent the printout straight to Pakistan, who instantly withdrew the independent umpires already appointed, replacing them with their own local men. The false statement entered cricket lore as a classic example of lack of tact. The Pakistan tour was now doomed; we could not possibly expect even-handed treatment after what I was supposed to have said, yet Bidwell refused to retract the statement when I confronted him. I rang Graham Dowling for assistance but none was forthcoming. I was mortified, to say the least. My intentions of creating some goodwill with the media and putting our cricket in a positive light were ruined by one piece of journalism.

Our tour goal of winning one match, either test or one-dayer, never eventuated. We lost the lot. The umpiring wasn't, however, totally to blame. Pakistan were, without question, a far superior side. Imran called us a 'B' side and never wanted to turn out; quite frankly, I had to agree. Badly depleted after the six withdrawals, we were arguably the worst side to leave New Zealand in over 20 years, if not more. The tour would be remembered mainly, however, for the ball tampering that went on throughout the test series.

In the first test, it was, we felt, simply a case of the Pakistani seamers, Wasim Akram and Waqar Younis, being too good, with their superb, and sometimes unplayable, fast swing bowling. It was not until late on the third day of the second test at Lahore, just before stumps, that I picked up something completely out of the ordinary. Standing at the non-striker's end while Wasim bowled to Trevor Franklin, I noticed, as the bowler ran in, that the ball he was holding had a different look about it. The side of the ball that faced me (or the off-side as the left-handed Wasim bowled over the wicket) was completely devoid of any colour or, for that matter, any leather. As the innings was only about 20 overs old, that was the first thing that surprised me.

As Wasim ran in with what I considered an out-swinger's grip, holding the shiny side on the on-side, I assumed that Trevor would need to judge the line carefully as the ball swung away from him. To my astonishment, the ball swung in sharply towards the pad, resulting in a huge in-swinger. Wasim used the same grip again, once more tried to bowl a big in-swinging yorker to the tall right-hander, and succeeded. The whole over was the same. Six supposed out-swingers turned out to be six lethal in-swingers. Somehow he was getting reverse swing for every ball he bowled. Reverse swing? I had never seen it before and immediately became very curious.

The last over Wasim bowled to me before stumps made me change my thinking about helmets and protection for the rest of my career.

Facing a bouncer, I prepared to sway inside the line of the ball, only to notice, to my horror, the ball change direction in flight and swing back towards my unprotected face; I wore only ear pieces on my helmet. I flung my head back outside the line to the off-side, swivelling in one quick motion but only just as the ball flew past, millimetres from my mouth. I settled into my stance, prepared for the next delivery and again Wasim bowled a bouncer. This time, though, the ball pitched on leg stump and I shaped to go outside the line, to the off-side, letting the ball go behind me and over leg stump. But then the ball swung again after pitching and started heading towards where I was moving. I was trapped as I had nowhere to go. I froze. Luckily for my teeth, the ball swung away so much towards the slips that it missed me again by a fraction. It was unbelievable! Both bouncers had swung while climbing off the pitch, and swung dramatically. I walked off the field a very relieved man. As the following day was a rest day I decided then and there to try a visor on my helmet for the first time in my career. I practised with it for an hour and satisfied myself that I would use it from that point on.

During the fourth day, while I fought hard to score 108 not out in just under eight hours, I finally found out why the ball was behaving so amazingly. At the end of an Abdul Qadir over, after having defended a delivery, I reached down and picked up the ball, taking a quick look at it before throwing it back. It was totally mutilated on one side, with two or three large scratches gouged out, presumably by some kind of sharp instrument. The other side, which had its full leather covering, was very red and extremely shiny. I complained to the umpires but they did nothing. I mentioned to the lads at the next interval that the Pakistanis were doing something with the ball and to keep an eye on them, and the ball, at all times. Later in the afternoon the ball was suddenly thrown from the field and replaced by another one. Mark Priest and Willie Watson raced to the boundary and grabbed the ball as it came off. They couldn't believe what they saw. Sure, it was out of shape, but it bore no possible resemblance to a normal cricket ball. They took it to Wally in the dressing room but the ball was quickly taken away by the Pakistani coach, Intikab Alam, and never seen again. At the conclusion of the match our manager, Ian Taylor, made an official complaint to the Pakistan Cricket Board about the state of the ball. They threw it out, saying that the rough outfield and the advertising boards on the boundary were responsible for the ball reaching that condition.

131

So, not only did we have the umpiring ready to get us at any moment, but we also had to counter ball tampering and the prodigious reverse swing that resulted from it. I had admired the brilliance of Wasim and Waqar so far, but I lost some respect for them due to the assistance they were getting during the series. Although we accepted that Pakistan were definitely the better team, we were not going to accept whatever they were doing with the ball.

The team met and decided that, as we had tried and failed to get the umpires and officials to do something about the problem, we might as well join the Pakistanis and try some tampering ourselves. This, we felt, would really bring the matter out into the open once and for all. I took a doctored ball to the next practice and ran in to bowl a few of my usual in-swingers with a normal grip, the shiny side on the off-side, only to see the ball curve the other way. Wow, I'd never bowled out-swingers in my life — wouldn't Frank Cameron be pleased! Turning the grip around, I then managed some big in-swingers but quickly changed again because I was having such fun. The lads were astounded to see me get such great results. Chris Pringle, deciding that this was definitely the greatest discovery since sliced bread, proceeded to bowl as he never had before.

The pitch for the third test at Faisalabad was green and hard, so it was important to win the toss, which I did, and send them in to bat. The next thing to do was to take a quick wicket so we could huddle round and get to work on the ball with our specially prepared bottle-tops. The first hour went quietly and then Chris Pringle struck. By lunch we had them in dire straits, with seven wickets down. The tampering made all the difference, as the ball swung everywhere.

When the umpires wanted to see the ball, we duly obliged, only to be left under no illusions about the whole shambles when they threw the ball back, saying, 'Well, now it's fair for both sides!' What a joke.

Leading on the first innings by 115, we found ourselves wanting 243 to win the match on the last two days. Needless to say, we were shot down by the umpires in a diabolical display of biased adjudicating, just as we were closing in on a win, with Dipak Patel hitting some form. The decision to give Dipak out caught behind was the last straw for us all.

Despite the results, we all enjoyed a tour in which we kept our heads up and enjoyed a superb team spirit. One man who contributed immensely off the field, mainly because he never got on it, was the

Canterbury fast bowler, Stu Roberts, one of the most jovial and funny tourists I've known. His greatest trick was imitating the muezzins who annoyed us often, chanting from nearby mosques as the sun came up. Stu would tie a handkerchief on his head and chant away at every opportunity. Another amusing incident involving Stu occurred when I was having a quiet knock-up before play in the first test. Stu, in his wisdom, decided to give me a bouncer, even though I had no helmet on, and the ball just missed my head as I ended up sitting on my backside. (A bad tour for the nerves, this one.) Asked by Wally why he did it, Stu replied enthusiastically, 'I'm just trying to impress the skip for the next test.' Cheers, Stu!

Our next goal was to reach the World Series finals in Australia with England, the other competing nation. John Wright and Andrew Jones returned to strengthen our top order, but our bowling still looked weak and in need of patient improvement. We fought game for game with England resulting in a two-all count, while the Aussies beat us both, oh so easily.

When it came to the final match in Hobart we knew that we needed a miracle and a win over Australia to make the finals. Scoring 194 was never enough in normal circumstances against the world champions but on this occasion I tried to deliver the message we needed before taking the field for the last time. Happily, it brought out the inspiration required, particularly when Wrighty turned to me early on and said, 'I've got one of those gut feelings.' When Chris Pringle lined up to bowl the final over with Australia requiring only one to tie, I wondered if that gut feeling might have been the result of a bad lunch. But Pring, one-day wonder that he was becoming, delivered six perfect dot balls in a row to Bruce Reid, and sent us through to the World Series finals. The whole nation woke up.

Prime Minister Jim Bolger was on the line within minutes of the victory, congratulating us on our marvellous spirit. So we achieved our first target and the satisfaction was evident. I was pleased that tactically I was able to make our thin resources work well enough, and before our crucial Brisbane encounter with England, Wally gave one of the best team talks that I'd ever heard. It was slowly but surely coming together. We went back for the finals, without Ian Smith in the squad, only to be spanked by the slick, ever-impressive Aussies. Ian had had big injury problems in the prelims and had given his spot to Bryan Young, who had batted well. So, when it came to selecting the finals squad, I insisted that Bryan be picked but that Ian make the squad of 14 as well. NZC didn't agree, allowing only us to select only 13 players for the three-game series, and naturally, because of the trend at the time, I took the rap for Ian's omission.

It was really starting to annoy me that, every time a player was dropped, I was portrayed as having fallen out with him. Shane Thomson was a classic example. He had struggled with injuries throughout the 1990 England tour, through trying to be both a quick bowler and a batsman. I felt he was better off going back to domestic cricket and learning to be a top batsman, so that in a year or two he would give himself every chance of succeeding. Instead, people talked about us not getting on and therefore he wouldn't be in the New Zealand side while I was captain. Shane and I are mates who have enjoyed good times together; my opinion was based on what I thought was right professionally. It was up to the selectors to make the decision — that was their job.

Ian Smith came back for the test series against Sri Lanka, and we began planning for the home series, our first in charge. Ian was a great support to me throughout. He encouraged my ideas and never bagged me when things looked grim. On his day he was the most devastating hitter of the ball. The year before, his innings of 173 against India at Eden Park, at less than a run a ball, was the greatest offensive batting New Zealand had seen. But Ian's great strength was as a wicketkeeper. He was outstanding in this role, a genius at work. Sure, he had his moments and moods, but by and large Ian Smith was, in my time, the finest keeper/batsman in the world.

Having lost to Pakistan three-nil, I was determined to counter that record by beating Sri Lanka three-nil in our home series. It was, however, a very unrealistic goal. I was underestimating the Sri Lankan batsmen and overestimating our ability to win tests, given our inexperienced bowling attack. In fact, at the start of the Pakistan tour, I had the second best bowling record of the entire team.

We had asked for greenish pitches so that our seam attack could make the advances we needed to set up possible victories. The problem was that we kept losing the toss. Sri Lanka made excellent use of the first test pitch at the Basin Reserve and on the second day we couldn't possibly have been in a worse position: all out for 174. In reply, by the end of day two, mainly through the efforts of Aravinda de Silva, Sri Lanka were in total command at 359 for three. De Silva played a blinder, punishing every single loose ball on offer — and there were thousands! They amassed 497 — de Silva was 267 — and had a further two and a third days to bowl us out again.

By now, though, the wicket had flattened out nicely and was easy-paced. Wright and Franklin gave us the solid start we demanded, batting through to stumps on day three. The next morning Simone woke me up and told me that I would score 120 not out that day. I joined Andrew Jones at 148 for two just before lunch and settled in very, very carefully. To bat out the match seemed, and was, much too far away to contemplate, so the instruction was to bat an hour at a time. From there we broke it down to a simple over at a time — Andrew one over, me the next. I began to slip into my automatic turn-on turn-off method of concentrating. Once a ball was bowled, I would turn off my concentration and conserve my energy by simply gazing at the sky or the crowd or my bat. Then, as the bowler turned to come in again, I would turn on the concentration and begin talking to myself: 'This ball, this ball, play straight, play straight, keep still, keep still, now watch the ball leave his hand, watch the ball, watch the ball.' This way I would eliminate any interfering negative thoughts that might enter my head and focus on what I had to do.

The final affirmation, 'Watch the ball leave his hand', was most crucial. This would give me the information early, as the ball was released, about its line or length or flight, so that as the ball arrived I would have gathered in the information and instinctively made a decision to move accordingly. I could get into position, wait for the ball to arrive and then strike it late, below my eyes, to gain maximum control and timing. I would go through this mental process of turning on and off each and every ball. It didn't matter if the previous ball was hit for four or enticed a mistake, as long as I was still there to face the next ball. The next ball or 'this ball' became the only thing in the world that mattered while the innings and the partnership with Andrew progressed. We just batted and concentrated, batted and concentrated.

By the end of the day we had added 221. Andrew was on 82, and I was on 126 not out. Simone had been wrong — I got six more runs! We had saved the match by not losing another wicket. We would make Sri

Lanka bat again but certainly had no time left to enforce a win. So, for the final day, we looked for personal aims and achievements.

I had never scored a double century, twice falling for 188, and so my sights were set on scoring a double. Away we went again, batting over for over, ball for ball. Andrew was superb, single-mindedly focused, fiercely determined to keep going and achieve the big score of which he knew he was capable. Tough, professional, always serious and always focused, Andrew was one very interesting character. He gave very little away but he could certainly bat. His style wasn't pleasing to the eye, but day in and day out the scoreboard showed A. Jones' contributions to be the most pleasing of any batsman I played with for New Zealand. If I were to choose someone to bat for my life, that person would be Andrew Howard Jones.

When we met in the middle after each over, very little was said except, maybe, 'Keep going' or 'Get stuck in'. By mid-afternoon I was nearing 200, enjoying the part-time bowling of de Silva. A six over square leg and then a delicate sweep for two brought me my first milestone of the day. Andrew passed 150 as I began to move into total offensive. Warnaweera, the off-spinner with a rather doubtful action, came in for some punishment when I decided to hit across, and even over, the boundary line as my confidence grew further.

I eyed up Glenn Turner's record score of 259 as my next objective. De Silva came on again, switching ends to rest the main bowlers for an over or two, so I took the opportunity to cash in. I started the over with a four through cover then a six over straight long-on, then another over mid-wicket up into the top of the bank, and then another four straight, which I thought went for six — although the umpire didn't agree. I did realise, however, that I had two more balls to break the world test record for most runs in an over — 24. So I lined up the next flighted delivery, swung too early across the line and sent the ball high into mid-wicket. Arjuna Ranatunga circled under the ball and, fortunately, dropped it, as I came back for two. I cursed myself for taking such a risk, as I was only 20 or so from the New Zealand record. Deciding that the over record could wait for another day, I proceeded to block the last ball back to the bowler.

The day wore on and, as tea approached, Andrew and I were beginning to tire. We knew that we had over 400, but we were content just to pursue our own individual aims, not taking too much notice of our partnership tally. By tea we were glad of the chance to sit down, sip a cuppa and replenish our reserves. Andrew had 200 in sight and I still needed a dozen to beat Turner's score. But, when we entered the dressing room we were pleasantly surprised with the excitement coming from the lads, but mainly Ian Smith.

'One more, lads, one more,' he cried gleefully.

'What do you mean?'

'The world record! You need one more to beat Bradman and Ponsford, Mudasser and Javed for the highest partnership ever!'

'Jeez,' Andrew replied, not being one for too many words.

'Hey, hold on,' I enquired, 'who's facing?'

'You are!' Andrew answered.

'Cripes!' I muttered.

The 20-minute tea break seemed to take an hour, and then out we went again, for the sixth session in a row, to attempt to create cricket history. Champaka Ramanayake ran in and for three balls I could only defend, nervously. Then, off the fourth, I tucked a slightly angled delivery off my hip into square leg and we scampered through for a marvellous moment: 452. Goodbye Bill and Don, goodbye Mud and Javed. We embraced in the middle, and Andrew was ecstatic. He punched me in the arm and said, with all the emotion he could muster, 'Bwilliant!' The letter R never was Andrew's strong point. What a moment.

We added a further 15 runs before Andrew aimed a tired drive off Ranatunga and was caught 14 short of a well-deserved double century. I needed only a few more for the highest score by a New Zealander. I drove a slower ball from Ramanayake and celebrated, hands and bat high, with 261 to my name. This was a dream I'd always wanted to fulfil. I had achieved the goals I had set myself as the last 45 minutes approached. All that was left was to try to score 300, but up to now that had never entered my head.

Paddy joined me. He had been padded up for nearly 10 hours and must have felt mentally exhausted from waiting. He pushed ones to give me the strike and soon I reached 290 with 10 minutes left. A four, a few more singles, a two, another single and then finally I stood on 298, with Ranatunga to bowl the last over. The crowd had tripled within the hour with the news of the world record and my chance of 300. Many Wellingtonians, sensing an historic day, left the offices, shops and pubs of the capital to rush to the Basin, even just to see the final run.

My legs were dead tired now, but my mind felt strong and I was still focusing and still talking to myself — 'Keep still, watch the ball'. I pushed for one and then Paddy did the same. I stood there, bat lying across my shoulders, left hand on my hip, looking beyond Ranatunga at the frenzied crowd gathering, chattering, fidgeting. Only one more. As the sweat rolled down my cheeks I thought, 'Three hundred, you've done it, you're the first for New Zealand.'

Then I settled into my stance once more and looked up. Ranatunga was on his way. He bowled, but I saw nothing, then a flash as the ball came into blurred view wide of off-stump. I hurriedly threw my arms and bat at the ball, and began to run. Looking behind, to my amazement and horror I saw little Hashan Tillekeratne dive full length and glove the ball a centimetre from the ground. I kept running, not believing what I'd seen, and then it hit me — I was out, caught behind for 299. My mind went blank, but then I heard the crowd, the roar as I approached the stand. As I snapped back into consciousness the realisation came that I had choked again. More applause, but as I walked through the gate anger overcame me. Shaking my head in disbelief, I smashed the nearest object, a sign, with my bat as I disappeared down the tunnel. I hit a fire hose to my right and then, as I stormed into the dressing room, hurled my bat skywards and screamed, 'It's not fair, this bloody game.' I hadn't seen anyone, but Wrighty ducked to avoid my bat while everyone else backed away. My head went into my hands again. I had choked. I didn't concentrate. I forgot to say, 'Keep still, watch the ball.' I didn't focus on the moment. Out for 299 — tell me it's not true! Tears streamed down my face as I realised that this opportunity might never happen again.

Before long, though, the champagne corks began popping and the rightful smiles returned. I concentrated on the achievement with Andrew and thoroughly enjoyed the emotions that went with it. We were beside ourselves with joy. As we posed for photos, and did the numerous interviews after match, we had to keep reminding ourselves that we were world record holders. It was a night to remember.

It didn't take long, however, for me to begin dwelling on the opportunity I had missed. For the next week I was shattered, mentally and physically. My arms ached, my legs were sore, but I also felt listless, devoid of energy. I would sleep intermittently at nights, tossing and turning, as I struggled to shut off the constant recollection of that historic match.

We had a one-day series of three matches against Sri Lanka and three against England to complete before the next test, and so we were on the road for a few weeks, cleaning up the Sri Lankans three-nil and coming back from one-nil to defeat England two-one in an exciting, pulsating contest. My form began to slip as my concentration waned. There was no question that, for Andrew and me, the Wellington test was a hard act to follow, but Andrew went from strength to strength as he continued to show his huge resources of commitment and application. Perhaps because he'd missed out on his double century, he retained his intense motivation to keep going. But then again Andrew Jones always kept going, a quality in him that I really admired. To confirm his greatness, and his status as, I believe, the finest number three New Zealand has ever produced, he went to Hamilton and became only the third New Zealander to score twin centuries in a test match. Then, at Eden Park, he scored his 500th run in a three-test match series, the first Kiwi to do so. As John Wright had been the previous year, Andrew Jones was now in the best form of his life.

While the Hamilton test proved the high point of Andrew's career, the Trust Bank Park ground provided me with my scariest moment. Late on the second day, with Sri Lanka halfway through their reply to our first innings, I took off from first slip to field a ball that had trickled down to short fine leg from the spin bowling of Dipak Patel. As I approached the ball, I moved into a position where I could bend down and pick up with my right hand. At the critical point when I began stooping down, my right leg feeling the strain, I scooped the ball up, only to slip and lose my balance. My right heel had skidded on the lush outfield and, as I attempted to regain my position, I lost my footing completely and somehow jack-knifed the leg as my body fell to the ground. I knew instantly that I had twisted and badly damaged my ankle. I lay there, clutching my foot, then my knee, as the pain exploded into unbearable proportions.

I was carried off and taken to hospital for X-rays, where doctors told me that I had suffered a massive flaking of the fibula bone near the ankle, to the extent that a sharp point was stabbing the main tibia bone.

Such a condition is called an osteochondroma and an operation was scheduled immediately. The knee joint had also been damaged. According to my surgeon, Barry Tietjens, the posterior cruciate ligament at the back of the knee — the one I damaged at school in 1980 — had been stretched an extra centimetre. The meniscus cartilage was tender enough to be a problem too. I didn't play for the rest of that season, missing the last test at Auckland.

After the ankle operation I began building up the leg muscles in an attempt to counter the weakening of my posterior ligament. The cartilage seemed okay and my knee and ankle responded to training. By September I had recovered well and was fit to take the development pre-World Cup squad to Adelaide for a two-week tour.

As soon as the season had finished in late March, Wally and I planned that the year leading into the World Cup would consist of a series of winter camps in Christchurch. New Zealand Cricket had just secured finance to establish a Cricket Academy, led by John Howell, the national director of coaching. We saw this academy concept as being an ideal chance for the team to plan and prepare over the winter months. Both John Howell and I wanted the help of outside experts such as podiatrists, sports psychologists and nutritionists, as well as our physical education trainers. So it was natural for John Howell to arrange the academy's schedule to suit our team and all the other age-group squads that followed. We would live in at the Christchurch Rugby Club, with its motel style facilities, and train indoors at the Canterbury Sports Centre.

Our main objective was to identify the weaknesses of our squad and begin improving the overall standard, particularly our one-day skills. The most obvious weakness was the underachieving of our semi-experienced middle-management players — players who were averaging under 20 in tests or one-dayers, players who weren't fit enough to sustain concentration and performance, players who had the ability but didn't appreciate the discipline and sacrifice needed to take their play up a level. In a nutshell, the attitude towards preparation was not sufficiently professional. We called for an improvement in attitude and demanded an increase in fitness standards. Jim Blair had looked after most of the Aucklanders, including myself, superbly over the years, but now everyone would be tested and monitored by Paul Carpinter at Canterbury University.

After the third camp, in August, we checked the results from fitness tests and still found the standard was down. We decided to set general criteria to be met in six weeks, by which time the development team would be picked. Another, more specific, area of concern was the lack of opening batsmen and spinners in particular. The side to Adelaide therefore needed to be selected with these issues in mind: the middle-management shake-up, the experimenting with openers and the encouragement of spinners.

The whole World Cup squad shaped up as follows: senior management — M.D. Crowe, captain, number four, I.D.S. Smith, vice-captain, J.G. Wright, opening batsman, A.H. Jones, number three, R.B. Reid, opening batsman, W.K. Lees, coach; middle management — K.R. Rutherford, middle order number five, T.J. Franklin, opening batsman, M.J. Greatbatch, middle order/opener, G.R. Larsen, medium pacer, R.T. Latham, middle order/opener, D.N. Patel, off-spinner, D.K. Morrison, fast bowler, W. Watson, medium pacer; junior management — C.Z. Harris, allrounder/medium pace, M.L. Su'a, left-arm fast medium, R. Petrie, medium pacer, C. Cairns, allrounder/fast medium, K. Wealleans, opening batsman, B. Young, keeper/batsman, A. Parore, keeper/batsman, G. Bradburn, off-spinner/batsman, S. Thomson, allrounder/ medium pace.

Richard Reid, the son of the legendary J.R. Reid, had come into the side during the season after an astonishing run of scores in the Shell Cup. Richard and I had opened for Wellington over Christmas, in what was my first season for my new province. With Andrew Jones at number three, it was felt I should go in first, as I had done the year before for New Zealand in the one-dayers under Wrighty. During this latest Shell Cup competition Wellington spectators witnessed the most amazing one-day batting, I believe, in New Zealand domestic cricket history.

At his best, Richard had the natural talent to play almost two shots to any given ball, such was his imagination on the offensive. Batting with him at the other end was the most enjoyable time I've had in New Zealand domestic cricket; we dominated every bowling attack in the country. Supporters would rush to the Basin Reserve upon hearing that we were batting first, just as they had for his father years before. Through Richard's sublime brilliance we easily won the cup, and thereafter the selectors had no choice but to include R.B. Reid in the squad for the World Series finals in Australia. He showed continued form and kept his place in the one-day side for the rest of the season. Halfway through the winter, though, he retired from top cricket to concentrate on business opportunities, which forced him to forgo selection for the World Cup.

So the side to tour Adelaide had become a difficult one to pick. We knew of the talents of Rutherford, Larsen, Latham and co. in that middle group, but felt that, particularly in Ken's case, being left out might jolt him into an improved performance — and into becoming a lot fitter. Trevor Franklin, too, was in need of a jolt, but we thought it was important to throw all our openers into the hat to see who would respond. Dipak Patel, also underachieving, was given his chance again, along with Grant Bradburn, as the spinners of the team. With John Wright staying at home, the rest were either certainties, such as Jones, Greatbatch and Smith, or young aspirants such as Harris, Thomson, Wealleans and Parore.

It was a low-key tour, just two weeks, and we discovered very little. No one really took their chance, particularly in the opening role. We did, however, get the response we were looking for from the three we left behind: Rutherford, Larsen and Latham. Although upset initially, they made the necessary improvements and by World Cup time were key members of the team.

On the tour of Adelaide I tore my meniscus cartilage and required surgery upon my return. My recovery took longer than I'd hoped and, through frustration, I made an overhasty comeback. It didn't work. I needed more time, but the England side had arrived for a full test series so I required some luck to be fit, and to find some form. England brought a balanced side, full of experience, with Gooch, Lamb and Botham leading the way. The tour opened with a bad loss for us at Eden Park in a one-dayer, but we always seemed to start slowly. The series opener the year before had been similar, but on that occasion we had shown great character to come from behind both times in the final matches to snatch a superb series victory. I felt we were beginning to build the belief that we could win, the sort of belief that would be vital in a month's time. In fact, for most of the series we and the media kept referring to the next month's cricket and the World Cup, rather than concentrating solely on the present, and on beating England.

The real truth was that we failed to focus at all on the first test at Christchurch and bowled, batted and fielded appallingly. After conceding over 500 and then succumbing badly at first bat, we needed to bat out the final four sessions. By stumps on day four we were 81 for one and by tea on the final day we were well placed at 211 for three, with John Wright on 99 and playing solidly. I had just joined him and, with the pitch playing easily, the drawing of the match seemed a formality. Instead, the final session must go down as one of our worst ever. Wrighty was stumped for 99 and then came a dramatic collapse, with Paddy, Shane Thomson, Dipak and Chris Cairns all getting out to Tufnell. Ian Smith came and went, gloving a ball from Chris Lewis to Jack Russell, so within an hour and a half six wickets had fallen for only 39 runs.

I stood in astonishment at the non-striker's end, trying to gee up my incoming batsmen, but they all looked so apprehensive. Chris Pringle joined me with 32 minutes left, or 22 minutes if we could score 18 runs and make England bat again. I knew I had to score all those runs, and quickly. I scrambled 14 and, with my score on 48, there was time left for four more overs, or a last one if I could hit a final four. Three overs would be used up with the break between innings and the match would be saved. Phil Tufnell was still bowling. I had six balls available to hit the single boundary and avoid the risk of giving Pringle the strike. I knew I couldn't live with myself if he had took the strike and got out.

The whole field was up. Robin Smith and Alec Stewart, fielding at short leg and silly point respectively, both piped up, 'You only need four to save it, you know.' 'Yes, yes I know,' I mumbled as I surveyed my options. Tufnell was flighting the ball nicely and gaining a little turn, so I decided against hitting across the line in case I hit the ball straight up. My option was to go to the pitch of the ball and hit him straight into the unprotected outfield. That was my plan. Tufnell looped up the first ball and as I saw it delivered high into the air I thought this was my chance to get down the wicket to attack. I stepped out and towards the ball, only to see it dip and turn slightly as I swung through the ball. I was too early. The bat moved up too quickly so that the ball connected high on the blade, ballooning out to extra cover where Derek Pringle ran round and pouched the easy catch.

The Englishmen ran and danced everywhere while I, head down, made for the tunnel. We'd lost, thrown the game away. I'd gambled, and failed. I'd made the final, fatal mistake. I'd choked once more. I couldn't look at anyone, as I slumped into my chair. I said nothing as I rode back to the hotel, where I flopped in a heap on the bed and again buried my head into my hands. Another choke! As I lay there the whole god-damned night, analysing why I had suffered yet another mental block, it finally occurred to me that, every time I had missed out in this way, I had been thinking of the consequences, the glory, the adulation, instead of focusing on the situation confronting me. The pressure had taken its toll. But I knew that if I could learn from those mistakes, absorb the pressure, concentrate on the basic plan, then I would succeed next time and break this mental aberration.

From there, the closer the World Cup came, the better the team started to perform. And when Ian Botham said to me in Dunedin during a one-dayer, 'You'll do well in this World Cup on these pitches', it made me believe that all the hard work and planning, all the heartache, would finally pay off for the team. We were ready for the 1992 World Cup.

CHAPTER 12
Taking Care of Business

During the winter of 1992, after the World Cup, Simone and I decided to spend some time relaxing in Italy, and in particular the beautiful city of Florence. When you walk through Florence you are forever looking around you, admiring the marvellous streets, the piazzas, the cafes, the architecture. Thousands of years of history and culture. Florence in May was superb, quiet, peaceful, coming out of spring and into an extremely warm summer. Simmy and I had decided to spend two months there, enjoying the lifestyle and the different culture. We had always wanted to visit, ever since we were engaged in November 1990. We actually considered holding our wedding in Italy, but there were too many problems. Simmy had talked often of visiting this lovely city as her mother's parents were born and bred there; in many ways Simmy herself has that Italian flair. We figured that if we hadn't managed to be married there, at least we could enjoy our first anniversary in Italy.

I had met Simmy back in 1985 during the winter when I hadn't gone back to England. I had decided to spend a quiet period at home to prepare for the Australian tour later in November. So we crossed each other's paths in June during a party at Franco's Restaurant in Auckland. Simmy was out the back having a cry over her boyfriend, whose surname was Eagle, so it didn't seem too odd that a Crowe should come to the rescue! I had spilt red wine on my sweater and was trying to wash it off when I heard her sobbing, so I introduced myself with the suggestion that we both seemed to have problems. As she relaxed and began to smile, I realised how incredibly attractive she was. She also had a very sexy voice, so we chatted for a while; I enjoyed her company immensely. I suggested perhaps we might meet up some time but meanwhile we had better get back to our partners. I noticed, as we departed, that we were both wearing pink. She had a pink dress, which was stunning, while I had a horrible pink golf sweater with red wine all over it. It was evident she didn't like my attire.

We saw each other the next week and then fell into one of those crazy love-at-first-sight relationships that lasted only one month. I had very rarely lost control of my emotions, as cricket had always dominated, so after one month I shied away and escaped, heading for England to play some cricket. Simmy had affected me as no other person ever had.

When I returned in late August she was convinced that my life was run by cricket. This was true, so I decided to stay with what I knew and we soon parted. Simmy and I still thoroughly enjoyed each other's company, but cricket always came first for me and I just hoped that we could remain at least friends. Simmy had gone to Japan for six months' modelling work, and I prepared for the tour of Australia.

Then we bumped into each other during the next tour across the Tasman, in 1987. Simmy had finished modelling and was working as an interior design consultant in Double Bay, Sydney. It was great to catch up and share our experiences and soon we were great mates, dining and laughing and battling over games of backgammon.

Four months later she flew home to attend my brother Jeff's wedding and I was shocked but delighted to see her again. Jeff had invited her without my knowing, which turned out to be a blessing in disguise. As I was Jeff's best man for the wedding I had the usual role of proposing a toast to the newly-weds, Jeff and Kath. I preceded to make a total and utter fool of myself as I delivered my speech in front of over 200 guests. In trying to be humorous I revealed a silly story of how it was, in fact, me who had looked after Kath for so many years, particularly when she came to visit me while I was in my first year at Somerset in 1984. Kath and I had always been close through our teens but when Jeff came home from Adelaide he not only took my New Zealand spot but also began seeing Kath as well. So a number of years later they got engaged, and then he had the audacity to ask me to be the best man!

Unintentionally, I did as much as possible to ruin the wedding with my embarrassing attempt to be funny. I felt so bad afterwards that I stayed away from the crowd for a while. Thankfully that was when Simmy came to the rescue and remained close to me. For the next two days I never left my bedroom, except when my godfather, Gordon Mace, came and gave me the biggest bollocking I'd ever had. That just made it worse. I sank into depression. Simmy saw me every day until I flew to back to Somerset, but before I left I asked her to join me there, in a month's time. She came and stayed with me until my back broke down and we returned home together. We lived in Auckland for two years before we decided to split as, once more, cricket was coming between us. I couldn't get used to the idea yet of settling down while there was so much travelling and playing to do. In reality, I messed Simmy around in order to satisfy my own selfish needs.

I spent a lonely six months until I realised, on the tour of Pakistan in October 1990, that I had been foolish and that cricket wasn't the be-all and end-all of life, especially when you had to tour places like that. Simmy was stunned by my sudden reappearance. As soon as I hopped off the plane I said that I had something very important to tell her, to which she replied that she had something to tell me. Naturally, gentle-man that I am, I let her speak first and Simmy proceeded to tell me of her new romance with a young Auckland financier. I couldn't believe it, but it served me right. After a few days I decided to go through with my decision and I asked her to marry me anyway. Besides, I had known Simmy for over five years, as opposed to this latest love affair which had been going for only five weeks! Following a very dramatic week, she agreed to marry me.

We were engaged on 17 November, my parents' wedding anniver-sary, and we married in 1992 on her birthday, 19 April, at Baradene College. We celebrated into the early hours with our closest friends and immediate family. It was a very special day, better than I could ever have imagined. We honeymooned on a farm in Arrowtown and then settled in Eastbourne, Wellington.

So while Simone and I were marvelling at the beauty of Florence, I took the opportunity to start planning and preparing for the future. I had received a couple of offers to play for English counties Yorkshire and Durham, and teams from South Africa and Australia had also shown keen interest. The money was very tempting indeed, but deep down I wanted only to play for New Zealand.

Having led my country successfully during the World Cup, I simply wanted to carry on and continue that winning feeling we had created. By September my contract with New Zealand Cricket would be up for renewal. This had always been a straightforward business: they offered you a contract and you either accepted or declined it. It was not negotiable. I felt that, over the last two years, I had earned the right to negotiate a decent long-term contract.

New Zealand Cricket contracts had started in the late 1970s when Richard Hadlee, Geoff Howarth and John Wright, all county professionals, were engaged to come back and be available for New Zealand. This was the result of Glenn Turner deciding to spend seven years in England playing for Worcestershire, since he and New Zealand Cricket chairman Walter Hadlee had fallen out. Apparently Glenn had asked NZC for assistance in the form of airfares to bring him back from England to play for New Zealand. That seemed only fair, but not according to the chairman. Glenn then turned his back on his own country and didn't reappear until 1982–83, playing just one more season. Oddly, as soon as Richard Hadlee became a county pro, NZC begin offering contracts!

New Zealand Cricket guaranteed a retainer for all the leading county pros to be available. I came into the scheme in 1984 when I joined Somerset. Then, in 1988, NZC decided to drop the whole system as I was the only pro left playing in England and they saw no need to continue paying me a retainer. I was disappointed, naturally, but accepted it as I was a lone player.

Then, in 1990, following the retirement of six players before the Pakistan tour, contracts were offered to all players who had appeared in a certain number of games or tours. By copying the Australian method of tiered contracts, the NZC Board was trying to maintain availability and postpone retirements. Apparently they failed to work it out properly, because it became costly to pay players who weren't always selected. I had been shown a draft of the contract two weeks before departing on tour, and it seemed similar to the Australian system in applying a tiered structure depending on your experience.

The contracts were to be drawn up and signed at least two days before we left for Pakistan. Then New Zealand Cricket ran into delays and the players received their contracts only hours before take-off. This caused a major panic, especially as 'new player responsibilities', which required each player to give 28 days of promotion or coaching, had been added at the last minute. As this had never even been discussed before, the players naturally demanded that it be deleted.

I didn't receive my contract until after I boarded the flight, but I was relaxed as I'd seen the draft. Some of the players were reluctant to sign as they wanted to have the legal jargon checked out by their own solicitors. I felt for them. It all seemed far too late now for signing; it should have been finished the week before.

The executive were in a mad panic, so I tried to assure the players that everything was all right, that I'd had the contract checked from a legal point of view, and that they should sign and then forget about it. The payment they would get was calculated entirely on experience, on the number of matches you had played. For example, John Wright, Ian Smith and I occupied the top tier.

When Ian Taylor, our manager, handed me my contract on the plane I just turned to the back section to check the schedule and then sign it. When I checked the payment schedule and dates, I began going down the list to see all was in order. Then I stopped. 'Hello,' I thought, 'they've made a typing error here.' Under the heading 'Retainer' I looked across to see that the figure was correct, and it was, except that it read 'for 24-monthly'. I couldn't understand this, as it was supposed to be 'per annum'.

I went to see Ian and show him the error. He hesitated, then, taking off his reading glasses, came out with, 'Sorry, Hogan, the original draft had a typing error. This is correct. If we had adopted a yearly retainer we would have doubled our cost and not been able to afford contracts at all.'

'No way,' I replied. 'This is half what I should be paid.'

'Well, I'm sorry, but everything has been rushed and there's no time to change now.' Ian looked sheepish.

'I can't sign this,' I snapped and stormed back to my seat.

Here I was in my first term as captain faced with the absurd situation of flying to Pakistan, and en route refusing to sign a ridiculous contract. It was so typical of our organisation and administration. I didn't know what to do. I certainly didn't want this hanging over my head while I was trying to play cricket in Pakistan, and I didn't want to pull out of the tour as I'd only just taken on the job of captain. New Zealand Cricket had no alternative, according to Ian, and so I was left pondering the whole sorry mess.

I decided to write a new clause on the back of the schedule saying that I would agree to sign the contract with an additional payment for the responsibility of captaincy. Also, the difference in payment between the top tier and the one below was too narrow, considering that we had nearly twice as many games as the next group, so I suggested that the top tier level be increased, and showed the new draft to Ian. He wouldn't agree until he had contacted head office on arrival in Singapore. After that he came back and said that New Zealand Cricket were prepared to offer only 20 percent more than the original. I had no choice but to sign. I felt cheated financially as I would receive only 60 percent of the figure previously agreed.

I decided then and there that when my contract came up for renewal I would get someone to put forward a professional proposal to negotiate a new contract with NZC.

Ever since I was 20 I'd always had a manager to help maximise the commercial opportunities available to me. When my first manager, Darryl Sambell, left for Queensland in 1987, I went into partnership with former test player, John Morrison. He had established close contacts with Ron Brierley and Selwyn Cushing of Brierley Investments Ltd. These two were cricket fanatics, always to be seen at the test matches, and John felt there were numerous possibilities within BIL's subsidiary companies, notably (at the time) Ansett New Zealand, Dominion Breweries and Whitcoulls. BIL became guarantors of our partnership, ensuring a minimum income if our earnings didn't reach a certain level. John and I enjoyed an excellent partnership. I was so delighted with the way things were going that, as a further incentive, I increased John's commission from 15 to 25 percent after three years. Added to our business success was the fact that we were also great mates. I enjoyed his humour and wit, as well as his advice.

Then, in 1989, our relationship became more involved. While working as a consultant for ATS Wilson Learning, John had met a woman called Pauline Ray. They had decided to break away and form their own human resources company and asked me to join them. Within months I had moved to Wellington from Auckland, and we had formed a new enterprise called Morrison, Crowe and Ray — Problem Solvers. John and Pauline brought some good clients from their former business, and the company achieved a pleasing result in its first half-year. I wasn't around much owing to cricket commitments, but when I returned I discovered that John and Pauline were more than just business partners. Under the circumstances I felt I'd best be out of the way so I resigned as a director and partner after one year, although I left my name in the company for a further 12 months. They then wound up the company and John and Pauline continued with sports management and marketing under the name Morrison Sporting Agencies. This company managed my affairs and was the marketing arm for the Wellington

Cricket Association. John at this time was also the coach of the Wellington cricket team. Our relationship went really well for nearly five years
until 1992, when we had a major misunderstanding over the way in
which one of my sponsorship arrangements was working. It was a very
serious matter which meant I could no longer work with John and
Pauline again.

Sadly, our friendship disintegrated. Not long afterwards John and
Pauline finished their work for the Wellington Cricket Association and
then failed in their bid for Wellington Dolphins to enter the Winfield
Cup. Ever since that period John has been out to ridicule me at every
opportunity on his Wellington radio show. The Wellington Cricket
Association has also taken some stick. Time and again people would
come up and say, 'Hey, I thought you two were great mates. Why does
he shit on you all the time?' I could only reply by saying, 'It's okay, he's
just got a bit of a chip on his shoulder.'

So by mid-1992 I needed a new manager and I immediately thought
of my brother Jeff. He had retired from cricket, had energy to burn and
was becoming involved in entrepreneurial activities around Auckland.
He would also be ideal in communicating with New Zealand Cricket as
he enjoyed great respect in the game because of his easy-going and
diplomatic attitude. I knew he was the man.

I wrote him a 12-page letter outlining the whole plan, from negoti-
ating the New Zealand Cricket contract to renewing old contracts from
John and creating new business with an innovative, upmarket
approach. I told him that I would be prepared to pay John his commis-
sions for the next six months and in some cases Jeff wouldn't be
involved until this time was up. Otherwise I could see some exciting
opportunities ahead for us both.

As well as a new New Zealand Cricket contract, I needed Jeff to find
a new bat and equipment deal. For 10 years I had endorsed and used
Duncan Fearnley, but I now learned that this company were having
problems and would be unable to renew their contract with me when it
expired in May. They offered to pay me in bats instead of dollars but I
refused. I found it hard to decline because I'd enjoyed great success with
the bats, but I thanked them and put myself on the market.

The first job for Jeff was to draw up a proposal for potential dealers.
He knew the Gunn & Moore people well as he had used their bats himself, so he proposed a long-term deal, up to five years, and then set

151

about convincing the New Zealand agents, Brittain Wynyard, that their British principals should sign me up and try to become number one in bats in New Zealand. They grabbed the deal, requiring me to use their bats for the next five years. I was thrilled.

Jeff had sold the concept so professionally that the deal was signed in six weeks, and he decided to fly to Italy and spend two weeks with us before we all flew off to London to sign on the dotted line. Next was New Zealand Cricket. While in London we arranged a quick chat with Peter McDermott, who was over for the International Cricket Council meeting at Lords. Jeff established areas of mutual advantage, concentrating on such issues as promotion of cricket and academy coaching, as well as playing and captaincy. Jeff had only to follow up on those initial talks with McDermott and we should have the next four years signed and sealed. Or so we thought.

As soon as the lawyers and board members got together, the whole process slowed up so that, by the last week before I was leaving for Zimbabwe in October 1992, there was still no contract. It was promised within five days, but when it showed up it needed a fair bit of simplifying. I passed it over to my support team to sort out. My lawyer, Dave Howman, who specialises in sports law and is the independent commissioner for the New Zealand Rugby Union, quickly began to make the contract as simple as possible. Dave, by this time, had become a hugely important part of my support team. Not only had he been a great adviser on legal and commercial matters but he also took on the role of watching over my public relations, something that became crucial later.

I also ran the document past my financial adviser and accountant Lyall Bunt, from Price Waterhouse, and together Dave and Lyall came up with the finished contract. Lyall has been an enormous help to me over the years, and has become a valuable member of the team that has worked my off-field business since 1982.

Dave Howman arrived at Auckland Airport with the legal document where Jeff and I signed it, just hours before departing for Zimbabwe. Graham Dowling, chief executive of NZC, was very reluctant to accept this new revised agreement without referring to his board but, as I was about to get on the plane and he could see no obvious problems, he signed. A complete turnaround from the last contract signing!

The schedule, of course, hadn't changed, just a lot of unnecessary clauses. The deal was for three and a half years expiring in April 1996, including so many days per year in promotion and coaching, where cricket allowed. It looked good from everyone's point of view. Despite the annoying delays and the problems, I was delighted to be tied up long term and looking forward to working with my cricket bosses. My wish now was that they follow up on all the other players who deserved recognition, particularly because of their efforts in the World Cup; otherwise I saw problems looming within the team.

What helped me in signing with New Zealand Cricket long term, from a financial point of view, was the continuing support of Brierley Investments and Dominion Breweries. DB provided me with the big commitment I needed to stay and play for New Zealand. As I was captain of the team which they sponsored, they again decided to invest in me for the same duration as my NZC contract. They saw their sponsorship of the team as having a better chance of success if I was still playing in New Zealand.

All I thought about now was scoring runs, and leading the team. I decided to set some long-term goals to ensure constant focus and a strong motivation to keep working all the time. Without these, I knew I would be too easily distracted, would become unmotivated with the same routine all the time, the training, the pressures. I needed goals to keep me in line, so I aimed for the top.

I wanted to become one of the dozen or so batsmen to score 20 test centuries or more. I had 13 at present, so seven more would place me within the elite. Whether I made it or not wasn't the issue — it was the process, the hunt, the day-to-day drive of trying to get there. I also fancied scoring a 100 against every country, and in every country, I played against. In the one-dayers, I simply wanted to lead from the front to ensure that, more often than not, I headed a winning team. This was my mission. I couldn't wait to get stuck into it, new bats and all.

My only concern was that, two weeks before flying to Zimbabwe, I had suffered a horrible glandular fever virus, caught in Hong Kong during the World Sixes Tournament. This had laid me up for 10 days, so I was feeling weak and washed out, desperate for some sun and exercise to put me right.

We arrived in Harare and I immediately struggled with the altitude. Trying to control my breathing as I eased into some training was hard work but, after a day or two, we all adjusted. I missed the first week's cricket, a one-dayer and a three-day match, before taking my place as captain in the first one-day international at Bulawayo.

Our itinerary was the most ridiculous any international side could ever encounter. In the next 13 days we were to play two one-day internationals and two tests with only a day in between the first and second tests to travel from Bulawayo back to Harare. There were no rest days during the tests, which is common enough these days, but we had to play the second one-dayer after the first day of the second test. This had never been attempted before and, quite frankly, I hope it never will be again.

Zimbabwe had just become the ninth test-playing nation and as soon as this was announced quickly arranged two tours to try out its new status. First, India played one test on the way to South Africa and then we followed straight after. Right from the outset we were greeted coldly and suspiciously. I couldn't imagine why, as New Zealand had been one of the instigators in nominating Zimbabwe for test status. We had backed them, along with Australia, so that we could expect their vote when it came to determining the next World Cup venue, which we hoped would be in England, as well as on other issues.

That was the deal, but Zimbabwe stabbed NZC in the back by voting for the opposition camp, allowing India, Pakistan and Sri Lanka to win the right to stage the 1996 World Cup. It seemed that India's dollars were preferable to our loyalty and support. By touring Zimbabwe we had helped to launch their test status but, in so doing, we had to agree to pay our own way, to the tune of some $85,000. We were keen for the competition, which would, in some ways, prepare us nicely for the more difficult Sri Lankan tour. New Zealand was in a sense investing the money for our own benefit, but to receive the kind of hospitality we were offered was quite upsetting. Their top administrators went out of their way to make life difficult, causing me to revise my impression that Zimbabwe was a great tour for barbecues, beer and good cricket. There was hardly time, with our schedule, for barbecues anyway, but we certainly didn't receive any invitations either. Perhaps Zimbabwe figured that they were now among the big boys and wanted to show that they meant business and a tough series. 'Fair enough,' I thought, 'let's give them some tough cricket.'

At Bulawayo, even the one-dayer produced only a small, partisan crowd to watch us beat the home team easily. Next day the test started and, to add to the letdown, only a dozen or so spectators showed any interest in the events in the middle. Not surprisingly, this led to an angry assault by our opening batsmen on their hapless attack. Play was delayed for two hours for overnight rain, the first rain for five years, which was why the farmers stayed on their farms instead of coming to the cricket. Greatbatch and Latham opened the innings for the first time together in a test, let alone opening themselves for the first time. After one hour the score had soared to 85, with Paddy on fire on 60. He just stood there and caned their pedestrian bowling. After only 15 overs there were four men on the boundary and only five up near the circle. This didn't seem quite right for a test match.

Just before the end of the first session Paddy was out for 87 off only 79 balls. I was a little nettled by his dismissal as he walked off proclaiming, 'Live by the sword, die by the sword'. I suggested that, no matter what he felt, no one was going to remember 87 and that a big 100 against Zimbabwe would have been appropriate for both sides.

Rod, on the other hand, dug in and carefully accumulated his runs while the carnage continued at the other end. Eventually he was run out for 119, his maiden test ton. After two sessions we had 205 on for two, stumps for the day, and next morning we carried on to 325 for three before rain washed out the rest of the day.

When we arrived on the third morning we noticed that the covers had not been placed properly and the run-ups were damp. Very little was being done to repair the damage until I suggested rather loudly that this was a test match and not a bloody club game. Dickie Bird, standing in his 49th test match, agreed and demanded action. Finally, after some three hours of very ordinary groundmanship, the surrounds were ready for play. Unbelievably, the Zimbabwe captain, Dave Houghton, then declared that his team would not take the field as they considered it was still unfit to play! How pathetic, I thought. Here is a new test nation and they don't even want to play. I couldn't take any more and promptly declared our innings closed. Obviously it shook the Zimbos because, by the close, they had reached 54 for one off 46 overs. The crowd had diminished to just the proverbial dog, for the man with him had dropped off to sleep. Who hadn't?

We bowled them out for 219 and quickly rattled up 222 for five, with Paddy holing out again in the 80s, to set them a reachable 329 in a minimum 75 overs. Typically, they never got out of first gear and after 80 overs had crawled to 197 for one.

There was no love lost between the two teams. Frustrations spilled into heated exchanges on field, and into the press conference. I felt that if Zimbabwe continued to play so negatively we were wasting our time and money, and would leave with no results, so I attacked them in the media. If I attacked enough maybe they would just have had enough by the end of the second test.

We went straight on to Harare and the second test where I won the toss and batted on an excellent pitch. Paddy continued his amazing form but Rod and Andrew went early so I joined Paddy and we took charge. After throwing my wicket away at Bulawayo in search of quick runs, I was really keyed up to knock off that first goal of mine. I had only two innings left so I approached my task positively, determined to get in. At lunch I was on four but by tea had reached my 14th test century and that special milestone. I had become the first man in test history to record a century against seven different nations. It was an innings that gave me a great deal of pleasure, despite the gentle attack offering. Then after tea, with Ken also playing well, we walked single after single as Houghton had all but three men on the boundary.

This certainly wasn't the way I had learned to play the game, but it worked for him as I holed out soon enough for 140 and then we lost two more to the new ball. From 300 for three we had slumped to 314 for six and then next day succumbed for 335. Zimbabwe trudged their way towards 283 and then, surprisingly, declared with nine down, still 52 behind. Maybe, just maybe, they were beginning to feel the pressure from all sides to make a game of it.

Then, to their credit, they attacked us, running in aggressively to reduce us to 77 for three. I realised I needed to stick around, so I quietly built an innings, unlike the first, to take us out of danger. Ken looked good, so again we built up a lead before I played across one and was lbw. I was struggling physically as, after the first day of the test, we had played the one-dayer and I had batted through in chasing 275. I'd strained an Achilles' tendon and then my left hamstring, as we rallied to knock off the runs in front of a stunned crowd. I could only assume that they were stunned, for they offered no applause to our remarkable reply. We had won with five overs to spare but I had picked up some injuries in pacing myself through 94. Now, in the second innings of the second test, the 11th day of 12, I had physically broken down and, in so doing, had missed the chance to score twin tons in a test.

We set Zimbabwe a very accessible 315 in 75 overs, and Andrew led the team in my enforced absence. He thought I was crazy with my declaration but I felt that, since Zimbabwe had never adopted a positive attitude, it would be difficult for them to change tack, let alone execute the task effectively. As I'd hoped, they didn't shut up shop straightaway. With half an hour to lunch they came out loose and wild and in no time were three down. Perhaps they had succumbed to the criticism for being so negative? They never recovered, trying to keep attacking instead of playing for time, and soon after tea we had bowled them out for 137. Dipak Patel had done the damage with his best figures of six for 50 and New Zealand had its first test victory since beating Australia in Wellington in 1990.

It was a huge relief finally to taste victory in a test after so long. Some might have seen it as an easy win but I felt it was worthy, particularly as Zimbabwe had demonstrated that they were hard to get out if they decided to defend. Our hard-line tactics had paid off. Better still, the win gave us heart for the next stage — we would now challenge the Sri Lankans on even terms.

CHAPTER 13
The Day of the Bomb

We jumped aboard the flight to Singapore, which didn't make much sense to me as we only had to come back on ourselves to reach Colombo. That's the way it works in Christchurch headquarters — a kind of extra challenge to travel as far as possible so long as it's cheaper. Forty hours later we arrived to a warm reception in Colombo. The Sri Lankans were really pleased to see us, particularly the charming and highly respected Chandra S.S. Perera, our liaison officer for every tour since 1984. We settled into the large Taj Sunadra Hotel, had a good sleep and then gathered for our first practice, indoors owing to rain late in the afternoon. We needed the exercise after our long flight and before hopping on a bus next day bound for Kandy, three hours away.

Next morning, 15 November 1992, I visited Mark Plummer at 8.15 for my usual early morning physiotherapy. As I was still battling my injuries, Mark decided on some acupuncture. There I was, lying face down, with six large needles protruding from my left leg, looking vacantly out over the Indian Ocean, when the earth shuddered. Suddenly, 60 metres up, the blast reached its height — smoke everywhere, debris, shards of glass, metal scattering in all directions. I jumped off the table, needles and all, standing in shock as the chaos settled, and the smoke clouds slowly drifted away.

Then, absolute mayhem. People appeared from nowhere, running in all directions in a mad panic, swearing, shouting as traffic screeched to a halt outside our hotel. Mark and I worked our way through a frenzied foyer and down the driveway 20 metres to the front entrance. To the right a mass of people stood in a square, just staring, some whispering, some trembling, fear on their faces. Around the other side of the street we stopped at a temporary roped-off area, just 15 paces from the scene. A black BMW had been blown to pieces, only the main frame intact, wheels, glass, bumpers, plates all scattered around. I stood on something and looked down to see human entrails, bloody flesh.

I clutched Mark's shoulder, tensing again as I recognised the remains of a body, no, two bodies, strewn among the debris, their white uniforms shredded, without arms or lower legs. Limbs had been completely ripped away as blood oozed out of mangled flesh. Dark skin stark against white uniform, no feet, no head, intestines all over the place. I felt my stomach heave and my breath shorten to a gasp.

I'd had enough and gestured to Mark that he could stay if he wanted, but I was out of there. I walked back towards the ocean, over the grassy park, gazing blankly out to sea. I kept thinking, 'What's going on here?' A huge bomb had just exploded 20 metres from our hotel. A bomb had gone off metres from our homeward route last time we were in Colombo. Is this meant for us? Is it some kind of scare tactic telling us to leave again? My head was spinning, trying to work out the motives. Why would it involve us, a goddamned cricket team? Mark caught up with me, turned me around and suggested we head back to the hotel.

As we stepped into the lift Mark turned to me and said, 'This makes this tour pretty interesting, eh? I can't see us leaving for Kandy in the morning now, can you?'

'No chance. It'll take them a while to clean up that mess first. Last time they put on a curfew for two days, so maybe we're stuck here for a while. Let's go and see Wally.'

Wally looked a mess. He was visibly shaken as the boys huddled around him. Adam Parore, sitting next to Wally, asked how it looked outside. 'Not too good,' said Ken, using one of his famous lines. When he was smashed in the face by a lethal Chris Lewis bouncer in 1990 he went down like a sack of spuds. When revived and asked how he felt, that's what he came out with.

Paddy strode in. 'This is bloody ridiculous. Any of us could have been jogging past that spot this morning!'

Dipak was behind him. 'Just like 1987,' he offered.

Ken interrupted them. 'There's still a bloody civil war going on with the Tamils.'

'The place isn't safe, never has been,' Dipak continued.

I told the guys to calm down as much as possible and that I'd speak to the manager. I mentioned to everyone to stick around as it was likely we'd have a meeting in an hour or so. It was 9.45 am as we filed out of the room. On the way out I noticed that Wally's bags were all neatly packed. Either he hadn't unpacked since we'd arrived or else he'd packed them up in the last 20 minutes or so, ready to leave.

'We can't stay here,' I heard someone suggest as I turned into my room.

The boys were certainly in shock. Some were angry and confused, which I could understand. The younger members seemed intrigued by it all, not knowing really what to think, but oddly excited as their first tour was becoming dramatic.

It was 11.02 am. I watched closely as the lads clattered into the meeting, trying to get a feeling for their thoughts, how they were coping. Leif Dearsley, team manager, then asked for attention.

'Gentlemen, the bomb that exploded this morning killed a naval commander and his three aides. Apparently a motorcyclist threw himself under the car with the bomb attached to his waist. He was one of the Tamil Tigers, obviously assigned to assassinate the commander. I've been on the phone to the British High Commissioner who assures me that this is an isolated incident, just a coincidence that it occurred in front of our hotel. The car was actually heading to the Naval Office, just down the road. As there's still plenty to clean up outside I've been instructed by Neil Perera, secretary of the Sri Lanka Cricket Board, that practice is cancelled and that we won't be leaving for Kandy today. It's possible we'll go first thing tomorrow. I suggest you stay around the hotel today and we meet at, say, 6.30 tonight to finalise our next move. The board will support any decisions we make. Any questions?'

Any questions? At once six or seven leapt to their feet. Paddy was first. 'Hold on a minute. How do we know that this place here will be safe from now on? That's two bombs going off close to the New Zealand team, if you take in the 1987 tour. What if someone was out jogging this morning when the bomb went off? Isn't there still a civil war with the Tamils?'

Paddy wanted some answers. He had been convenor of the players' committee since just before the Zimbabwe tour. This group is designed to meet with the board before the start of each season. At our October camp, a week before departure, Paddy had run into huge problems first time up. I had had glandular fever so missed the camp, and almost the tour, while all the others were finalising contracts and outfits as well as practising. In fact all new contracts, except Andrew's and mine, had been put on hold for six months, causing obvious resentment and envy.

The board had introduced a new level of tour payments called the 'rookie level'. Anyone on their first tour would receive less than those on a second trip, but the figure hadn't been circulated, until, at the last minute, Paddy demanded to know it. It was only $600 a week minus tax. That was probably the lowest figure since the early 1980s and the players were made very aware of it straightaway.

The protest was partly on account of the low figure, but also because it looked as though the board were trying to hide it. The players' committee met and decided the team would boycott the tour unless the rookie level was cancelled. Leif Dearsley had to inform the board of this ultimatum, but they said that if that was what the team insisted on, then they would go pick another team. The players' committee backed off but their relationship with the board was severely strained; Paddy had an open row with chairman Peter McDermott.

It was a two-edged sword — the board was at fault for not admitting the new level and the committee was wrong for failing to request another meeting to solve the problem rather than threatening with an ultimatum. Time was running out and again the board expected everyone to agree to their proposals only hours before departure, when players should have been concentrating on practice and training. It was typical of New Zealand Cricket. So unprofessional.

The players also felt let down by Leif, who appeared to be totally pro-board. Compared with Ian Taylor, the previous manager, this was a big difference. It seemed that Leif had been appointed to keep the board informed of everything — which was certainly his job — rather than actually get alongside the players and support them. Even at this early stage some of the players couldn't relate to him, which didn't make for a pleasant environment. The team room, normally next to the manager's, was traditionally a place where the boys could congregate, but so far on this tour it had almost always been empty. I had tried to chat with Leif to help him understand but he simply saw his job differently from our previous manager. So there was a huge adjustment for everyone — and most of them didn't want to make it.

Leif paused for a minute before replying to Paddy's string of questions. 'I'm looking to arrange a meeting with security and the embassies, hopefully later this afternoon, to explain the safety here. Only then can we get a feel for what's happened. The important thing is that you stay in the hotel until further notice.'

'Has the news broken yet back home?' I wanted to know.

Wally spoke. 'Yes, Waddle has been on the radio. It's major news at home, especially as it's our early morning. Everyone is saying we should come home on the next flight. I've checked the airline and we can leave around midnight.'

'Hold on,' interjected Leif, 'let's just see what this meeting tells us, please.'

'Fair enough. When?' Paddy demanded.

'Oh, I'll arrange the meeting in two hours. Cancel the 6.30 time and we'll meet back here at 1 o'clock.' The boys moved out the door, now very confused. More meetings! The media were waiting impatiently outside but we walked straight past them.

It was now 1.10 pm. The whole team met in one of the big conference rooms. In strode the British and Australian High Commissioners, plus two highly ranked army officers, and Neil Perera. They sat at a long table facing us as Leif introduced them one by one. The meeting lasted two hours. We listened to all the information and the comparisons with bomb blasts in London and elsewhere. They stated emphatically that there was no danger and that the Tamils, as always, had got their man without killing any civilians. At least, not since 1987.

The Australian High Commissioner actually put it to us that, if we went home now, then surely that would mean we wouldn't tour London either in future. I quickly suggested that, to be fair, we had experienced back-to-back bombs within hours of each other, even if on separate tours. Maybe it was coincidence, but it had a larger significance than some underground explosion in Shepherd's Bush.

After the top brass had left I decided to address the group. 'Lads, I've taken everything in and I honestly believe the situation isn't like it was in 1987. Then I was convinced there was a civil war around us. Although, as they've explained, there have been bombs since, they've been isolated and targeted. No civilians have been killed and so I believe we're safe. If I was a professional businessman working here in Colombo I'd have no hesitation in staying on. However, if as a team we decide we have to go then we should all go. If only one or two want to leave, the rest can stay and continue the tour.'

It was 6.17 pm. The votes came in as we sat around the room looking at our feet or biting our nails. I gathered 18 bits of paper and started to unfold them. I read out each in turn: 'Stay, leave, stay, leave, stay' and so on. Soon it became apparent that too many wanted to go. The final tally was nine-nine. I announced the result and confirmed that as there were nine who wanted to leave we couldn't carry on with only half a team. We would all return home as soon as possible. Leif Dearsley nodded his approval and said, 'I'll tell both boards of our decision and inform you when we may leave. Thank you.'

Next morning the phone rang. 'Marty, it's Leif. I've spoken to our board and they're not happy with our decision.'

'But they said they would back us whatever we decided.'

'Sure, but after hearing what the High Commissioner said, the board are upset that we still want to come home and Peter McDermott is flying up to talk to the team.'

I sighed. 'Oh, my God. When does he arrive?'

'Late tonight, so we'll meet him first thing tomorrow morning. Naturally we won't be leaving until he's checked out the situation.'

'Beautiful, bloody beautiful! The boys will really love this! Why have they changed their attitude?'

'The Sri Lankan Board are furious. They say it will cause worldwide repercussions. No more tours here, and in reprisal, not many to New Zealand either.'

'Bullshit!' I was aghast. 'A goddamned bomb has just gone off outside our door and that isn't real?'

'Well Marty, there are wider implications and now the governments are involved. Peter is on his way to assess it all and, most likely, to try to persuade those who want to go that they must stay.'

The word soon spreads that McDermott is riding up 'on his big white horse', as Paddy puts it, to save the tour. I'm trying to relax, to calm down, for I'm agitated and frustrated. The problem is that the whole team is split. Nine-all, remember. I hope the boys can keep their heads, think clearly enough for themselves to decide what's best for them. I do want the team to go home as the split is too large. I can't captain a side that's depleted of its talent. As an individual I still believe that it's perfectly safe to stay, so I start working out which players are wanting to leave, and why.

The first are obvious, those with families. Wally, Dipak, Gavin, Rod and Ken all have young families and all have expressed a desire to return to them. Their families back home are really concerned and won't be convinced that their men, 12,000 kilometres away, are perfectly okay. I feel for these five especially, as they are constantly on and off the phone. I worry, though, that they may also be convincing the others that, no matter what, they're going, and that everyone should be leaving together. As captain I agree we should all go if we lose too many, but I can't agree that they should be influencing the younger players. It's important, from this point on, that each individual has his own say. I have tried to instil a policy of being fair to 'the team', but with McDermott on his way I know it will come down to each person. So we wait.

I ring Simmy, who instinctively feels that it's safe, and that I'm doing the right thing. I explain our dilemma and she suggests I work on my gut feeling. Trouble is, I can't find one.

Peter McDermott arrived after midnight, checked into his hotel and grabbed a few hours' sleep before he summoned Leif, Andrew and me to his room. He was reasonably calm and relaxed and also seemed well informed. Leif had already briefed him on arrival, reporting on the general feeling, our safety and, most important, the nine members Peter needed to address.

The first five were already obvious, and I had spent much of the previous afternoon working out the positions of the others. Both Chris Harris and Blair Hartland had lost their fathers in the past year, so naturally the families at home were desperate to see their sons. On reflection, Blair decided to carry on. Adam Parore had already thrown in his lot with the senior players but, after we discussed it, he accepted that he would be better to keep his place in the team. He had no special need to rush home. The other two were Willie and Paddy. Willie had received word from his parents that he should return. No matter how hard he tried, he couldn't console them enough to stay on. Finally to Paddy. From the outset he showed he had the team's interests totally at heart. And, as at the camp, he was adamant the team be treated fairly. Once we had decided as a team to return, then that was that — Paddy was going home with everyone else. I admired his loyalty, but I felt that maybe he was sacrificing his own personal position and that, in so doing, he was beginning to act very stubbornly.

By now Peter was aware, through Leif, of those individuals he needed to talk with. First he addressed the team, expressing an understanding for those with families, and assuring all of us that no one need feel under any pressure. Consequently, everyone did. He then decided to speak to each of us individually before asking for a new vote. Most significantly, he wanted to speak to Wally. Before leaving New Zealand Peter had heard Wally saying on the radio that no matter what the team did, he was coming home. This was a kneejerk reaction which didn't go down at all well, so Peter called in Wally first. It was a disaster.

I was playing a board game with Andrew and Mark Plummer when Wally appeared at the door, crying. He just couldn't control himself and broke down completely once inside. 'This is terrible, awful. He's calling everyone in and demanding to know what reason we have for going home. But he won't accept our reasons. He's asked me to resign right away. He says that I have no feeling for what we've achieved in the past and that I don't care for the future. He also wants those going home to write a letter of resignation from the tour. He just doesn't understand!'

Wally felt he had no choice but to go home. The night before his son Gregory had screamed down the phone, 'Come home, Dad, please!' Wally had already lost his first wife tragically when he was on tour in 1976 and he didn't want to put his family through any more worry.

We three were nearly speechless. I could only mumble how sorry I was. I felt angry and I felt useless. It seemed that, after all, Peter was going to put pressure on the players. I didn't like the look of this.

Finally the interviewing ended and Peter called Andrew and me in to discuss the outcome. He got straight to the point. 'Wally, Gavin, Dipak, Rod, Willie and Paddy are all adamant about going home. Ken and Chris Harris are still thinking about it, although they, too, would like to return. I want this tour to continue as there are huge implications if it doesn't. We stand to lose our tour guarantee if we quit, plus there are Sri Lankan Board threats of political repercussions. I think we can replace those who want to go. What do you think, Hogan?'

'If you think you can replace seven players, forget it. It's too tough. I understand the implications. I want to stay, but when my team is down to nine players and a physio, you've got to be joking,' I replied.

'So what say Ken and Chris turn round? Have we a team then?'

'Shouldn't we find that out first?' I suggested.

'Yes, I do. I'll see them again in five minutes after Chris has called home again.' He busied himself with his papers.

After another hour Peter had the final list. Ken and Chris Harris would stay. Some of the others were furious, deciding that these two had been offered a contract by the end of the season in return for staying. Paddy was livid with Ken for being a turncoat after he had been

165

adamant about going home. There was an air of tension and distrust among the boys.

Now the tour was on, despite my concern at seeing the team split and some of the boys extremely upset. I told Peter that we should continue but that it would be extremely difficult. We started talking about some possible replacements, but right then I needed some time alone.

Later that day I went to visit Wally and found him sitting sadly among his untouched bags. He was so angry with Peter, almost violently, and it was hideous to see the whole team in disarray like this. Wally and I discussed replacements but, no matter who we considered, we still looked weak. John Wright had agreed to come but there was no mention of another coach, unless Ross Dykes joined the side. Peter wanted Wrighty to oversee the team while I concentrated on captaincy and coaching. As this plan unfolded I slowly began to believe that perhaps something could be fashioned out of all this, so I cheered up a little. Peter asked me to speak to Willie and Paddy one more time.

I pleaded with them to forget the team decision and concentrate on their personal contribution. Willie had to go back to his parents, so I didn't argue further. Paddy, however, wanted to stick to the original principle. He despised the arrival of McDermott, saying he was going home whatever. He dug in his heels, and there was nothing I could say to budge him. I asked him to be perfectly clear in his reasons, once he returned. I told him I'd miss him immensely and he apologised for not being able to help. My best mate walked out and I swallowed hard, for he was my confidant.

Paddy and I had grown up together, played cricket together since I was 10. We were team-mates at Cornwall and then through our Auckland Grammar days. We became really close, however, when I persuaded him to come to Central Districts in 1986–87. I felt he needed to get out of Auckland, much as I did, and to find some direction playing with me. We were like brothers, having already spent a lot of time together in England in the early 1980s. I loved Paddy. A man full of passion and energy, hugely proud and loyal, when he batted for New Zealand he showed a spirit greater than that of any other Kiwi I've played with. He would put his body, his heart and his soul on the line. Deep down, I admired his stance on going home. In all probability, if I hadn't had a contract or hadn't been the captain, I might have done the same. But I felt, at the same time, that there was no right or wrong, that it was a hard one to call.

Those returning to New Zealand watched as we climbed aboard the bus to take us south to a beach resort for a couple of days' rest before the replacements arrived. It was a hollow, sad moment. I tried not to think about it, not looking back as we pulled away after wishing them a safe journey home. It was over. The team was split, but the tour continued.

After three days at the Triton Hotel, a splendid resort on the coast, our replacements John Wright, Justin Vaughan, Michael Owens and Grant Bradburn arrived. Only Wrighty was experienced, the others being pretty much untried. Our itinerary had to be changed, with two practice one-day games at Matara before heading back to Colombo for two tests and three one-day internationals. We would be home a week earlier and it was pleasing that both boards were able to resolve this amicably.

The practice games were a disaster. We were beaten in both, with no one showing any sort of form or determination. We looked resigned, deflated and tired after a hectic and horrible week. I was struggling to find the drive to lead from the front and pump the boys up. Wrighty looked terrible with the bat, hardly surprising after a winter off. He spent a lot of time practising, trying to work out his game, but that left little time to help or oversee the others. I had to forgo personal preparation while I took on the dual roles of captain and coach. Peter McDermott, who stayed on for the opening games, could see that our spirits were pretty low. He told me to hang in there and play well but he knew that we were really up against it from the start.

In the end I believed that the tour had to go ahead for the sake of keeping the game alive in Sri Lanka; it was important, also, for the game of cricket. But it was vital that there be no repercussions from recent events. Everyone had good reasons for their views, as did Peter, but he should definitely have had someone else attending all the interviews to try and balance the pressures. The fact that six players had already made up their minds to return meant there was a fair amount of anxiety, particularly in Wally's case. He knew that, by going home, he ran the risk of losing face and possibly his job with New Zealand Cricket, particularly as he and Peter had crossed swords.

We returned to Colombo and checked into the Taj again. This time

I was given the key to Room 309. As I unpacked my bags it dawned on me that this would be my home for the next three weeks and that would be a long time in the same hotel room. Practices were ruined by persistent rain and the test ground was under water before the first test. The pitch at Moratuwa looked damp and green so when Wrighty, Andrew and I met to discuss the team our first thoughts were to opt for a seam attack. As Wrighty was still concerned about his poor form, he felt we should stack the batting, playing Parore at number eight. Andrew and I felt a spinner and three seamers would be better balanced, but I wanted Mark Haslam because he'd been the first choice spinner for the tour. Andrew preferred Bradburn because he could bat better, supporting Wrighty's theory. I wished Wally were around to give us some feedback. Wrighty was dead keen to play his Auckland team-mate Justin Vaughan instead of a spinner, for he could bat six or seven and bowl seamers, while I was feeling that we should be more positive and think about winning the game. In the end I was outvoted and we selected a long batting line-up and no spinner.

On the first morning I inspected the pitch and tried to delay the start. I was now in a totally negative frame of mind, especially as Wrighty urged me to prolong the delay at least to lunchtime so he wouldn't have to bat for a short period before the break if we lost the toss. I understood Wrighty's request, but we had to look as though we wanted to get out there.

The New Zealand media were noting that we seemed to be as negative as Zimbabwe had been when we had criticised them. They were right, of course, and I felt foolish that I hadn't taken the bull by the horns. We lost the toss and were soon in trouble, not to the seamers but to the Sri Lankan spin. They had included two spinners in their side because they thought the pitch would turn.

One of the Sri Lankan spinners was Warnaweera, an off-spinner with an extremely peculiar bowling action. After facing him for one over I was convinced that he was a blatant chucker, spearing the ball into the turf and making it climb and turn off a length. I questioned the umpires on the legality of his action but all I got in reply was, 'He toured New Zealand in 1991 and he wasn't called then.'

'The difference is he's throwing it now and you know it.' As far as I was concerned this was cheating, so I decided to try and take him out of the attack myself, but Ranatunga dived full length at mid-wicket and somehow plucked the ball out of the air with his right hand. It was a silly tactical error and I was beside myself with guilt. Fortunately Ken and Chris Harris played superbly and so we reached a respectable total, but the Sri Lankans proved their ability and passed us with only two down. We managed to draw the game, and receive some justified criticism, as rain curtailed play.

Rain washed out the first one-dayer but the weather cleared for the second test. The pitch looked great, smooth and white, certain to take spin at some stage. We included a spinner but I lost the vote on Haslam again because Bradburn could bat better. This annoyed me as Haslam, I felt, was the better bowler and after the first test I knew we should attack more. We needed to take 20 wickets and although it was suggested we needed seven or eight run-outs, I still wanted to be positive.

We lost the toss again and Sri Lanka smashed our poor bowling everywhere, reaching a total of 394. When we batted we looked good for a time until the ball really started turning, so from 57 for none we slumped to 102 all out, and had to follow on. I went for nought. I played at a ball outside my off-stump, which spun back, missed my bat and pad, and bowled me around my legs. It turned all of a metre.

I lay awake all night battling with the negatives. I was convinced I'd finish with a pair of ducks. I kept seeing myself dismissed in all manner of ways, so I worked on visualising different, positive scenarios. It took me hours and hours. Finally I begin picturing myself scoring, slowly at first, then dominating, hitting the bowling, taking it to the spinners and going on to score the century I wanted so badly.

In nine test innings in Sri Lanka I'd scored only 155 runs at the miserable average of 17. This was my one last chance to do something worthwhile, so I visualised for another hour, well into the night, finally dropping off to sleep around 5 am, only to wake again at 6.30. I was tired but somehow relaxed. Under my door was an envelope which I opened, only to find it was a chain letter: 'If you send 20 of the same letter to 20 different people then you will have extremely good luck.' What did I do? I raced down to the reception desk and had 20 copies made, asked for 20 envelopes and addressed one to each member of the team plus a few back home. I couldn't believe what I was doing, but anything that might bring some luck was worth trying.

By the time we reached the ground all 20 letters had been posted or handed over, although I insisted no one need open them. So, with that off my mind, I began to focus on the job in hand. I felt so relaxed and prepared that I was keen to get out there. When the second wicket fell I was on my way to give it a real go.

This is the way I remember it. Second ball I turn to square leg and call Wrighty through to get off the dreaded pair. He's backing up well, so the fielder throws the ball to my end. I sense danger and stretch out, only to see the ball fly past everything and run to the fence. Five not out, and the luck is running my way. Except ... as I stretched out to make my ground I felt my hamstring strain and now I know I'm restricted if I try any more quick singles. Instead I'll have to strike out at anything within reach. The ball is really turning but it doesn't stop me from striving to dominate. I race to 39 and stride in to lunch. Wrighty's there, doing a great job, running into form.

After the break I play myself in quietly, when suddenly I feel my luck's running out. I defend a ball from Warnaweera, bat to pad, and then down to the ground just short of Asanka Gurusinha at silly point. As he scoops the ball the fielders appeal for the catch and even before they've finished the umpire raises his hand.

Gurusinha at this point hasn't even appealed but, on seeing the umpire's hand up, he turns to celebrate with his team-mates. I can't believe it! I stand there, looking straight at him, and say, 'Come on, Asanka, you didn't catch that, it bounced first. Look at me and tell me you caught it.' By now Wrighty's coming down the pitch, probably to tell me to move on, when I appeal to Gurusinha once more, 'Come on, you guys, play the game!'

Wrighty turns to the umpire and asks, 'What's your decision, umpire?' The umpire has just spoken to his colleague at square leg and thankfully he crosses his arms and reverses his decision — 'Not out.'

I breathe a huge sigh of relief but keep my eyes on Gurusinha. Why the hell would he want to cheat anyone out so blatantly, especially as they were cruising to victory? I get down the other end and the umpire walks over and says, 'I'm very sorry for giving you out. Thankfully, I heard the fieldsman tell his team-mates he didn't take the catch.'

'Thank you,' is all I can say.

Now I'm really pumped up and I start lashing out, reaching 50 with a series of boundaries. I notice Gurusinha has left the field and I wonder if he's beginning to regret his action. I know Asanka quite well and regard him as a nice enough person so the whole episode bewilders me.

I guess the Sri Lankans are so eager to force their first test victory over New Zealand that their normal instincts desert them.

I'm going strong, taking their three spinners apart. I go after Warnaweera especially, for he is the man I've branded a chucker, and it pleases me to see the ball sail over the ropes a few times. Wrighty and I are into an excellent partnership, with him so solid in defence and still encouraging me to stay positive.

I've no intention of changing styles at this point although my hamstring is tightening badly and I'm relying totally on boundaries. On this pitch, with the ball turning sharply, attack is the best method of defence. The risk is a bat-pad chance and Ranatunga keeps two or three fielders close until I approach the 80s. Then three are dropped back to the leg-side fence but I blaze on, ignoring the nervous 90s until, on 99, I go for a short single only to have to dive to make my ground.

I pick myself up, brush off the dust and raise my bat high to the applause for my 15th test 100. The joy is overwhelming. Wrighty covers the length of the pitch to congratulate me with a huge bear hug. I'm so happy tears are streaming down my face. At last I've broken the drought in Colombo! I last only 10 minutes longer before edging to short leg, right on the tea break. As I limp off I feel that, under the circumstances, I've played my best test innings to date.

The boys kept on fighting, taking us right into the last day. It was a good performance and I was pleased beyond words. After the test Asanka walked in and apologised profusely. I told him to forget it.

My hamstring was in trouble, however, and I asked Mark Plummer about the risk of continuing to play on it. Two one-dayers were coming up, but if I played I would jeopardise my chance of being fit to play the Pakistanis as soon as we returned home. He left it to me, so I informed Leif and Wrighty that I couldn't play.

So, after 24 long, unenjoyable days, I was relieved to pack my bags at last and leave Room 309. It had certainly been a torturous nine weeks. I reflected on what might have been for this New Zealand side, after the successful build-up in Zimbabwe. At home we would have to start all over again with the Pakistanis touring first, and then the Aussies coming for a full test series. The team split had horrified me but only time would tell if the effect would last. At least I could enjoy Christmas and look forward to 1993, knowing that my own performances were still on target, and hope that the team had not lost any ground.

CHAPTER 14

Who Can You Trust?

> If I were asked to give what I consider the single most useful bit
> of advice for all humanity it would be this: Expect trouble as an
> inevitable part of life and when it comes, hold your head high,
> look it squarely in the eye and say, 'I will be bigger than you.
> You cannot defeat me.'
> — ANN LANDERS

Christmas Day 1993 was perfect. Simmy and I had joined our two families out at Grendon Road for most of the day, thoroughly enjoying the magnificent food Audrey had arranged.

Rodger Curtice, Simone's father, known as 'Croc' after Crocodile Dundee, is a great guy, a real salt of the earth character. Whatever the situation, Croc always has a smile, keeps his sense of humour and retains his faith in people. He's had his share of ups and downs, but always remains himself and I admire him greatly. He has become, like Dad, a close mate, someone to whom I enjoy talking and who helps to keep things in perspective.

Judith, my mother-in-law, is a true Italian, always talking, expressing her opinion, full of life and energy. Gerard, Simone's only brother, is a handsome, genuine person who has followed his father into the landscape architecture business. He's like a younger brother to me, even though he is completely different — quietly determined rather than openly competitive.

The Curtices all get on well with our family. Aud and Jude will discuss anything; Goose — Dad's nickname because he acts like one now and then — and Croc are quite happy to chew on a cigar and sip on some good local red wine. It was a wonderful Christmas, everyone sharing the joys of being close and loved, and of being together. It never happens enough.

Sometimes we all meet at Piha, where Rodger and Jude live, and where we own a bach nearby. These are the times when I truly feel at ease, because these are the people I can really trust, from whom I can ask advice, and to whom I can express my frustrations and emotions. I know, too, that these breaks are all too short and that soon I'll have to get back to work, to my job of cricket.

On Boxing Day I packed again and flew to Wellington. New Zealand Cricket had invited Pakistan, who were free for two weeks during their involvement in the Australian World Series, to play three one-dayers and a one-off test. Pakistan snapped up the offer, as their alternative was to travel around Australia, but I'm afraid the idea went down like a lead balloon with us.

Initially we were due to arrive home from Sri Lanka on 23 December, enjoy Christmas and then play Pakistan on 27, 29 and 31 December. This was ridiculous. Thanks to the bomb, dare I say it, our revised schedule saw us return home a week earlier to rest and be with our loved ones. We had felt the original schedule was unreasonable and had said so in no uncertain terms before the season began. Now, since the bomb had changed the programme, I figured that maybe it wouldn't be such a bad thing to get back together as soon as possible, and put the Sri Lankan tour behind us.

The team selected for Pakistan included those who had come home early, and this pleased me because we needed to have our best team — we needed some good results. I was determined to lead from the front against the world champions. Our administration had arranged for all the players, plus wives or girlfriends, to fly to Wellington for practice the afternoon before the first game. Typically, only half the side arrived on time and practised, as travel arrangements weren't circulated quickly enough from HQ. It wasn't the sort of preparation I had hoped for, but after a team dinner and some rebuilding of our old team spirit we looked forward to the challenge ahead.

Pakistan had been struggling in Australia, so I sensed that if we applied pressure early on we had an even chance of winning. We won the toss, sent them in and produced a bowling and fielding display quite the equal of anything we had accomplished in the World Cup. I made more than 15 bowling changes and thoroughly enjoyed having my old team back together again. We bowled them out for 158 and walked in with good spirits. Then Wasim Akram cleaned us out.

He produced a devastating spell of five for 18 and completely dominated the afternoon. I managed top score of 28 but paid the penalty for not being sufficiently patient and batting through the innings. One incident was so typical of the way the Pakistanis could annoy you time and again. I had driven Aaqib into the hands of Aamir Sohail, their left-hand opener, at cover about 25 centimetres off the ground. As he completed the catch he yelled at me, 'Fuck off, you motherfucker!' I hadn't provoked him in any way during the match but he still had a go at me. I know he was still incensed because I had hit him for plenty in the Hong Kong sixes last October. In fact, I had reached 26 off only five balls, the last two balls from Sohail going for six each, when I hit a shot that landed just inside the rope for four. This took me to 30, one short of when you have to retire. Sohail, though, insisted to the umpire that the ball had gone for six and that therefore I should retire on 32. While he was arguing I suggested to the umpire that he ignore the little prick; the umpire agreed. I hit the next ball, my last, for a huge six and proceeded to walk off, mentioning, as I left, that my grandmother could bowl better than that. He ran after me screaming that I was nothing but a so-and-so motherfucker and that I should shove off — or words to that effect. At the end of the game, which they won, he offered his thanks by sticking his middle finger into the air, in my direction.

As soon as he caught me at Wellington and vented his feelings I decided to hold my ground and check with the umpire if he had in fact caught the ball fairly, which I knew he had. With that, about four Pakistani players came running towards me in a fit of rage, claiming that I was setting them up — which I was. It was just like the ball tampering: I wasn't going to let them walk over me, or anyone else. It's fire with fire when you play the Pakistanis.

Unfortunately, we lacked sufficient fight in our reply, relying too much on the next person to score the runs. No one took responsibility and I worried that, after the Sri Lankan disaster, the stuffing had been well and truly knocked out of us. We were good in the field because we were together, but while batting we looked exposed and frightened, as though we didn't want to be out there. I knew that in our next match I had to be there throughout to show the way.

At Napier we repeated our excellent bowling and fielding. Pakistan never got going and were all out for 137. Although Paddy went early again this time, there was more resolve from all the remaining top-order batsmen and we triumphed quite comfortably. I played it tight, determined to be there at the end, even though I didn't feel in great touch. The Pakistanis' bad behaviour continued; Aaqib Javed was suspended for one game for calling umpire Brian Aldridge 'a fucking cheat'. Later in the inquiry captain Javed Miandad claimed that Aaqib was only talking to himself, calling himself 'a fucking cheat'. Well, I cracked up laughing when he said that as you'd expect. As I was a witness to the incident, the Pakistanis really had it in for me, with talk about how Waqar or Wasim was going to run through the crease and bowl off 15 metres next time we played. Anyway, we levelled the series and headed for Auckland for the final match.

The Eden Park pitch looked bare and brown and logic suggested batting first if we won the toss. I played a hunch against logic and made them bat again. It was the same story: early wickets, outstanding bowling from Gavin and Dipak and excellent fielding to back them up. They made only 133 but we needed to work hard this time to hold out their pacemen, Wasim Akram and Waqar Younis, whether off 15 or 22 metres.

We had learned from Wellington and, by showing great concentration, we won by six wickets with overs to spare. It was an excellent performance all round and I was delighted with the boys for coming back together and showing all the critics that our one-day game was as good as ever.

During their innings I had jammed my ring finger between the ball and my knee, causing a bad cut and hideous swelling. I had managed to bat, in some discomfort, to take the boys home with 57 not out but the finger worsened and I was now in doubt for the test at Hamilton in three days' time. I didn't make it. The finger became infected on the top joint, so I pulled out on the morning of the match, and Rod Latham replaced me. As Andrew Jones had resigned the vice-captaincy the selectors naturally chose Mark Greatbatch to stand in for me as he was the vice to Andrew in a couple of matches on the Zimbabwe tour. NZC then vetoed Wally's endorsement of Paddy and selected Ken Rutherford for the job. It seemed that Paddy was being punished for returning home from Sri Lanka.

It was a huge blow to Paddy, who now saw any future leadership opportunity flying straight out the window. He was bitter, really bitter. I was furious, totally opposed to this latest decision, but there was nothing that I could do. I tried to tell Paddy that this had been exactly what I was trying to get through to him in Colombo. He took it hard, but vowed to get stuck into his work just the same. So Ken Rutherford became captain upon my late withdrawal.

This was an incredible transformation in Ken's position; only 12 months before he had been asked to take a more professional approach to his cricket, and now he was the boss. Ken acknowledged the responsibility and believed he had the tactical acumen to do the job well.

Right from the word go he looked in control and his bowlers, especially Murphy Su'a, backed him to the hilt. Pakistan were bowled out cheaply and then Paddy strode out there and played one of the great knocks for New Zealand. Obviously stung by his demotion, he showed enormous character and commitment to put his side in front with a magnificent innings of 133. Wasim and Waqar tried all sorts of tricks to remove the big man but he was too motivated to stop.

New Zealand had a sizeable lead on a pitch that offered plenty of encouragement and with the very first ball of Pakistan's second innings Danny knocked over Sohail's poles to give him a pair and us the perfect start. It couldn't have happened to a nicer guy! The boys did well despite resistance again from Inzamam, and bowled them out to leave us only 127 to win. With two and a bit days to go there would certainly be a winner.

Tragically, Paddy had a finger broken in the early overs and was then dismissed a few balls later. The rest looked too tense and failed to attack, allowing Miandad to set aggressive fields for his two key men. By stumps the score was 39 for three and I had returned to Auckland, having relinquished my room and expense allowance to my replacement, Rod Latham. I had to watch from a seat in front of the television.

It was going to be a fascinating struggle with so few runs to get, but up against the best bowling duo in the world. The key to success was Andrew Jones and Ken. We had already wasted one night-watchman and so Ken needed to come in next ahead of Rod. The attitude had to be positive. Unfortunately, Ken waited until number seven, which was far too late. Andrew was dismissed by a freakish catch at short leg and there went our chance. It was a real shame; we deserved a win for the way we had bowled and fielded. I felt for the guys, who had come up against the best bowlers in the world and lost.

It was no disgrace, of course, but there was a certain lesson to be learned again: that everyone had to take responsibility, and had to want to get out there and take on the challenge, no matter the strength of the opposition. It was encouraging to see the lads bowl so well and a big plus came from the media praise of Ken's captaincy in the field. He earned plaudits for his first-up effort but the wave of enthusiasm for him to remain as captain after my return built to such a pitch that I began to suspect there was more to it.

Only when I was away from the international spotlight did it suddenly dawn on me. The media, in particular those who had travelled to Zimbabwe and Sri Lanka, had become puzzled and disillusioned with aspects of my leadership. I realised where I'd lost them, especially Don Cameron of the *New Zealand Herald* and Bryan Waddle of Radio New Zealand, plus the New Zealand Press Association correspondent Sri Krishnamurthi. After verbally attacking Zimbabwe for negative play, I had turned around and adopted the same attitude when our post-bomb revamped side took on the full Sri Lankan team. In their eyes I'd turned full circle. I should either have carried on positively from Zimbabwe and backed our team or I shouldn't have been so high and mighty to Zimbabwe in the first place.

I felt at the time that I should have backed us against Sri Lanka, particularly as we had nothing to lose, but I wasn't strong enough at that stage and the whole bomb episode had left me with a sense of regret. I know it had made a negative impression on the media, who had witnessed my weakest moments. Certainly, when I stood my ground in Colombo, Don Cameron seemed to lose all faith in me whatsoever. Waddle, who has always been a supporter and a friend, was definitely confused and puzzled and slipped into neutral gear. The media were now relishing Ken Rutherford's performance, which was good from a long-term viewpoint, but I felt I deserved a reprieve after the hardships of Colombo.

I still felt that I took the right aggressive approach toward Zimbabwe. We had been shunned in many ways, and were also desperate for results and a test win. I tried to snap Zimbabwe out of their negative mentality, to give us a game. As it turned out, it worked.

By mid-February the Australians had arrived for a full test series. They began the tour with a match at New Plymouth in which I captained the President's XI and felt in great shape, scoring 163. John Wright had just announced his availability for what would be his last test series but the shock news was that Bruce Taylor, the New Zealand selector who was bursar at a Dunedin college, had been charged with fraud and theft. This was a huge shock and an embarrassment to New Zealand Cricket.

Either a new selector had to be found in a hurry, or the three remaining selectors, who included Wally Lees (appointed after the World Cup), would be enough to do the job. So Don Neely, Ross Dykes and Wally sat down to pick the side to play the Aussies in the first test in Christchurch.

Having played at Lancaster Park a couple of times already in the season, I suggested that we select four quick men plus Dipak Patel, with Chris Cairns and Adam Parore batting six and seven. We all agreed that those two had matured enough to handle higher batting positions but the cry went up that it was foolish to go into a test with only five specialist batsmen. We hoped our three allrounders would cover that contingency. What we really needed, though, was enough bowling to contain Australia's superb batting line-up.

We had three days, plenty of time, to prepare for the test. I told the media that we expected to do well even if, as usual, we were the underdogs. Persistent rain kept the pitch damp and green and I began to worry that it would be slower than expected when we chose the team, and that perhaps we would need a stock bowler like Willie Watson. But it was too late, so we had to go all out with our quicks.

Wally wasn't his normal self. He was starting to whisper in little groups about his contract renewal in April. After the loss to Pakistan in the one-off test he was taking the flak from John Parker, a former test player, who attacked our practice procedures and called for his mate Geoff Howarth to take over. Depressed after the Pakistan loss, Wally needed reassurance. We had a long talk in which I asked him to forget about his contract, forget about Sri Lanka and pump the boys up for the Aussie series. Then he came out and said he was annoyed that Wrighty had returned to the team: 'He's stuffed us around so often about whether he'll play, that I can't be bothered with him any more.' Really, Wally was nervous because he feared that Wrighty, like John Parker, believed that Howarth should replace him.

So Wally and Wrighty were at loggerheads — in fact, they weren't even acknowledging each other. I hoped that this would not affect the rest of the team and that both men would knuckle down to help me motivate the boys enough to give the Aussies a game. There was also a nasty feeling about the contracts again. The boys were unhappy about NZC's lack of action in this area. They were told that there was no money left to set up any more contracts, which immediately put Andrew and me, the only contracted players, under the spotlight. There was a lot of bitterness building within the dressing room, particularly, I felt, from senior men such as Ken and Dipak, who had played so well during the World Cup.

Happily, though, we won the toss and I could ask Allan Border to bat. This was our big chance to catch them on the back foot, knowing they had just come off a hiding from the West Indies at Perth. We went out full of good intentions and opened up with Danny, three slips and a gully, short leg and a normal attacking field. Then, for some absurd and absolutely stupid reason, I did away with the short leg and put in a third man. I was somehow thinking that runs would be at a premium and that any edges through slips would go for four. So Danny was operating with a seven-two off-side field. There's nothing wrong with that on occasions, particularly if you're attacking with four slips, but a third man in the first over? Idiot! Almost on cue Boon edged to fourth slip and I dived from third slip, and only fingertipped the catch. Fool!

Danny subconsciously began bowling wider of the off-stump, to his field, but the batsmen didn't have to play while the ball was new and the pitch was green. It wasn't Danny's fault, it was mine. The whole session had got off on the wrong foot and we had all become anxious, especially when no breakthrough eventuated. The harder the bowlers tried, the worse they became. By lunch we had picked up only one wicket, and heads were low.

I realised my mistake and asked the boys to start again, but got no response. No one was really listening. I looked at Wrighty, but he was lying on his back in the corner, reading a book. The room was dead silent, the mood utterly resigned. As we went back out Wally said that the ball was still new and the pitch green, so we must bowl straighter and give support from the field. His words fell on deaf ears.

Life in the middle got worse as the Aussies reached 210 for three at stumps. We had let them off the hook entirely and most of the blame lay with me. Still, it was disturbing to see the team so down and out.

Next day we were all pretty nervous; something had to happen before lunch. Wally and I tried to fire the boys up, then Wally asked Wrighty to say a few words. It had no real effect. Our focus was at an all-time low, and we lost day two by the proverbial country mile. Australia amassed 485, with Allan Border becoming the highest test run scorer, so we had to show some fight in the hour's batting before stumps. Two quick wickets fell immediately, and so it was up to Wrighty and me to survive. I was grim-faced as I walked into a solemn dressing room. I decided I needed to speak to the selectors so I asked Chris Harris, our 12th man, to find Don Neely. We meet 15 minutes later, in the empty stand.

'Don, I don't know what's going on with this team,' I began. 'I mean, I know we bowled badly and I stuffed it up yesterday, but I can't believe the attitude. No one wants to say anything, no one wants to listen, and I'm buggered if I know what to do. Wrighty's hardly said a word, Wally's so worried about this and that, and half the guys can only mutter about contracts and stuff.

'I want to make a suggestion. Why don't you selectors drop me as captain for the next two tests? That might put a bomb under the whole team. I don't want to resign, as I don't believe my standing down would have much effect, but if I'm dropped, well, that may work.

'I'm worried that the guys think I'm untouchable, what with this contract and so on, and that I'm not accountable if we stuff up. I am accountable, and I want them to understand that they are too. Maybe it's best if Wrighty leads for his last two tests, so we can get them performing again. When Wrighty retires, I'll come back.'

Don said that he understood my concerns, but still believed I was the right man to do the job. He finished by saying he'd check with the other two selectors and come back to me. The whole situation since Colombo had become a bloody mess. From a professional point of view I felt that our meeting was important, even just to assess things, to gain reassurance. Even though I hadn't had much faith in Don since that pre-World Cup meeting, I needed to speak to someone within the management system. To be honest, I didn't know who to trust.

Next morning, after a fairly sleepless night, I opened the Christchurch *Press* to find that some hack named John Coffey had gone for my throat. Not about cricket, but about my character, my personality and my so-called inability to make friends. He had read an interview I did with the English magazine *The Cricketer*, in which I had described my 'Life Lines'. I'd been asked for my favourite this and that, best and worst moments, likes and dislikes, and so on. This Coffey had combed through every detail of my answers, taken them out of context and ripped me to shreds. He was particularly sour about my comment that 'newspapers destroy society'. I had become really hot under the collar about the tabloids, especially the Fleet Street mob, and the 'destroy society' remark had been aimed at the way the gutter press was treating the Royal Family, and others.

I headed for the ground, keeping very much to myself. I wasn't in good shape. Apart from Simmy, I just didn't know who to turn to, who, in the cricketing world, I could trust.

I struggled to play a single stroke in the first 40 minutes. I was very defensive and very negative and when Merv Hughes found the edge we were in all sorts of trouble. Only Ken looked assured as we crashed to be all out for 182, well short of the follow-on. Our second innings was only slightly better but Ken went one better by scoring a brilliant century to add to his 50 from the first innings. But we lost by an innings and the press conference was packed with eager vultures ready to pounce.

I expressed my concern about our recent test record, dearly wishing it could improve. I suggested that, like any leader, I was accountable and responsible, and not untouchable because I had a contract and no one else but Andrew did. I hoped that we would improve in Wellington but that we had to work hard, starting with a tough practice the next day. I added that it was up to Wally as well to give us a good dressing down and then pick us up so that we played to the best of our ability.

When I was interviewed for the *Evening Post* I gave Lynn McConnell much the same material, emphasising that I was always accountable if we failed, upon which he asked if there was to be a change of captaincy. I hoped there wouldn't be, I replied, but my record wasn't good and I needed the guys to be more supportive and communicative towards each other.

Meanwhile Don Neely had returned to me and insisted that I carry on. Wally gave us the full build-up speech in the dressing room and we filed out to have a drink with the Aussies. We had a great little session with the victors and, as I left, I turned to Allan Border and said, 'I promise you, AB, that we'll give you a tough series from now on!' He looked at me and nodded. He knew what I meant.

CHAPTER 15

Private Investigation

Checking out the reports, digging up the dirt
Well, you get to meet all sorts, in this line of work ...
... So what have you got, to take away?
Bottle of whisky, new set of lies,
Blinds on the window and pain behind the eyes
Scarred for life, no compensation. Private investigation.
— DIRE STRAITS

First thing next morning I called home. 'How's Dad, Aud?' I asked.

'Not great, Marty. I'm taking him in for some tests this morning so we'll know in a couple of hours.'

'Can you give us a call as soon as you know?' I asked.

'Yes, of course,' she replied. 'Hasn't been a great week, has it?'

'No, it's been hideous, but I just hope Dad's okay.'

Dad had suffered a minor heart attack two days before the test match, and Simmy had had to break the news to me next day. The family didn't want me to be alarmed, especially with the test due to start, but Debbie and Simmy felt it only fair to let me know. It certainly affected me over the next week as I battled to deal with that worry, plus the rest of the débâcle.

I rang Wally and excused myself from practice. I decided to wait for the call, and also to speak with Simmy, who was getting really annoyed with the events of the previous three days. She was mortified that I had discussed with Don Neely the prospect of being sacked. She said I was being stupid, that maybe I needed to spend more time with the team, and that maybe it wasn't a good idea for her to come to Wellington. I had no desire for practice just now, despite my call for hard work the evening before. The tests came through and Dad was okay. He didn't need surgery and so declared he was coming to Wellington to watch me score a century! I was pleased to know he would be there so I relaxed a little and chatted with Simmy. She decided to head back to Auckland, via Wellington for one day, so we agreed and it turned out to be a good morning after all.

On the TV news that night I was severely criticised for failing to attend practice. I assumed that Wally hadn't told anyone my reasons; I didn't want the news about Dad to get out but he could have covered for me. Next day we flew to Wellington where the media turned out in force. I was surprised by the number of journalists as the test had finished two days before and there was surely nothing new to discuss.

To my utter horror, splashed on the back page of the *Evening Post* in bold type, I saw the headline 'CROWE OFFERS TO RESIGN'. I read on to see that Don Neely had exposed everything that we had said in our confidential meeting. I was stunned. Neely was quoted as saying that 'it was a marvellous, courageous gesture to resign, as he has always expressed a huge desire to captain New Zealand. He has made the offer in an attempt to put a bomb under the team.' I couldn't believe it. He had gone to the media and given away everything I had told him in confidence. Maybe he felt he was seeking revenge, after I had mentioned in a TV documentary *Crowe on Crowe*, after the World Cup, that I had been asked to stand down from the captaincy in that infamous meeting at the Basin Reserve. Perhaps he felt I'd broken his confidence. Now the media wanted to know if it was true. I had no choice but to admit that I had made such an offer, but that it had nothing to do with resigning; there had been no mention of the word 'resign'. I told them that if the selectors agreed to sack me then it would show everyone that I was accountable and not untouchable. I said that the selectors had told me to carry on, which I appreciated, but that I was shocked and upset that this had been made public. The press loved it. On top of the test loss, here was a new source of controversy. Just when I thought I was getting over all the negatives, I now had to face the media again and explain myself.

We were waiting for our bags to come off the plane when I finished doing a second retake of a TV interview with Peter Williams of TV One. The cameraman had failed to put in a battery, so I was asked to repeat the whole thing. I obliged, and then noticed Peter race straight over to John Wright. I sensed that something was up but Wrighty refused to do the interview with Williams. We travelled back to the hotel and, as we waited for the lift, Wrighty asked me to come to his room. He looked upset. I sat down while he paced up and down.

'Williams tells me you said I hadn't supported you in the test?'

'That's not right. I never mentioned your name. I said I needed more support from the team whether they were playing their first or their 80th test, and especially from the senior members. Bloody Williams is trying to stir things up as always. You know what he's like. Anyway, I do need far more support.'

'You and Wally never asked for any. I assumed you didn't want me involved. You never asked me to speak at the team meetings.'

'Hey, hold on, since when do we always have to ask you? Shouldn't you be wanting to help?' I was indignant. Wrighty was getting really emotional and I thought we'd both better back off.

Eventually, he spoke: 'Of course I want to help but it's your show, Hogan. You've got to say what you want.'

'I realise that you and Wally aren't communicating much,' I said.

'I don't trust him, Hogan, but listen, we've got two tests to play and I'll help you, anything you want, but you've got to ask more. I want to see this team play well, I'm not in it for much longer. I'll help, you can bet on it.'

'Thanks mate, it's really important. Everyone looks up to you still, so I need you to be the Wrighty of old. Hey, I'm sorry, it's been a tough week.' I shook his hand and left.

It had been a vital meeting and I felt so much better as a result. For one thing, Wrighty was absolutely right. I needed to ask for more, to delegate more. I decided to sort it out for the next team meeting, and to explain to the team about Dad and why I'd missed training. I'd tell them that I hadn't offered to resign but was looking for ways to shake us all up. Even more, we needed to help each other.

Adam Parore had pulled out after he was struck over an eye at nets and needed eight stitches. His eye closed up completely so we called up Tony Blain, who was near selection anyway. Wally and I had felt that we had it wrong in Christchurch with Cairns and Parore at six and seven, and that Tony could give us more stability and experience. The selectors had decided against any changes; now the change was made anyway.

Our team meeting went really well, even 'Chill' Blain adding something. There was more chat and more encouragement so I knew that we would improve in this test. Having lost the toss, we batted first, but this time the Aussie bowlers sprayed everywhere. Paddy and Wrighty put on over 100 to start, with rain ending play early. Paddy was more positive this time out, taking the initiative before he departed for 61. Next day, Friday, Andrew didn't last long so I joined Wrighty to set things up again. I was hit in the back of the head early on by Hughes and this shook me into playing some shots. After all the drama of the last few days it was good to be out in the middle doing what I knew best. We'd lost Wrighty by stumps but I was still there on 62.

About 11 pm the phone rang, waking me from a deep sleep. It was Simmy and she didn't sound good. 'Marty,' she sighed. 'They're saying I'm interfering with the team.'

'What do you mean?'

'On TV3's *Mobil Sport* tonight a panel of so-called experts, led by Eric Young, were talking about you as captain and whether you should stay or go. Then this Murray Deaker speaks out. He said, "Here we see the Australian team all decked out in their blazers and ties, and then we see the Kiwis looking shabby in tracksuits, being led off the plane by Martin and Simone Crowe. Who the hell's running the show?"

'Then they had a vote on whether you should go or stay as captain. Trevor McKewen from the *Sunday News* says you should go, Martin Snedden says you should stay, as does Phil Gifford and finally Deaker yells out, "Martin stays, Simone goes!" '

Why would they make an issue out of Simone walking off the plane with me when several of the others also had their wives with them? To suggest that Simone was 'running the show' was just plain stupid. Sure, the two teams looked different in their respective dress, but what had that to do with my wife? I couldn't work it out. I really liked Murray, he was a good friend of the family, a close mate of Jeff's, so why had he taken a cheap shot at Simone? He had become a radio talkback host a few years back and had worked up great popularity around Auckland. He was outspoken, and passionate about sport. I had always been available for interviews, even allowing him into the dressing room after matches for comment. He got a fair go when it came to dealing with me or the team, so why turn on my wife? It didn't make sense.

My sister, Debbie, rang him up immediately and gave it to him straight. Taking it on herself to speak for our family, she held nothing back. Murray hadn't realised that there were in fact four or five other wives or girlfriends travelling with the team. He had been caught up in the hype. He apologised later, which I greatly appreciated.

I wasn't handling this very well. No sleep, constant worrying, wondering what would be next.

I walked out with Ken to resume our innings on the third morning and began to attack like a wild cornered tiger. I lashed out at everything, scoring 33 runs in 25 minutes, racing into the 90s. Ken then went, followed by Tony Blain and so I was joined by Chris Cairns. For the next five overs I faced four deliveries as Chris couldn't turn the strike over. At the end of each over I would walk down to him, encourage him, and then hope he would take a single. He took one all right, off the last ball of each over! After another 35 minutes I was still on 95, and Chris had gone to Hughes, driving and edging to slip. I managed a two and a single off Warne, but in attempting to quell my growing frustrations I nearly got out taking one risk too many.

Finally, for the first time in 45 minutes, I faced a quick bowler, Craig McDermott. First ball, pitching on off-stump, I groped forward too late, beaten for pace. My stumps were uprooted and I stormed off, threw my bat in my bag rather than at the wall, and disappeared into the physio room for some solitude. Chris had really messed me up but I couldn't be too hard on him as he was still a young player, trying his heart out. I tried to calm down and forget it.

At the end of the third day, 6 March 1993, a Saturday, a press conference was held, as usual, for the benefit of the Sunday press. My duty was to answer questions from all sections of the media about the cricket being played. Beforehand I sat in our dressing room keeping pretty much to myself, contemplating what would happen in the following hour. I had had enough. I was sick of being treated without any respect and had decided I would speak out. There was a knock on the door and I got up to go out, knowing it was Richard Hadlee ready to take me to the conference. I felt quite jittery and nervous as I wandered down the tunnel and into the lunchroom.

The place was full. Thirty-odd chairs were assembled facing the top table where numerous microphones were positioned in front of the hot seat. There was plenty of chat and buzz about the room as I sat down, surveying the gathering. Bryan Waddle got into position to interview me as was the normal procedure, but I quickly put up my hand and asked if I could have everyone's attention as I wished to ask a few questions myself before the conference began. All eyes immediately turned in my direction as pads and pens were lifted and dictaphones and TV cameras were clicked on. I took a deep breath and noticed, as I began, Wally Lees slide into a seat at the back. He was obviously concerned that

I might announce my resignation as captain, but he needn't have worried — I would never resign in the middle of a test match.

I turned to my left and asked Trevor McKewen from the *Sunday News*, who was sitting a couple of metres away, 'Trevor, do you think I'm a homosexual?'

After hesitating for a few seconds he spat out, 'Ah, no.'

Good answer, I thought, as I had been ready to climb over a few seats and smack him one, if he had said otherwise.

'Right. Then why did you imply in a *Sunday News* article that I am?' I was referring to his mentioning that I had a mystery virus, when everyone knew I had had salmonella. Was the mystery virus Aids? That's what I was trying to ask him, but I don't think he understood what I was on about, although the question was a little obscure.

'Ah, now, hey, I'm just the sports editor, I don't know what you're talking about,' he replied.

'Doug Golightly?' He nodded in my direction. 'You mentioned in your latest *Truth* article that the New Zealand team didn't lunch together during the Christchurch test. Where were we supposed to have lunch, Doug?'

'Hey, I'm sticking to my story,' he replied.

His article had implied that the team didn't eat together because the players weren't getting on. What he had written was untrue. During the first two days the bowlers had rested and lunched in the dressing room after bowling, while everyone else went to the lunchroom — the same thing that's happened since the game of cricket began. It seemed unbelievable that someone within the team was feeding *Truth* the line that any disharmony in the team was my fault. It wasn't difficult for me to work out just who that could have been.

My brother Jeff told me that one of the players had dined with Doug during the test match in Christchurch, which wasn't unusual, but he suggested that what he had to say may have given an angle on the spirit within the dressing room. In his next article, 'Sack Crowe!', Golightly ran a story accusing me of polarising the team. I couldn't believe it. I couldn't work out why one of my own team-mates would turn on me behind my back and go to the media. So when Golightly said that he was sticking to his story, it told me that he was definitely protecting his source.

Now, every time I walked into the dressing room I could sense the distrust and resentment. I would think, as I looked around, 'Who else wants me out?' Through my offer to be sacked, I was searching for ways to change things. I felt I couldn't operate successfully if people were working against me. Like every captain, I needed support. If only they knew how hard the job could be, then maybe they would understand and accept that you sometimes have to make decisions that don't please everybody. Deep in my heart I knew that I was trying to do what was best for New Zealand cricket. I needed to focus on getting a competitive unit all working towards a common goal, all working for each other. Then, from a selfish point of view, I could enjoy the success that came with it — along with everybody else. In other words, if each individual could identify what he had to do to help the team and carry it out, then everyone would benefit. That was our secret in the World Cup, that was what I'd taken 18 months to work out, but now it was falling apart. This was happening because some players weren't being rewarded as they should have been after the World Cup. But I still could not condone the backstabbing that was going on.

I stopped my questioning and dropped my head, not now knowing what to think or what to do.

The room was hushed. Finally Don Cameron suggested that perhaps we should all put this behind us and try and get on, a comment I appreciated but found hard to accept just at that point. Then Bryan Waddle, a tiny grin on his face, said, 'Shall we talk cricket then?' I smiled. Just before Bryan started, Jeff Longley, a reporter from the Christchurch *Press*, asked if I felt I was being victimised. I responded with an honest and frank affirmative.

After it was all over I walked out of the room, feeling absolutely devastated and empty. I couldn't believe that, having given my best for my country for over 10 years, I would end up feeling like this — that anyone could feel like this. I felt as though something within me had died, and that I didn't really care any more. I had suppressed my feelings for so long, particularly the rumours and gossip about my sexuality. It was when they started to drag Simmy into the spotlight that I cracked. I felt very sensitive and therefore spoke out. It was an upsetting time; I would come to regret the action I took.

I had questioned Trevor McKewen in particular because I felt the *Sunday News* reporters were going completely over the top in their quest to sensationalise my life. One of their reporters, Scott Cordez, had phoned me after it was discovered I had salmonella, and stated that he had heard from three reliable sources that I had Aids. When I said I wouldn't answer such a stupid question, he replied, 'So you won't deny you've got Aids!' I hung up. He had therefore implied that I was gay, a rumour that had been hanging around ever since Darryl Sambell was my manager.

So when Trevor McKewen, in an article entitled 'King of Pain', said I still had a mystery virus and other physical complications that had affected my career, I bit back. Maybe I had overreacted to the 'mystery virus' comment but on top of the phone call and then another article, the attacks were happening too often. The other article had been print-ed a fortnight before when Simone gave an excellent interview, over the phone, to Radio Pacific. The editor of the *Sunday News* rang to ask if they could transcribe the interview. Simone denied the request, explaining that she could not accept the innuendo in regard to the 'mys-tery virus' comment. The editor said he had recently been appointed to clean up the paper's reputation so, after he had pleaded with her, she agreed, provided they took nothing out of context.

Next Sunday we were mortified to see front-page headlines: 'CROWE'S WIFE HITS AIDS SLUR'. The 'clean' editor had taken a small piece from the radio and blown it up out of all proportion. This was why I had confronted the situation in the only way I knew how — front on. The annoying thing about all this was that I didn't know what it was I'd done to antagonise these reporters or their papers. I certainly had no personal animosity towards McKewen or Golightly; in fact, on the few occasions I had met him Doug Golightly had seemed a reason-able bloke. McKewen I'd never really met. Deep down, though, I knew I should have taken no notice.

The rest of the media were great. I really enjoyed working with the likes of Lynn McConnell of the *Evening Post*, Duncan Johnstone of the *Sunday Star*, Bryan Waddle and Ron Snowden of Radio New Zealand, Murray Deaker of 1ZB, Sri Krishnamurthi and Dave Leggat from NZPA, Geoff Bryan, a fantastic frontman for the cricket broadcasts, and Don Cameron of the *New Zealand Herald*. Other media personali-ties whom I admired and worked well with, although they weren't directly involved in cricket much, were people like Keith Quinn and Phillip Leishman from TVNZ, Ron Palenski from the *Dominion* and Tom Scott. One of my favourite commentators was the energetic Peter

Montgomery, a top man. I thoroughly enjoyed chatting with those outstanding current affairs presenters Paul Holmes and Ian Fraser.

So in most cases I felt good around the media, although I knew there were others out there who didn't like me or my professional attitude. Men with chips on their shoulders, out to cut you down, they would label you as being this or that, but would rarely offer any credible supporting facts or details. Or, if you had done something years before, you were saddled with it for life; you weren't allowed to change in any shape or form, to improve from your mistakes.

One reporter made a thing out of how I was 'unpopular in the team', or that I had fallen out with so many players, but he only ever came out with names like John Bracewell or Mark Priest. Mark and I had in fact never had an open disagreement, but because he was dropped from the team for Dipak Patel while I was captain, those who wanted to believe it decided that Mark and I did not get on. As with the Shane Thomson non-selection, I was only giving the selectors my professional opinion about what I thought was the best team at that time. Surely that's the captain's job. The selectors then go ahead and pick the team with the information they have.

After the press conference I left for the hotel, wound up and defiant one minute, ready to give it all away the next. I dined with Ian Smith and Richard Hadlee, who were there as commentators, and poured my heart out to them. I described the problems that I felt existed in the team and explained that I also felt I had become a target for the tabloids, that *Truth*, for example, was being fed nasty stuff about me. Richard understood all about the media and jealousies — he himself had gone through similar trials — but he told me to be rational, to take time out and think it through. Their support was excellent and I thanked them profusely for their time.

I also sought out my old Somerset team-mate Peter Roebuck, in town writing for top English and Australian papers, but spoke to him only about the media problems and my own form, not about team difficulties. He knew me well enough to suggest I hang in there, that the situation would turn round.

I felt for Simmy, who was going through murder handling the backlash in Auckland. This whole drama was putting huge pressure on us both. She knew I wasn't coping very well, despite my telling her I had it under control. This only made her more upset and so our conversations became shorter and shorter as the tension increased. There was no time to slip away and put it all back together; we simply had to keep going. One thing was for certain — Simmy would never forgive me if I quit. I had to agree with her, and so decided to carry on. My father, though, was filled with fury, which really worried me because of his condition. You could see the bitterness in his eyes as we met and talked things over. Audrey just couldn't understand how you could be giving everything for your country one minute, and then be crucified for doing nothing wrong the next. They were beside themselves with anxiety and concern.

When the test ended in an even draw I felt the team were on the way back. Wrighty and Wally had been excellent, putting their problems behind them and working together for the good of the side. I had, for one half-hour period, given the captaincy to Ken, first because I was very tired and second to see how he would respond. It was no big deal but it became an issue with the commentators. Jeff told me that it was a foolish decision, given the circumstances. He was probably right. Nevertheless, with our improved performance, we all looked forward to Auckland and hoped to have a little luck.

As I checked into the hotel I was handed a bundle of letters. They were all from caring New Zealanders who had been disturbed and disgusted by the tabloid media attacks. They wished me the best, asking me to play on and maintain the pride and passion of the last 10 years. One letter said that at least the focus on me meant someone else wasn't suffering from the tall poppy knocking, for there must always be a victim somewhere, sometime. This was a very interesting observation, one that made me feel so much better. I was overwhelmed by this caring support. When I felt surrounded by enemies on all sides, those letters gave me a huge lift.

Practices went well, and we sensed that we could pressure the Australians into some mistakes. Two nights before the test the Bank of New Zealand, our series sponsors, took us all out on a harbour cruise. The host was the brilliant comedian David McPhail, who soon had us smiling and laughing. It was just the medicine we needed, at just the right time.

191

CHAPTER 16

Fighting Through

Danny Morrison charged in, showing perfect rhythm and balance. He was at the height of his powers, swinging the ball late and at pace. He had struck form at Wellington, taking a career best seven for 89, delivering some balls that were simply unplayable. Now he was in the groove again.

It was 12 March 1993, the opening hour of the third test at Eden Park against Australia, our greatest enemy. The lads were determined to continue our improvement since Christchurch and a positive aggressive start to the test could see us cause an upset. Allan Border won the toss and, after some deliberation, decided to bat. That suited us as we had to exploit any initial movement in the pitch. Also, the weather was very humid, helping to retain the moisture in the pitch till the afternoon. Our bowlers were dead keen, highly motivated to get into their work. The man to lead the way was Danny Morrison.

He was our main hope at this point, as we desperately needed a breakthrough before Mark Taylor and David Boon became settled. He got it. It was a beautifully pitched in-swinger to the left-hander Taylor, who jammed down in trying to catch up with the late swing, missed and was plumb leg before wicket. Willie Watson, as if not wishing to be outshone, completely outdid Boon, also trapping him in front lbw. Then Danny again.

This time, using all his pace, he ripped one past Langer, who was caught behind. Then Willie. Bowling the unplayable leg-cutter, pitching middle to miss off stump, and Damien Martyn became Australia's fourth victim as he, too, fell to the waiting gloves of Tony Blain. Finally, to complete the perfect hour's bowling before lunch, Danny reached his ton of wickets in test cricket by dismissing the best, Allan Border. Building up full steam, Danny moved in for the kill. This was the most prized scalp, the greatest run scorer in test history, and Danny wanted him, wanted him badly. First he beat him outside the off-stump, the left-hander groping in hope, then, relying on his key delivery, the in-swinger to a left-hander, he beat Border through the gate and clipped the top of the off-stump.

Immediately after play on the second day of the first test against Australia at Lancaster Park in 1993 I suggested to Don Neely that I be sacked as captain.

Press conference time, my least favourite task, but I always tried to satisfy the needs of the media. Here Wally raises his eyebrows at another interesting question.

Test victory over Australia, Eden Park 1993, and the best send-off for John Wright (in the white tracksuit).

Above: Finding form again during the exciting one-day series against Australia, 1993. Here I cut Shane Warne for runs.

Right: During the same innings, hitting Allan Border clean out of the Basin Reserve. The sound of my Gunn & Moore bat was heard at the Beehive.

Ken Rutherford has always enjoyed a happy relationship with the media. Here he's pictured with David Leggat (NZPA) and Bryan Waddle (Radio NZ).

Above: A sad Geoff Howarth. Geoff was never properly prepared for the job as national coach, and was rushed into the position following Lees' sacking.

Right: Brace yourself! Following major surgery, the only way I could continue my career was by wearing a titanium brace.

Playing at Lords is the greatest experience I've had as a cricketer. Here I hook Angus Fraser for six in the second test of the 1994 tour to bring up 5,000 runs in test cricket.

Incredibly, the bail didn't fall as the entire New Zealand team roared a spontaneous appeal. Border, hearing the fatal click behind him, turned and walked away, thinking he was bowled, only to look down and see his castle still intact. He stopped, knowing he wasn't out, and looked back down the wicket in surprise. As he did so, the umpire, Chris King, raised his finger, believing him caught behind. Australia were five down for 31!

Over breakfast that morning I had read in the *New Zealand Herald* that Border was calling for more positive umpiring, by making more decisions to move the game along. It was a brave statement to make at any time, let alone on the morning of a test match. At lunch, Border must have been rueing his outspoken remarks. But the real key was the outstanding bowling of Morrison and Watson, who played with real skill, maximising their talents, reaping the rewards. It was the dream start we needed and, with it, we had the luck.

We continued to keep the pressure up, snatching Healy's wicket after the break before Steve Waugh and Hughes fought back. Merv had looked quite effective against the quicks so I gambled on Dipak sucking him in. One huge six and two fours were the trade-off as Danny swallowed a good catch at long-on. Off came Dipak and back came Willie to join Danny for the clean-up. Australia all out for a very modest 139 — Danny six for 37, Willie three for 47.

Beginning our reply, Paddy and Wrighty set about their task in a steely, determined fashion. Almost half their total was reached when the first wicket fell. Ken and I took us past 139 with only three down but Steve Waugh turned me round once too often and Taylor held me at slip off the back of the bat. From there we crawled forward to 200 for five but our lower order lacked conviction and we led by only 85.

As we changed for fielding I threw the room into a turmoil as the call went out, 'Dipak and Danny to start.' Throwing the new ball to Dipak always got me pumped up, because I knew it was truly a gamble. Mark Taylor seemed pumped up, too, for he took off down the pitch in a rage to hit Dipak and then quickly retreated, too late, as Tony Blain whipped off the bails. Then, to throw panic into the Aussies, Langer padded up to Dipak and received a shocker of an lbw. Langer had made a pair and Australia at two for seven were in despair until Martyn and Boon led a counter-attack. They quickly added 107, with Martyn forcing superbly through the off-side, until Paddy dived right at short point, off Dipak, to end Martyn's masterly 74. Steve Waugh, ever the nervous starter, stayed on the crease line to another from Dipak, who snared his fourth victim in a row and the lead was only 34.

Now we needed to be patient, bowl some maidens, apply pressure and wait for the rewards of our hard work. On the verge of tea Murphy Su'a felled Boon with a skidder, lbw for 53. In the last session only Healy went, controversially caught off his chest as umpire King was showing the strain. Dipak had his 'five for' while Border, rock solid, kept Australia alive with the lead now 140 and four wickets left.

Next morning the New Zealand team filed out in a fashion I hadn't seen in a test since we last beat the Aussies in March 1990 — focused, highly motivated, desperate to see the job done. The goal was to restrict them to a 200 lead. Blow me down if it wasn't realised exactly!

Sitting in the dressing room next to Paddy, I sensed something dramatic. He was dead still, deep in contemplation. Then he jumped up, grabbed his weapon and marched onto the field. Within an over he was down the track to Craig McDermott, slotting him high into the terraces. The beans were rattling, the blood was boiling, the curtain was down and the red rag was fluttering in the breeze! Hold onto your seats, folks, this could be a rocky ride.

Hughes, big Merv, that gorgeous creature known by his team-mates as Australia's largest pest, zeroed in on his heavyweight opponent, not with the ball but with his turbo-powered, fuel-injected spit. One gob landed on Paddy's pads, and first blood was drawn. Attack and counter-attack were in order, but no one knew the rules to this game; it was as close to big-time wrestling as you would ever see on a cricket pitch. When the bell rang to end the fight, it was Big Merv in front on points as he sent Paddy's stumps flying everywhere.

I thought Hughes' whole performance pathetic. Watching his antics to the crowd, his constant spitting at the batsmen and his childish sledging made me feel sorry for the bloke. He's a good bowler, no question, but he acted disgustingly on the field and did nothing but place the game in disrepute. Merv could be good fun off the pitch, but his behaviour while he was playing had me wondering why it took so long for the code of conduct to be invoked in series that followed. I could never understand why Allan Border condoned Hughes' actions, as they only encouraged newcomers such as Shane Warne to start acting like idiots as well. So when Greatbatch was bowled by big Merv for 29 to leave

New Zealand at 44 for one, it stopped the child's play and meant we could get on with what was turning out to be a fantastic, evenly poised match.

Watching all this, from the neutral corner, was one John Geoffrey Wright. In his debut at the Basin Reserve in February 1977, he had faintly nicked his first ball in test cricket to Bob Taylor off Bob Willis, but, receiving the benefit of doubt, had then battled on, all day mind you, for 55. He didn't add to his overnight score, but he had shown his obvious commitment for his country from the outset.

So, 82 tests, 147 innings, 5301 runs and 12 centuries later, Wrighty walked out to open the innings for the last time. From the time I first played with him against Australia in 1982, nothing much had changed. His pre-innings routine still had the 'going to a funeral' look about it. His face would be etched into one big frown of concentration, determination and worry. Wrighty always looked worried. Had he had enough water? Had he relieved himself enough? Had he stretched those hamstrings enough? Had he got the right bat? On the other hand, he never worried about the shirt he wore, whether it was this year's allocation or that of four years ago, whether it was hanging out or dyed a subtle pink in the wash, whether his shoes were dark grey or badly off-white, as long as they were well worn in. His gloves would be different brands and styles, his trousers loose enough to accommodate all the thigh pads you could think of, plus his cute little pot belly. Unless it had something to do with him scoring runs, or more precisely, occupying the crease, it didn't matter at all. What did matter was that he was playing for his country. He wore the silver fern with more guts, more pride and more determination than anyone who has ever represented New Zealand.

His job at number one in the order was never easy but he fashioned a record, especially on New Zealand wickets, which should rate up there in the Graham Gooch and Desmond Haynes class. At times the job became so difficult that it bogged him down and tormented him. He fought and fought with the opening role until, finally, in the first half of 1990, he broke free and showed the stroke play of a master batsman, a cricketer in control. His hundreds against India and Australia were sublime. At that point John Wright, captain of New Zealand, was at the very peak of his powers. It says a lot that he continued for three more years but by now he was back to where he started, looking only to survive, to endure. If you went by his last five tests this summer he would be remembered as dependable, solid, durable John Wright. I, though, would always remember the moments of greatness when he let go and played without a worry in the world, the moments when it couldn't get any better.

Wrighty was run out for 33. So stubborn had he become that it took a third umpire and a red light to remove him. From 1977 to 1993, in 16 years of devoted service, Wrighty had gone the distance. He walked off Eden Park to the most heartfelt, emotional ovation and disappeared into the tunnel for the last time.

Now the whole team felt it was only right to play for our man, to send him home with a win. Andrew Jones and I knuckled down and took the score past the halfway mark. With Shane Warne operating, I sensed it was time to take the initiative, to attack. I couldn't believe the transformation in this bowler's form since the opening tour match at New Plymouth. There he had seemed so out of control and inexperienced that I thought he could be just another flash in the pan. But over the next month I watched closely as Border used him cleverly, encouraging him into bowling leg spin as I'd never seen it before. Not only was his control outstanding but he began to unleash a brilliant variety of destructive deliveries. It was so exciting to see such a talent, even though he sat on the other side.

I was a little annoyed that Border hardly let me face him in the first two tests. This meant that I was facing him only when it really counted, but I devised a plan to combat his growing confidence. I tried to play him in the mind. I would keep a close eye contact with him to check to see what his body language was, how he might be feeling, whether he was struggling. With any top spinner I would concentrate mainly on what length the ball would be, and then quickly position myself accordingly. With Shane, though, I needed to treat him as a straight bowler first, so as to negate his superb flipper and top spinner. That meant I only had to pick his leg-spinner, which was quite easy. Once I'd picked the leggie, I would position myself to play horizontally, shaping to either sweep or pull depending on length, or cut if the ball was directed outside the off-stump. In between I'd keep out any good deliveries by using my bat only, if pitched on the stumps, or my pad if pitched outside leg-stump. I would always be playing with his confidence, knowing that if he ever pitched short he was gone.

I raced to 25, three fours off Warne through the leg-side, and then, while I contemplated another change in the field placing by Border, I was undone by a superb wrong 'un and caught in close. It was magnificent bowling. In this innings he had the better of me and had earned my respect as being the best leg-spinner in the world.

Unfortunately Andrew's luck ran out again, but by stumps the target was down to 33, with Ken and Tony Blain looking good. This time there were no ugly nervous collapses as there had been in the Pakistan test. No, we polished them off in 25 minutes to allow more celebration! When Tony turned Hughes to fine leg via the pad, the boys had given Wrighty the perfect gift. Wally and I embraced, and came out crying with joy and relief. We deserved this win. It felt as though we'd been to hell and back to get it. The enemy was beaten.

We joined the Aussies for a drink or 10 and then I asked them all to drink a salute to Wrighty; they loved and respected him too. Back in our room, the New Zealand team and sponsors stood once more to the Rigit, and this time there were tears. He replied as only he could. He would be missed. We celebrated from 11.30 am to 4.45 pm and then adjourned to the Cricket Society, where the entire bar rose to Wrighty and the boys. By 8 pm the DB boys had arranged a dinner, so, appropriately, we ended the day and marked our victory with DB coming out our ears.

It's hard to describe how the last three to four weeks had affected me emotionally. Certainly, to be on the verge of flagging away the captaincy during the second test had left some scars. It felt as though there were enemies everywhere — Aussies, tabloid media, selectors, one or two players — but the victory at Eden Park, our first really meaningful win for three years, filled me and the team with further faith that, despite the odds, we could triumph and reach our expectations. It was pure glory.

Immediately afterwards the selectors announced the squad for the one-day series. Michael Owens and Murphy Su'a made way for Chris Pringle and the new golden boy, Jeff Wilson. Rod Latham returned to open the batting for the now retired John Wright. Jeff was delighted, if surprised, at his inclusion. He is certainly a great athlete but whether he was ready for international cricket was a question New Zealand Cricket weren't prepared to delay. Peter McDermott had told Don Neely to get him in the team before rugby snapped him up. I was dismayed at the reason for his selection, but was assured by Ken that the boy could play. It staggered me also that Chris Cairns couldn't make this team but he did need a break, maybe to come back for the last couple of games.

So off to Dunedin we went, cock-a-hoop with our win and ready to turn it on in the wham-bam version of cricket. We decided to find out about Jeff Wilson straightaway so we picked him to make his debut in front of his home crowd. He opened the bowling with Danny but proved expensive as Mark Waugh and Mark Taylor cut us down to size with a fast and furious opening stand.

We never got into the game and finally fell over, leaving Danny and Willie to entertain the crowd after the regular batsmen had failed. It was a poor effort, typical of a New Zealand side coming off a huge win. But it was also typical that we bounced back at Lancaster Park and deserved a tie when Chris Pringle had Paul Reiffel plumb lbw, only for rookie umpire Dave Quested to miss out on a routine decision. All the Aussies sympathised with us as we angrily filed back into the dressing room, cursing the fact that so often New Zealand umpires are too scared to give out visiting batsmen in case it is seen as bias. Deep down I admire our umpires' integrity, but in this case it didn't help our desire to keep the series at one-nil.

Off to Wellington, where we looked more at home on a low, slow pitch, especially after amassing a respectable 214. I was due for some runs after successive singles, even though I felt my form was at a low ebb after a dreadful net the day before. This prompted Don Cameron of the *New Zealand Herald* to propose that I be dropped, such was my mood and my form. I delivered the perfect answer to everyone with 91 not out on a poor pitch. I was beginning to feel in control again, enjoying the thing I do best: batting and scoring runs.

I continued my better form into the next game but we were soon in trouble at four for 94, chasing 247. I decided to go all out, first to entertain the superb Hamilton crowd and second to see if we could get close enough to put Australia under pressure. Tony Blain joined me in the fightback but once I was run out for 91 only Jeff Wilson was left to perform a miracle. He did it with ease, launching a magnificent assault on the faltering Aussie bowlers and, with Gavin Larsen in support at the end, finished off the game in grand style to send us to Eden Park at two wins each. It was magic, pure brilliance. Eden Park would surely be packed the next day.

It was back to World Cup atmosphere as cricket fever reached amazing proportions for the final match of an unforgettable season. I was thrilled to have led from the front, despite damaging my old posterior cruciate ligament behind the right knee, which was now out of control. It was a blessing that we had only one match to go as my body was rather fragile and sore.

Both sides went at it hammer and tongs for the whole day, with the Aussies always just a trick or two in front. But, encouraged by a crowd of almost 40,000, the boys edged their way towards a victory. Chris Pringle and Gavin Larsen staged our last fight, and when it came down to nine runs off three balls, it was anyone's game. Gavin hit a great shot toward the cover boundary but Tony Dodemaide dived full length to restrict a sure four to just two. Instead of five off two balls, we needed a difficult seven. A single was taken next ball leaving the big fellow 'Pring' to swat the even bigger fellow, Merv Hughes, into the stand. The larger motor won through as Chris could only jam down on a perfect yorker, run two, and we lost a great game by only three runs. Only later did we learn that the fifth to last over was a delivery short!

The season was over at last, but the finish would have all cricket fanatics throughout New Zealand itching for next summer. We had shone through and, despite losing a fantastic one-day series on the last ball, we had proved that the team's unity and spirit were alive and well.

For all the drama, and the insecurity, of the season, there was a feeling of satisfaction inside our cheerful, relieved dressing room. The players had put some of their problems behind them and responded when needed, and Wally had drawn the best from his charges. Surely now the Colombo episode was over and forgotten. Surely now Wally and I had responded sufficiently to satisfy the powers that be. Surely now we could confidently plan the future, leading up to the next World Cup in 1996?

The next day I set off to walk the Milford Track with Jeff. It took us four days to tramp the most wonderful track in the world. The peaceful tranquillity of being away in the bush, instead of at another cricket ground, made it a marvellous experience.

I decided also to go to South Africa for a six-a-side Airlines tournament along with Paddy and another good mate, former Australian cricketer David Hookes. Before leaving, while I was spending a couple of days with Simone, who had stayed away from the tensions of the past month, I rang New Zealand Cricket headquarters and indicated to Cran Bull, deputy chairman, that the players were adamant Wally should have his contract renewed; he had established a bond of understanding and trust that couldn't be ignored. There were calls from outsiders, as well as a few within the board for Wally to go, for leaving Sri Lanka and for untimely remarks on his return, but the players knew that Wally's results as a coach were the best reasons for keeping our merry band together. I had no doubts — Wally was the best coach, easily ahead of all other available contenders.

I left for Johannesburg confident that the board would ignore the cries for change, or punishment if you like, and would contract Wally again. The board meeting was scheduled for 17 April, so I noted the date in my diary to ring home for the news. We enjoyed an excellent 10 days playing heaps of golf in Sun City and on Johannesburg courses, especially at the Wanderers where the famous cricket stadium stands. I looked forward to the opportunity of playing on the great ground when we toured there in the future. On the due date I rang Auckland and Dad answered, summing up the situation instantly: 'The bastards have sacked Wally! They've dumped him, and they're trying to say it's nothing to do with Sri Lanka.'

'Come on. It's got everything to do with Sri Lanka. That's unbelievable, just unbelievable. I suppose Howarth's in?'

'Yeah, he's in and he's already come out and said Paddy shouldn't be opening!' Dad was livid.

I rang Wally to express my shock and sympathy. He was devastated. I told Paddy and he was mortified. We had a few drinks that night, saluting a good man who had been done the worst possible injustice. I found it hard to shake the impact of the news from my mind. I was just glad I was in South Africa and not in New Zealand, so I didn't have to hide my disgust. It could have been pushed aside, this whole bomb thing. Couldn't they just let it alone? Personalities were getting in the way and the casualties were proving to be the men who had served New Zealand so well.

I headed back home to get ready for a couple of quiet months in Italy. Simmy was relieved it was all over so we could be back together with no hassles for a while. I was looking forward to a stress-free winter, getting fit again and recharging my batteries for a hectic season starting in October. I realised I would need to start over with a new coach and that I'd have to make it work, even though I knew the right man was no longer there.

CHAPTER 17

Adding Injury to Insult

Our greatest glory is not in never falling, but in rising every time we fall.

— CONFUCIUS

It was a hot, steamy morning in Hamilton, the sort of weather that, once you were outside, would open your pores and give you a glow for the whole day. I really liked this kind of heat. It got the arms and legs working, the blood pumping. For me, on this particular morning in Porritt Stadium, it was vital that the body responded.

I had flown up from my new home in Arrowtown to have a fitness test just before the selection of the team to tour Britain. The one-off test versus India was underway, so the selectors were on hand to assess my situation. I hadn't played any cricket of length since the previous November, when, on the tour of Australia, my right knee blew up in the match against Tasmania. I had played the first test in Perth a week later, but it had been useless to continue. The posterior cruciate ligament had gone again and, in doing so, had put horrific strain on the knee joint. As a result I had damaged a bearing surface that protected the femur and the debris floating about had caused dreadful swelling and pain. I had no choice but to return home for further surgery. We had tried cortisone injections and even, during the test match, a local anaesthetic to ease the discomfort. But I was in trouble and my surgeon, Barry Tietjens, advised me to fix it up immediately so I would be fit for the home series later in January 1994.

Immediately the criticism came forth — why hadn't I had an operation over the winter so as to be ready for a full season coming up? The simple answer was that there had been nothing to operate on after the previous season. I had seen Barry to assess whether anything needed to be done but he had insisted that there was no damage to repair, but that I needed to work hard on building up the muscle groups surrounding the knee joint. I spent eight weeks working daily with weights in an excellent gym in Cesena, Italy before completing my time in Europe by hitting the roads to build up some stamina. I arrived home in great shape and came second behind Adam Parore in the New Zealand squad fitness tests at the Cricket Academy.

Then my problems began. After a test to determine our lung capacity, we were asked to do two 20-metre sprints to test our speed. Just as I completed the second sprint I felt a sharp pain come from the front of the knee as I slowed. It swelled up straightaway and I was sidelined from training for two weeks, only a month or so from departing for Australia. There was no time to undergo surgery at that point, not that this was diagnosed because the knee did settle down in the final lead-up to the Australian games. It was only when I scored that quick 100 against Tasmania, putting the knee under huge strain by running aggressively to chase a target, that the knee actually gave out. The problem for everyone was simply that it came at a dreadful time, so early in the tour. I saw a Perth surgeon, Keith Holt, a specialist who had done over 60 posterior ligament reconstructions. He suggested that the chances of success for a reconstruction, using an Achilles' tendon to replace the damaged ligament, were 50-50 and that I would take possibly 18 months to recover. Keith thought I was better off having arthroscopic surgery, checking the damage and then countering the problem by working harder still on the muscle groups.

So, within 48 hours of the test finishing, I had undergone arthroscopic surgery from Barry Tietjens, who had operated on me previously. The complicated operation revealed permanent damage to the surface protecting the femur. Barry cleaned out the joint, handing me a jar of at least 60 to 70 pieces of cartilage and gristle. The knee was incredibly sore. It took five weeks for the swelling to go down so I could begin exercising. I had no chance of being ready to play Pakistan. I ordered a newly designed brace, made of titanium, from a Californian company called Innovation Sports and was so excited with its quality and function that I took a gamble and decided to play for Wellington in the Shell Cup mid-January. I had been incredibly frustrated and was dead keen to resume playing. There had also been a lot of pressure on me to return to the New Zealand side, such were the fortunes of the team in Australia. Under Ken Rutherford, the team had suffered humiliating defeats in the remaining two tests at Hobart and Brisbane. Then, after looking certain to make the World Series Cricket finals at the expense of South Africa, somehow, unbelievably, they blew it and missed out altogether. The media crucified the team's performance, but enjoyed and praised Ken's leadership, his openness and brutal honesty in defeat.

So, while I struggled to find fitness, the big issue was who should become captain once I was back in the team. Although it was obvious that the media preferred Ken, there was plenty of support for both alternatives on the talkback phones around the country. Finally, while I was attempting my comeback for Wellington, Ross Dykes, the convenor of selectors, announced to the public that it was me they wanted to lead the team. My comeback failed, as the knee just wasn't strong enough; the muscles surrounding the knee had simply wasted away. I spoke again with Barry, then rang New Zealand Cricket and confirmed that I needed another eight weeks to work the leg into shape. Simone and I flew straight to Auckland where I had meetings first with Barry and then with Bryce Hastings, the physio in charge at Les Mills' Fitness Centre. Together we formulated a rehabilitation programme using a 'one on one' personal trainer from Les Mills, a man called Vince Powell, who had successfully trained Susan Devoy in her last year as world squash champion. I also went to my good friend Mike Byron-McKay, a yoga master who operated in Herne Bay. He had helped to heal my back, and got me up to full fitness after I returned from Somerset in 1988. For eight weeks Simone and I lived out of our suitcases, staying at friends' and families' homes, and set about rehabilitating my right leg once and for all.

At 7 o'clock each morning I'd wake and dive into one and a half hours of yoga with Mike. Then it was off to Les Mills with Vince for two hours before lunch, and another session in the afternoon, mainly in the pool. We concentrated on building up the quads, and surrounding muscles, before I even tried to run again. Six weeks later, when I did try, the discomfort was there, but the progress was evident. I remained patient, sticking to the plan set out by Bryce Hastings. By early March I had announced that I would miss the remainder of the season in order to be fit for the England tour. On 12 March I had a preliminary fitness test at Eden Park. I was struggling. I couldn't get out of a hobbled jog and experienced too much pain in doing so. I asked for more time, but there wasn't any. The selectors would pick their side on 23 March and they needed to know if their possible captain was fit enough.

So there I stood, on 21 March 1994, sweat showing on my brow, a knee warmer covering my troubled joint. I was very, very nervous.

Mark Plummer, our physio, was to put me through a physical test under the watchful eye of Ross Dykes. I wanted, at this point, more than ever, to prove that I was okay, to convince everyone that my cricket career wasn't over. It was the most agonising period of my life.

As we set off around the track, slowly at first, I felt the leg responding. The knee seemed to be working well. As we stretched out a little I began to believe that I could finally crank up the speed and feel normal again. Away we went into a series of sprints and, as I reached top speed with just slight discomfort, I felt free and alive again. Only when I began to slow down did I have any problems. So Mark tried me doing some running of twos and threes, turning as if running between the wickets. I passed fit. I was overwhelmed. For a moment I felt like breaking down and crying, to release all the agony, to turn off the pain and frustration. I would play for my country again.

Ross Dykes was delighted, genuinely happy for me. As we walked back to the car, I turned to him and gave him a piece of paper. 'Dykesy, I don't wish to be the captain any more. I've written out a statement so I can announce it to the media, with your endorsement.' As I explained my reasons regarding my need to concentrate on my own personal fitness and form, and for the team to have a captain who would be certain to take the field, he reluctantly agreed. He was really understanding, really caring, and I noticed that we were both becoming quite emotional.

We drove back to the ground and I asked if I could make a statement to the media. Richard Hadlee arranged for it to be done straightaway. I read aloud my statement explaining my decision and my huge desire simply to play for New Zealand again. As I finished I felt the biggest sense of relief I have ever experienced. I was no longer the captain of New Zealand.

All I wanted was to get back to playing the game I loved so much. The time away had fuelled my passion to play once more, to go out and bat against the best, to score runs again. I didn't want or need any more innuendo, character assassination, comparisons — and nor did the New Zealand team. Giving up the captaincy was the hardest, and the best, decision I could make. I felt free, and that felt good.

A few weeks before I had had a long, thoroughly enjoyable lunch with my long-time mate Grant Fox, and asked him for some advice about the captaincy. He then told me what he did to ensure that his last years as an

All Black were successful. When he decided to give up any official responsibility within the team and concentrate solely on his game as first five and goal-kicker, he proceeded to play some of the best football of his life. He thoroughly enjoyed his final fling and retired a man on top of his game, the best in the world. He advised me to do the same, to enjoy my cricket and finish happy.

I had told Grant of my concern over my working relationship with Geoff Howarth. When we had toured Australia the previous year I had decided to let Geoff try some of his ideas and theories from the start, to get him involved and part of the set-up. He began by insisting that everyone warm up each morning on their own, in their own time, before the start of play. Usually we warmed up as a team before doing our fielding practice, which also gave us a chance to have a morning chat. Geoff's idea lasted four days. It was a disaster. No unity, no discipline, no communication resulted. He also decided to give each player one cricket ball and told us that we were to look after that ball for the whole tour. This was ridiculously funny. It was like something out of the late 1960s, probably stemming from his days in county cricket. When he spoke to the team he tended to accentuate the negative too much for my liking, instead of outlining what needed to be done. I felt NZC never prepared him for the job, giving it to him without analysing his strengths or weaknesses. This really annoyed me as I knew from other coaches just how hard the job was.

So when Geoff slept in and missed the bus and the start of training one morning in Tasmania, I'd had enough. What he did after hours was his business but this team, any team, needed a coach who was totally professional in all aspects. After a while the players began to lose respect for him and, in doing so, they couldn't develop their own disciplines well enough to encourage better performances. Our form in that first month was dreadful. I became so worried about the lack of man management that I began spending most of my time staying as close as I could to the players. My own game went out the window as a result. Used to a totally different approach, I began to get very stressed out. When I left the tour for knee surgery, I noticed that the performances hit absolute rock bottom.

While I was recovering from surgery I also took the opportunity to have dinner with my brother Jeff and Peter McDermott. When I enquired if NZC were happy with Howarth's job so far, Peter indicated that they were, although he had personal reservations. In fact NZC had just offered Howarth another two years in office, based on positive reports written by manager Mike Sandlant and physio Mark Plummer. When Jeff heard this from Peter, he said, 'Are you serious? A two-year contract based on a report from a manager on his first tour and a physio? Unbelievable!' New Zealand Cricket had decided to make their decision two months before the end of Geoff's current term. The team's results were appalling, so why a sudden surge of confidence? What was the motive? No one could work it out. It seemed that the only reason for an early announcement was to end the pressure and speculation that were mounting as the season's end approached.

It was disappointing that Glenn Turner still wasn't among the selectors. He had been appointed to the panel three years before, but only under Don Neely. As he so rightly suggested when he withdrew, what was the point of a new face on the panel while the convenor remained who had been in charge for the past six to seven years? The policies would remain the same. Glenn should have informed the board of his unwillingness to work under Neely from the start, but he had assumed that Neely would go anyway. Glenn was ideal for the job but New Zealand Cricket inexplicably let Neely continue when it was obvious that we needed a change. The board, too scared to give the reins to a strong personality such as Turner, employed a yes man instead. The following year Glenn reapplied, but only as long as he could continue commentating as well. They bluntly refused. Once again a good man was left on the bench.

The big picture was being ignored and we weren't capitalising on the high profile of cricket since the 1992 World Cup. In my opinion NZC badly missed Martin Snedden, who had decided that he didn't have enough time to continue serving on the board. Martin had been excellent at liaising with the team and especially with me. For the first time that I could recall, he gave the board some balance and understanding of our needs. It was no coincidence that, since his departure, the board's reasoning had narrowed. It was critical that everyone start facing facts, and the imminent tour of England would force them to do just that.

Part Four

The Final Chase for Runs

CHAPTER 18

Brace Yourself!

The secret of success is being crystal clear as to your purpose
and directions, and having the courage to act accordingly.
— J. DONALD WALTERS

A Journal of the 1994 British Tour

23 March

The selectors announce a 16-man team to tour Britain. The balance of
the squad is questionable. They've gone for eight batsmen including
three openers, and Mark Greatbatch, surely one too many. Paddy, it
seems, has given up opening and is gambling on forcing his way into the
middle order. Eight batsmen means only one wicketkeeper is picked.
Adam Parore will have a huge task playing almost every game, which
will test his keeping ability, but probably improve his excellent potential
as a batsman. Only one genuine spinner is in. That's because five quick-
ish bowlers plus Gavin Larsen have got the nod. Gavin is in because he'll
bowl a lot outside the tests, and be the vice-captain, but to select Heath
Davis, a raw rookie, is once again like sending a lamb to the slaughter.
What's happened to Willie Watson or Dipak Patel, the ex-county all-
rounder, whom I regard as one of two of the best off-spinners in the
world? Still, I'm happy to be making my fourth tour, this time just as a
senior pro. While I'm supportive of Ken Rutherford's leadership, the
continued appointment of Geoff Howarth as coach makes me a little
nervous. On the other hand, Ray Illingworth and Mike Atherton have
joined forces to resurrect England's fortunes. Illingworth could prove to
be an inspired decision, such is his respect and standing in the game.

11 April

The final fitness tests are completed. Paddy and I fly to Christchurch to
prove that the recent operations on our knees will last the tour. I have
no problems, having proved myself two weeks ago. Paddy can't even jog

so there's interesting debate on that. They decide to risk it. The other players were put through a quick casual assessment last week, and the only concerns are Blair Pocock's and Simon Doull's shoulders. Neither is asked to bowl or throw during their physical, which I find incredible. It seems my test is the only thorough one, probably because they thought I might fail!

21 April

Ken, Simon Doull, Paddy and I all assemble at Auckland airport ready for departure. The rest are already in Sharjah playing a two-week tournament. Ken rightly decided to rest. But I can't work out why Danny Morrison hasn't as well, especially now that he's torn a groin muscle in their first game, and could be out for weeks. Paddy and I have been granted special medical clearance to have comfortable leg room for our 30-hour flight via Frankfurt to Gatwick. Typically, New Zealand Cricket didn't stress the urgency and necessity for our request to Air New Zealand, so we all sit cramped up in economy, reminding flight officials of the fact that their employer is actually sponsoring the tour! The word comes back that business class seats are set aside only for New Zealand Cricket officials.

First Week: 24 April–2 May

We have a short gathering once the team from Sharjah arrives. Geoff Howarth hands out a sheet with his goals for each person for the tour, which I'm not sure about. Setting personal goals is for the individual to decide, and should not necessarily be made public to everyone in the team. The boys want to know more about what the tour goals were.

Our first game is a casual affair, although as it's my first game back I'm a bit nervous. We play three warm-up one-dayers, win them all comfortably and prepare to play our first county, Surrey. It's only another one-dayer but I see it as being an important morale booster if we win. I graft hard for 40 before Shane Thomson scores an outstanding 90 not out. He's really come on in the last two years, working on his batting mainly, while giving up seamers to learn to bowl off-spin. Ken experiments too much with our bowling and Surrey rub off our total of 259 very easily. The bowling looks ordinary without Danny and Chris

Cairns. I'm still a bit tentative on my knee, lacking some confidence, but I'm putting in some solid weight training sessions to keep the muscles strong. What's saving me, though, is this knee brace I'm wearing. Lightweight, brilliantly designed, it's probably the very thing keeping me in cricket. So, as they say, brace yourself!

Second Week: 4–10 May

The weather packs in, very cold and miserable. This makes it difficult to get the body moving, and I struggle for any form at all, scoring just three and four. I enjoy an excellent evening with Michael Parkinson who is interviewing me for the *Daily Telegraph*. He wants to know why all this personal rubbish has being written. I suggest to him that I'm not that comfortable talking about it, but I fill him in on what's happened. He does a nice article, I have to admit, helping to make people here or at home in New Zealand understand the problems of celebrity status.

We move to Somerset in search of better form and come away with worse. Our bowling is pathetic and our batting just woeful. I graft out a first innings score reaching 56 and then pad up to a ball probably hitting middle and leg! That's twice now in three innings — it's obvious I'm not watching the ball. I'm bloody furious with myself and head out for a walk, to blow off some steam. I spend 45 minutes wandering around but by the time I get back we've gone from three for 162 to 182 all out and batting again. Luckily it's just turned lunch. I'm determined to have a crack at the 100 against Somerset goal that I set myself before the tour, but our openers bat well second time and are still there at tea. Then Blair Pocock retires hurt so that gives me my chance. Ninety minutes later I return with my fastest century ever in 76 balls. Such a special moment against my old county. I now feel a lot more confident. The other guys, though, are beginning to feel the strain, as the counties are making us look like nobodies, while the media have no hesitation saying we're just that.

Third Week: 11–17 May

The team spends a couple of days practising at Lords. What an environment to hone your skills in. I've been rested to allow all those who haven't played at Lords a chance to experience the hallowed turf. Middlesex field a second-string bowling attack, as most counties do, so it's time to post a big score for once. Alas, only Stephen Fleming looks in control. I watch him closely, soaking up his style, his pure striking of the ball, and I begin to think this man is a potential genius. I saw him play last year, scoring his maiden first-class 100 against us for Canterbury, and commented then that no young player excited me as much. I'm convinced he'll go on to become one of New Zealand's greats. Also, as I've been sharing his company a lot, I find him to be positive, mature person. 'Flem' is cool outwardly, and maybe a little less calm inside, but he has an excellent temperament and his intelligence will serve him well. He scores in this match, his first at Lords, a stunning century.

Everyone else struggles, especially Paddy, whose knee is troubling him, and so by match end, where rain saves us from a certain crushing defeat, the injury list is growing — Danny Morrison: 50 percent fit, groin; Simon Doull: going home, shoulder; Dion Nash: 60 percent, side strain; Mark Greatbatch: 60 percent, knee. Actually Paddy is really struggling with body and soul. After scratching around before stumps, getting dropped two or three times, he comes into the dressing room and slumps in his chair. Our manager Mike Sandlant, a lovely person, approaches Paddy and says in a genuine way, 'Keep going Paddy, you'll get through it, I know you will.' Paddy, obviously not in a tolerant mood, responds, 'Oh, yeah, scored a few runs at Lords have you, pal?' Ouch! The manager walks away a bit shocked.

Danny's told that if he doesn't come through this match and then the build-up games to the first one-dayer, he'll be going home too. I protest. Surely Danny should be left to come right for the first test in three weeks' time, not these one-dayers. Geoff Howarth wants success for the side now, which would be nice, but the tests are the priority and we need to stay patient. Anyway, at the end of the Lords match Howarth gives the team its third bollocking in as many matches for another poor performance. You can just see the confidence slowly erode. And we're still to have a cricket meeting to discuss cricket! I can't believe what's happening.

Then, to add insult to injury, Michael Owens arrives as a replacement for Simon Doull, only to be found totally unfit and out of condition. Didn't NZC do a fitness test back in Christchurch before confirming him to tour? Apparently there wasn't time comes the reply. Mark Plummer, our physio, is absolutely livid, immediately sending his

213

feelings back to headquarters. Owens won't be ready to play for at least 10 days.

We defeat Northants and Leicester in two pathetic one-dayers. The pitches and opposition are typical of the way touring sides are being treated. Ironically, maybe that's what we deserve at present. I'm thinking that we're not prepared well enough or haven't been pushed, especially in our batting, as the victories are achieved by eight and six wickets respectively. It's a false sense of security, as we're definitely not battle hardened, even though our one-day bowling is manageable. We head off to Edgbaston to face England.

Fourth Week: 18–26 May

The night before the first Texaco Trophy match, the management calls a meeting. Shock, horror! Surely we're not going to discuss cricket? Yes, this is our first official cricket meeting of the tour since our quick get-together on our arrival four weeks before. The coach lays out the plans for defeating England. He speaks for about 12 minutes, pointing out that, as we've done all the talking, it's now time to deliver. I look around the room and honestly believe these youngsters don't know what's going on. It's not their fault, of course. They're wide-eyed and beside themselves with fear. But they're all so promising and I feel genuinely sorry for them. Ken talks a bit, and I add that the game will be decided at a critical pressure moment; we need to identify when it is. I'm pleased that Ken agrees we should field first, no matter what the pitch condition is, as it gives us two chances to win. Chasing has become our only option in the last year or so.

Having restricted England to 224 in a good bowling and fielding display, we are poised to take hold of the match as we approach tea. Bryan Young and Adam Parore have put on 76 and only need to take it to 90 for one by tea to have control. Instead Adam gets too clever and lets England in when he backs away to off-spinner Udal and is bowled. Then just on tea Ken is out for nought, and the game disappears from our grasp. Our lack of discipline, and the fact that the game plan was never really communicated very well, and we're beaten — and easily.

The Lords one-dayer is rained off so England take the series one-nil and all the cash. Danny didn't last the Edgbaston match, his hamstring tearing because he wasn't 100 percent fit. He'll struggle to be right for

214

the first test. What a bloody waste. I decide to drive up to Leeds immediately and spend some time with Gordon and Shirley Chadwick. They've always offered me invaluable support and encouragement, and spending a few days in their company is an excellent break from the touring and hotel life.

After a disappointing meeting, when Geoff reads out everyone's 'goal' progress, the lads try to prepare to take on Yorkshire at Headingley. The game is hardly worth recalling. Crushed by an innings and plenty. One moment is worth recording, however. After Ken and I were out in the first innings, I asked him for a chat. I said openly and honestly that, although I had respect for him, I was devastated with the way the team was heading. I said I'd never seen a New Zealand team so poorly prepared, and pleaded with him to take charge of the tour and stamp his authority on the side. The youngsters, and I, were in desperate need of his leadership; we needed to hear him, and him only. He agreed. He had felt the same but was too afraid to confront a situation about which New Zealand Cricket had given him no choice. At this point Ken took over, while I crashed back to bed with influenza. This whole mess was getting to me, mentally and physically. I felt stressed and upset. But I was relieved to hear Ken respond.

I'm also delighted to have received such strong support and encouragement from Don Cameron of the *New Zealand Herald* since I've been back in the side.

Week Five: 27 May–1 June

We travel to Essex, east of London, and discover some sun and warmth. Alive again! Ken and I go out together and have a good chat over a pint or two. It's amazing that, after all these years, we're actually starting to get to know each other. Most important, we talk out all the ups and downs of the past, get things off our chests. It feels good to have this session, even though he drinks far too fast for me! Next day he scores a great century, as does Bryan Young. He speaks to the team constantly, and must have suggested that Geoff relax a little, so there's only one voice. The boys start responding with spirit, but actual playing confidence is low and may take a while to rediscover. Still, the match goes quite well, even though we lose Chris Pringle, to a back injury. He's been overworked, no doubt. We head to Nottingham.

First Test: 2–6 June

The 11 to play England at Trent Bridge is announced at our third crick-et meeting of the tour. Unbelievably, there are only two survivors from the Perth test seven months before, Ken and I, and only one left from the Hobart defeat — Ken. I find this staggering. What's happened since then? Sure, we've had injuries on this tour — Morrison, Pringle, Owens, Doull all out — but all of them should have been better pre-pared or they shouldn't have come at all. Like Chris Cairns. He needed an operation, so he had it. Pringle's injury is a result of overwork while all around him crumble. So our bowling line-up is Dion Nash, Gavin Larsen and Heath Davis. Only Dion has played before, with a total of two test wickets to his name. Gavin and Heath will make their debuts. Heath has gone for seven an over on tour, averaging one no ball an over. His whole confidence has gone, and now he has to open the bowling to Atherton, Stewart, Gooch and Smith!

The rest of the line-up is predictable. I suppose when I look at the fact that one player has survived six tests, it means that the turnover of players has been far too drastic. I mean, there should be at least four or five players, injuries granted, involved just to help the transition of bringing in new players. Almost all these guys are from the post Lees-Crowe era and are therefore learning to play first-class cricket in test matches.

I admit to feeling the pressure, hence my request to drop from three to four in the order after the Yorkshire match. My preparation has been thorough pre-test, through extra nets to find my footwork, but I haven't had a score for a while and I'm edgy.

Thursday 2 June: Lunchtime, First Day

My edgy feeling is confirmed. Literally. Caught down the leg-side flick-ing at a nothing ball. We're three for 66 and the game is sliding downhill fast. It's in the air. Only Stephen Fleming plays with any confidence and freedom. In only his third test innings he cruises to a delightful half-century. Stephen was introduced to test match cricket in the ideal way. The selectors, having lost Andrew Jones to retirement after the Pakistan series, decided rightly to blood the youngster against an Indian side

with little to fear, and on a good, easy-paced Hamilton pitch. It was perfect. He responded with a sublime 92 in the second innings and, in
doing so, gained huge confidence. It was just the way this marvellous
talent should be treated. He was on his way. With Stephen Fleming, the
selectors were spot on.

Monday 6 June: Lunchtime, Fifth Day

We've lost by an innings and 90 runs. Not even a contest, to be honest.
God, our confidence is hideous. England weren't extended one iota.
Actually, that could be a positive thing as they can't gauge their form
properly, while still trying to organise their own strategies and make-
up. Their management are putting a lot of pressure on Robin Smith and
Graeme Hick, which is backfiring as neither looks comfortable. I find it
astonishing that a player of Smith's ability is even questioned when you
look at what he has achieved. The way Robin describes it, I get the feeling that the England coach, Keith Fletcher, has no idea about man management. Anyway, from our point of view we can't get any worse.

Week Seven: 7–15 June

As soon as we arrive in Swansea, Ken calls a meeting. First a selection
meeting, then a full team meeting. In the first meeting, manager Mike
Sandlant and Geoff insist that we instil a few off-field disciplines.
Things like wearing our blazer and tie to each day's play, a possible curfew and so on. I just cringe. Thankfully Ken and Gavin give it the big
no! I suggest that maybe our discipline could be shown in our practices
and warm-ups. The upshot is that sanity prevails and Ken starts
demanding better work habits and moderate off the field habits. He
then facilitates a superb meeting, speaking directly to each player,
informing everyone of their role and responsibility, including his own,
from this point on. I'm impressed. You can't help but be inspired somehow.

The wicket at Swansea, where we're playing Glamorgan, is a poor
one but the boys knuckle down and create an excellent win. Ken and
Stephen Fleming strike masterful centuries, while Shane Thomson hits
some form. As Simone is flying in during the match, management
allows me to miss the game and drive to London to pick her up and

spend the night, before meeting up again in Bristol for the next match. It's good to get away, and obviously I'm over the moon to see Simmy again.

I'm far more relaxed now and display my improved mood with a quickfire 73 in 50 balls to the delight of Simmy and my folks, who have followed me and the bad weather since Somerset. Once I'm out I'm shocked that we don't declare behind Gloucester, to kick the game along. Paddy then gets out and I ask for an explanation from the coach as to what we're doing. Inexplicably he deliberately ignores the team's suggestion to stop wasting the match and declare. Instead we bat on till tea, pass their total and naturally rule out a decent run chase tomorrow. Next morning Geoff decides to put me in my place by lecturing me that cricket is in fact a team game. No kidding! We then have a heated exchange before I join the others for warm-up. We spend the last five overs of the match defending for a draw after Gloucester set us 360 in 68 overs, which was impossible. Interestingly, I sense that my anger is helping my focus. I certainly batted well at Bristol and can feel the killer instinct growing. Simmy has also bought me some perspective and, I hope, some luck. I'm looking forward to Lords.

Second Test: 16–20 June

I've practised well. So have the others, I think. To be honest, I haven't noticed what the team has been doing. Since that confrontation at Bristol with Geoff, I've just focused inwardly, slowly drawing the right inspiration. Yet I also feel low-key and relaxed. I know Lords, it can tease you. It can make you a man or a mouse.

We win the toss and bat. I watch the first over only to see Bryan Young depart. I don't watch again until I face up to Paul Taylor for my first ball. I'm sure Ray Illingworth has lost the plot in dropping paceman Devon Malcolm for left-arm dobber Paul Taylor. This had to be the decision of the year!

I feel good, not too tight, happy to play the odd shot before lunch arrives. I change my shoes, preferring spikes on this first-day pitch. After lunch I just keep building, scoring in 10s, encouraging Stephen Fleming to be positive. I'm 48 not out at tea, still building it up. Then, after a cuppa, Atherton brings on off-spinner Peter Such, pavilion end, bowling down the slope, no protection. I attack. Four, six, four, four, four and I race into the 70s. Shane Thomson at the other end is playing superbly. We hit top gear. Into the 90s, up to 98, then Gooch bowls short and a hook for two to reach three figures. I'm happy. Then, all of a sudden, I'm overwhelmed. Shane Thomson shakes my hand, and I burst into tears. I'm choking up. This is pure, utter elation. All that hard work over those last five months has meant something. Another 100 at Lords, and the first New Zealander to score two tons there. I'm struggling to see, my eyes are so full of tears of joy. I ask Shane to give me 10 minutes to come right.

Five minutes later I swing Angus Fraser high into the stand to bring up my 5000th run in test cricket. Then a cover drive that even Fraser can't refuse to acknowledge. At over's end Shane strides down and says, 'I thought you wanted 10 minutes!' At stumps we walk off 313 for four, I'm 133 not out, Shane 68 not out. What a day! I reach my chair and explode with emotion again, mumbling, 'I can't believe this, I just can't believe this!'

The next morning is overcast, and the new ball is due. I expect a tough time for the first 40 minutes and so dig in accordingly, but we lose Shane to a brilliant run-out. After an hour the English bowlers are still keeping the screws on, so I wait, and wait, and wait. Only one loose ball in 75 minutes. Then Phil DeFreitas bowls fractionally short and I position myself to pull. Alas, there's too much bounce and pace and I splice to mid-wicket. Out for 142, the greatest innings of my life.

The rest of the match belongs to Dion Nash. Enter the young all-rounder from Dargaville. Batting at number nine he takes our total up to 476, with a very effective 56. Then, taking the new ball, he spends a few overs finding his length and, just before stumps, produces a jaffa to Alec Stewart to give us hope.

First over following morning Dion strikes. The key man, Graham Gooch, pads up first ball and the boys explode. Dion is on fire. He runs in from the pavilion end, and amazingly manages to bowl away-swingers and leg-cutters back up the slope of the pitch to give every Englishman trouble. We just fail to make them follow on, so embark on setting them somewhere near 400 in four sessions. We lose two wickets quickly, then I inexplicably use a wrong leg-stump guard instead of middle, to DeFreitas for one delivery, and leave a straight ball to be bowled. Bryan Young, however, is in top form. He carves the bowlers relentlessly through the off-side to give our innings some momentum. We struggle before tea, however, and so the declaration is delayed 40 runs, leaving England 407 in 430 minutes.

The final day of this absorbing test match is a beauty. Dion claims Atherton and Gooch in successive balls to throw their chase into neutral. After lunch Dion claims Robin Smith again while Alex Stewart caresses on. All the while Ken is calling a brilliant tactical game: bowling changes, subtle field placements, encouragement, the works. The whole team respond to a man. Dion Nash is the one, though, who's playing the loudest tune. With six wickets already in the first innings, he snatches his fifth in the second to become the only man ever to take 10 or more wickets in a match and score 50.

But Steve Rhodes, their doughty keeper, holds firm as the light fades and, in the last five overs, Ken has to resort to spin from both ends. Matthew Hart keeps wheeling away heroically as he has for 85 overs in the match, but the victory is denied. For the first time on tour we've shown our potential, our true talent. Why so late? As we down some sponsor's product, the real romance of the test emerges. Dion's father, having flown all the way from Dargaville to watch his son play in a test for the first time, let alone at Lords, stands in a New Zealand blazer under the visiting bowlers' honours board in the dressing room alongside his now famous son and toasts our 'bloody Kiwi pride'. The emotion of the past week is catching up on Paul Nash — a tear drops into his champagne. It's been a great Lords test, mainly for the fact that from it has emerged an allrounder, but particularly a top-class bowler, who will grace test grounds all over the world with superb skill and fierce determination, and, crucially, he will be wearing a silver fern over his heart. Dion Nash has come of age.

Ninth Week: 21–29 June

It is no shock that we wake the day after the test slightly hungover. The boys, and supporters, enjoyed a good night out. So while the team gets ready to board the coach for Cambridge, Simmy and I join my parents, Audrey and Dave, for a day at Wimbledon.

It turns out to be an eventful day in more ways than one. First it is cold and rainy, and Audrey and Dave haven't been well during the test so this climate is only going to worsen things. In fact, Simmy seems to be going down with whatever Audrey's had. This is happening while we sit in centre court, huddled up in raincoats, witnessing the most dramatic upset of the decade. Unseeded Lori McNeill, a solid serve and volleyer, is challenging the biggest favourite anyone can remember, Germany's Steffi Graf. There is an eerie feeling on this dark day as the world's number one concedes the first set. Entering a tie break second set, Graf gets anxious and the whole centre court senses the impossible. Steffi Graf is beaten, and we are there to see it!

We then drop the folks at Heathrow and wind our way towards Cambridge, where we know we can enjoy a quiet three days. After the gorgeous setting of Fenners we then have to endure the stark and unsettling Derby Cricket Ground. This match is marked by the fact that I pick up Simmy's and Audrey's flu and worse. I try batting on the second day to help us pass the follow-on, but last only two balls before retiring, such is the fever I have. By now, we all just want to head to Manchester and get the final test underway. I manage to surface the day before the match, to have a 10-minute net and announce I'll be okay to play. The team meet for five minutes that night; with little talk, and a lot of hoping, we can grab some early luck. Finally Paddy sees the light and has decided to open, so is replacing Blair Pocock who, also finally, is doing something about his shoulder.

Third Test: 30 June–4 July

I'm still feeling hideous, so I hope we can field first. But also because it's our best chance if we can bowl England out for 300 or less. We lose the toss and will bowl anyway. It's an excellent day's test cricket for us as we bowl one side of the wicket and keep them to 199 for four. I head back to bed, wake at 4 am and can hardly breathe. I seem to have had a relapse — my throat and chest don't work, and anything I eat or drink doesn't stay down or in long. Apparently the antibiotics have had a reverse effect. Once at the ground I plead with Mike Atherton to allow me a substitute, but, to be fair, there's only one answer. I take the field. By 3 pm I ask again, as my condition is getting ridiculous. We bowl them out for 382, after having had them in trouble at 235 for seven, but DeFreitas and Gough, in his first test, play well as the bowlers tire.

To finish the day I'm required to bat the last 25 minutes, lose Bryan

Young at the death and walk off having somehow, because I can't remember, thumped 33 not out in a handful of overs. After my first 10 balls I had scored 27, all this in the intensity of a test match. By stumps we've lost four for 84.

The two sleeping pills I took overnight have shaken something up, instead of calming me down, because in the morning I continue to blaze away like a lunatic. Jumping down the wicket, smashing the fast bowler back over his head, hooking anything short, yes I'm really enjoying myself. I have to, as I can't enjoy the way I'm coping with this virus. Unfortunately it doesn't inspire my colleagues. We crash and burn for 151, and are asked to follow on.

Within two and a half hours I'm batting again, but this time with total control. No reckless hooks, just a nicely balanced straight bat. I produce what I feel is also one of the best innings I have played. Technically I can't fault it. As for concentration, I'm highly motivated, organised and focused. It's amazing when I look back to my preparation for this test. Since the Lords test two and a half weeks ago I've calculated that I've had no more than 10 minutes' batting practice going into this match. Yet I've probably spent well over 10 hours visualising, removing negatives, clearing my mind and focusing on the present to enable me to play like this. So who needs a training session when you can do it all in your mind! It's a great lesson. I've especially managed to black out any negative tones that are clearly existing in the dressing room. I've always thought visualisation valuable, but this example has just blown me away. By stumps Adam Parore and I have fought back, the total five for 205 with 50 and 65 not out respectively.

We bat on for only 90 more minutes on day four because of persistent rain. So, by the final day, we have a chance to salvage a draw. I go from 94 to 115, despite some early anxious moments. As I drive Peter Such to long-on for my 17th century I look towards Simmy in the stand, blow her a big kiss and thank her for the support and the luck she's brought me. Despite my illness, she's managed to keep me thinking clearly and precisely about what I have to do. I'm so thankful that I've been able to draw strength from her to finish my final innings in England with my best 100.

We fight on. The weather in the end has the last say as the match is drawn. England one, New Zealand nought. It's a fair result, although two-one to England would have been better. The horrific first six weeks have determined this series, but there are some bright points in the finish. I'm excited about the nucleus of this young side, its talent and potential. Young, Fleming, Thomson, Parore, Hart, Nash and Pringle are all set for distinguished careers. Add in Cairns, Morrison, Rutherford and me, along with Pocock (if fit) and Greatbatch (confidence restored), and you've got something to work with, for the next two years and beyond. But the obvious necessity is a support system, with a coach skilled in man-management who will complement and bring out the best in this bunch of Kiwis.

I'm pleased to have played my last series in England to the best of my ability. I leave this tour knowing that the last six months have been worth it. It's good to be back.

CHAPTER 19

High and Dry

'Sex, drugs and rock'n'roll' was the theme for the team's Christmas party in Durban on our tour of South Africa. Why this was so I'm not sure, but everyone, except one player, entered into the spirit of the things as we dressed in all sorts of costumes ranging from drag, to drug addicts, heavy rockers and even a priest and a nun. Ken Rutherford wore jeans and a T-shirt. It was clear to everyone that he wasn't himself, and hadn't been for a week or two. From being very much one of the boys, he now appeared disgruntled with his team-mates. He'd had a frustrating and testing period as captain, since our return from the England tour in July 1994.

Only weeks after we returned from the tour, NZC called all players into a debriefing in Christchurch. For the whole of the first day we were asked to listen to a number of people, ranging from the chairman, to a communications expert, down to the selectors, all expressing their opinions and concerns on why the team wasn't functioning properly, and what needed to be done to fix things for the coming season. We all sat there during the day and absorbed the full wrath of their criticism, much of which was justified. Yet not once did any of the speakers admit that they themselves could have done their job better and that the players weren't the only ones who needed to look at the recent performances. Instead, the players felt totally alone, and totally to blame. Even the selectors stated that, given the chance, they would still pick the same team that had toured England. This, for me, was just about the last straw.

Over the next day the team went through a series of meetings discussing medical problems and training programmes before we were gathered together by the new cricket director, Rod Fulton, and given a questionnaire to fill in. The document was not to be discussed by the team, but was to be completed privately and left anonymous, unsigned. All the players filled in the 36 questions and then left. Throughout the camp neither the team manager or, more important, the coach, Geoff Howarth, were in attendance.

PATRICK EAGAR

Above: Steering a short delivery from Graham Gooch to fine leg for two to raise the finest test century of my career, Lords 1994.

Right: Sharing the emotion with Shane Thomson. At this point I'm overwhelmed, and tears roll down my cheeks. Shane respects the moment.

PATRICK EAGAR

Enjoying the spoils. Dion Nash and I stand under the Lords Century Board, saluting my second hundred at the ground and his amazing feat of being the first man to score 50 and take ten wickets in a test at Lords.

PATRICK EAGAR

In the third test at Old Trafford, 1994, I scored 70 and 115. Here I swing and miss, only to be struck above the eyes, flush on the helmet where the silver fern proudly sits. How dare Craig White remove the fern!

PATRICK EAGAR

I retaliate by hitting a six off the same bowler in the second innings.

Finishing the book on an island in Fiji, one of my favourite places to relax.

New Year's Eve 1994–95, Cape Town, South Africa. Shane Thomson, Danny Morrison, Bryan Young and I try out new helmets, courtesy of room service.

Right: Stephen Fleming, the finest New Zealand batting prospect I've seen. He has the talent and the temperament to become the greatest runscorer in our history.

Below: Striking a four off Allan Donald through backward point in the centenary test at Eden Park, 1995. This is the last professional photograph taken of me scoring runs. Will there be any more?

Three weeks on, in late August, another camp was scheduled and the national squad returned to Christchurch, this time, though, to undergo some training and practice sessions. Before we entered the nets at the Canterbury Sports Centre, we were ushered upstairs into a cold room for another meeting. This time Geoff Howarth spoke to us. He started by saying that he was surprised but thankful for our open and frank comments in the questionnaire. He said he was determined to change and work hard on improving his own performance as coach, a job he intended to keep until at least after the next World Cup in 1996. He spoke firmly and sincerely. In fact it was the best I'd ever heard him speak in the 13 years I'd known him. But the players were confused. We didn't know what all the questionnaires said, only what our own individual thoughts were, so everyone was curious to find out exactly what Geoff was on about.

Then Geoff went downstairs and was replaced by Rod Fulton and Ken Rutherford. The questionnaires, Ken announced, showed that there was a 75 percent vote of no confidence in Geoff Howarth. Seventy-five percent! I was stunned. I knew the senior boys, especially Ken, Gavin, Danny, Paddy and I, had reservations, but 75 percent? This was serious. Even Geoff's old Northern Districts players — nearly half the team came from ND — were saying that it wasn't working. Ken stated that after reading the results, the board wanted the team to reassess their views and to express them openly in front of Rod Fulton.

There was total silence. Then one player spoke up saying that he didn't think Geoff was responsible for his own poor form in England. But still no one was willing to now come forward and expose himself as being the one to vote against the coach. Finally I suggested that it was difficult for young players to stand up and speak their mind, and that if anyone wanted to rewrite their questionnaire then they should do so, privately and anonymously, as before. Again no one moved or spoke. In other words, everyone's views stood.

Ken then concluded by stating that it seemed clear to him that the team's feelings remained the same, and that 75 percent wanted a new coach. Another player then asked why the board wasn't acting on what was a pretty obvious situation to everyone within NZC who had read the questionnaires. Fulton mentioned something about contracts and legal problems as the reason for the board wanting the team to reconsider. The boys filed out, bitter and twisted about the whole situation and, suddenly realising that they had to knuckle down to some net sessions run by Geoff himself.

Later that day Geoff called me to his room to discuss things. He wanted to know what was going on. Telling him that I could only speak for myself as the team had never discussed anything collectively, I proceeded to lay my cards on the table. I told him that I thought his practices were unorganised and dragged on too long, that he didn't have the man management skills I felt the job demanded and that, deep down, I didn't have a lot of respect for his professionalism, especially in terms of preparation. I said that 75 percent of the team was a lot to turn around in such a short time and that he should spend the next year or so learning some specific skills so he could come back and have a better chance of succeeding as a coach.

Geoff wouldn't have it. He expressed a firm resolve to keep his job and to make it work, so determined was he to see out his contract. He said he refused to give up under any circumstances. I stressed that, although I admired his stance, I felt that he had been rushed into the job simply because the board wanted Wally Lees out. I said that I was disappointed that a number of players who had been developed over the last three to four years, men such as Patel and Watson (let alone the negative attitude towards Mark Greatbatch) had been discarded so swiftly that it looked as though you had to be from ND to get into the team. I felt that we were throwing away experienced players who had something to offer, especially in the one-day game, and that there were now far too many youngsters who had too few senior players to look up to or learn from. I finished by saying that who was coach didn't affect me personally, that I would try to continue to score runs anyway, as I'd done in England, and that it was up to Ken and his deputy to decide who they wanted as coach. I had nothing further to say about the coaching position. As I said to Geoff, I was sick of being criticised for having an opinion on the subject and, to be frank, I really didn't care any more; it was Ken's problem. All I wanted to do was continue my chase for runs.

It was here that Rod Fulton, in his capacity as cricket director, took it upon himself to report to the board, in no uncertain terms, that NZC should not appoint Howarth for the upcoming tour of South Africa. Roddy and Geoff were old mates and Rod found it extremely difficult to forward this recommendation, but believed that he had to. The board then met and threw out Fulton's report. It appeared that to sack Geoff would cost NZC a huge amount of money under the Employment Contracts Act, which stated that a number of warnings have to be given before dismissal, unless of course NZC made Geoff an offer he couldn't refuse. I rang Ken and suggested that, if he felt strongly enough, he should make it very clear to NZC that he needed another coach, otherwise he would be the one who would suffer most if and when the wheels fell off. Ken understood what I was saying but didn't want to act and be seen as the one who caused Geoff's dismissal. He left it to the board to decide. Geoff Howarth was appointed the coach for the tour of South Africa.

As the team was due to be named in the afternoon of Monday, 10 October I waited patiently at home for the news. Around 1 pm, two hours before the announcement, I received a phone call from Ross Dykes, convenor of selectors. He got straight to the point. 'Martin, we need you to be the vice-captain — we've got nobody capable of taking over if Ken gets injured or can't play for any reason. I know you don't want to do it, but we're left with no alternative.' I asked Ross for an hour to think about it and spoke to Simone, who gave me a quick, firm no! I could see what Simmy was getting at, that it would take the enjoyment out of playing, as had happened in England. But I knew I had to accept the position, as that's what the team needed, especially now that Gavin Larsen had made himself unavailable to tour. I rang back and agreed to be Ken Rutherford's vice-captain.

The only problem, from a team point of view, was that, two weeks before, I'd received permission from NZC to bypass the 10-day Indian tour and instead go straight to Johannesburg to prepare. My surgeon, Barry Tietjens, felt it was a great risk going to India and playing in one-day internationals straightaway, without giving my knee a gradual build-up of cricket. He could see it blowing up in the first sharp single I ran. I knew it wasn't ideal for me to be missing the first stage of the tour but we had to weigh it up against working the knee in slowly, considering that such a big season lay ahead. So I left for South Africa the day after the team flew to India.

My immediate impression of South Africa was that it had certainly changed a great deal since my first visit back in April 1993. Obviously, since the election of Nelson Mandela as the new president, the vast nation had settled down and there were no obvious signs of racial unrest. The only real problem that we could see was the large number of homeless black people wandering around, especially within Johannesburg. We heard of the horrific number of murders that occurred in the city every day — an average of 50 — and those were only the ones that were reported. The crime rate throughout South Africa was something of which we became quite conscious. For example, when we drove around the inner city area of Jo'burg, we did so with our cars locked at all times, and at night we didn't bother to stop at red lights for fear of an assault.

The other obvious thing I noticed was the massive construction taking place all over the country since the elections. New hotels, shopping malls, high-rise apartments and business blocks were all rising rapidly. So in many ways it was a positive, buzzing, happening place. I quickly found the locals to be warm, hospitable people, delighted to have us in their country, to share the lifestyle, the great climate and all the outdoor adventures. Whether it was enjoying the magnificent golf courses, or a day on a game reserve, or a lie in the sun on those superb Cape Town beaches, South Africa appealed immensely.

Judging by the way the various stadiums were set up for huge crowds, corporate entertainment or night matches, the South Africans were incredibly keen sportspeople. In fact, I felt the supporters went over the top when reacting to results from their national sporting teams. While the Springboks were winning in Britain and getting hysterical support, the cricket side, struggling in Pakistan, was being dumped on from a great height. Therefore the pressures on players were quite overwhelming.

I noticed that the South Africans tended to be very disciplined, very ruthless and yet very conservative in their approach to international play, almost openly acknowledging a fear of failing in front of their own people. I felt we had a good chance of succeeding if we could attack South Africa early on, while they were not receiving positive backing from their own people. In the meantime it was vital that we boost our own confidence by making use of every opportunity leading up to the tests.

By the time we had finished our build-up for the first test against South Africa at the Wanderers, I felt everything had gone perfectly for both the team and me. Six players had scored 100s in the lead-up games and our confidence was excellent. The management team had worked smoothly and Geoff, in particular, had knuckled down and prepared the boys well in practice sessions. Having gradually built up some form, and confidence with my knee, I felt as good as I ever had going into a test match.

Before the team arrived I had spent a lot of time practising and walking around the Wanderers, visualising that I would score the magical 100, and become the first player ever to score a 100 against every test-playing nation in the world. Also, I needed 105 more runs to beat John Wright's record of 5334 runs as the most scored for New Zealand in test cricket. This was a big reason for wanting to spend extra time in Johannesburg — to familiarise myself completely with this magnificent stadium. I felt that if I could achieve the 'Royal Flush', and the New Zealand record, in the first test, then the pressure would be off and the milestone behind me, so I could relax and enjoy the remaining tests. If I didn't, I knew the expectations would become stronger and stronger as the series went on, and the task that much more difficult. I could not have been better prepared for the start of the historic test that marked 33 years since New Zealand last played on South African soil. It was to be a huge occasion.

Before the test we had noticed the pressure on South Africa to win since they had lost 11 internationals in a row, and had changed their captain and coach. They were vulnerable, but we needed to put them on the back foot from the word go. The first decision was the toss, and Ken not only got the call correct but also made the brave though sensible decision to bat first. The pitch looked a little sporting but noticeable cracks were appearing and they would only widen and become worse to bat on.

Somehow we survived through till lunch, losing just the wicket of Bryan Young. The newly gained confidence of rookies Darrin Murray and Stephen Fleming saw them through some anxious moments. This was a vital session to win. First ball after the break signalled my chance to enter the fray, as Fleming was bowled by an excellent delivery from Fanie De Villiers.

In many ways I felt that the whole day was set up to nail the 'Royal Flush' there and then. I began slowly, determined to see off their best performer, De Villiers, and lay a foundation to bat all day. If I was there at stumps then I would surely have reached three figures, particularly as the outfield was fast and the wicket was drying out under a hot blazing sun. That was my plan.

Ken joined me half an hour into the second session and we proceeded steadily to build a partnership, with the skipper in an aggressive mood. I was content to wait for the loose delivery but, to the home side's credit, they fed me little; I could work only singles for the first 90 minutes. Then my worst fear was realised. Running through for a three to a shot played into the outfield, I overstretched on the final turn and felt my bloody knee go again. This time, though, I felt it collapse under the pain of more cartilage tearing away from the bone. I knew this was more trouble. I struggled through to tea to be only 23 not out after two hours of batting. I iced the leg, swallowed some anti-inflammatory tablets and a large glass of calcium to prevent cramping, showered and headed out again, trying to stay positive. Mentally, I was battling, unable to keep a clear picture, a tight focus, now that the knee had gone again.

Ken played really well, dominating the run scoring, encouraging me to remain patient. Before long the bowlers started to strain and my score jumped up to 50 with a succession of boundaries. Unfortunately, Ken lost concentration and got out to a rash stroke when set for a big score. This was so typical of his batting during his career. By now I was really starting to feel the heat and the high altitude and, almost in desperation, began to lash out, hoping to get the 100 before the body said enough. It wasn't to be the big day; time ran out with my score on 81. I'd survived two sessions but, as I walked up the 40 steps to the dressing room, I couldn't recall feeling so exhausted, so sore, in my life.

Then the little mental pressures started to emerge. 'Only 19 more, Hogan, only 19!' Messages of goodwill were scattered under the door as I walked into my hotel room. The phone started to ring from home, and all of a sudden I began to feel a little nervous about the whole thing. You know that feeling when your guts start churning, you can't eat, your breath shortens? Still, I felt confident that if I played sensibly for 45 minutes then it would happen.

Shane Thomson and I resumed the innings, with me taking strike to De Villiers. He bowled an immaculate maiden over, aggressive and on line. At the other end Richard Snell bowled loose and Shane picked off him nicely for an early boundary. The thought crossed my mind that his was the better end. De Villiers' second over was again spot on, and I sensed that they were determined to stop me, no matter what. I managed a couple of singles but still couldn't get on strike to face Snell. After 25 minutes I stood at the non-striker's end on 83, when Fanie, walking back to his mark to bowl the final ball of his over, turned to me and said, 'This will be the longest 17 of your life, mate.' First ball next over, having finally got the opportunity to face Snell, I smashed a full-blooded straight drive back down the pitch heading for the boundary when the bowler stuck out his hand and somehow managed to stop the shot. Two balls later he got one to shuffle low and I was gone, lbw Snell 83. What a long walk back. 'Next time, Hogan, next time'. I wasn't sure, though, that the leg was going to give me a next time.

The lower order rallied well with Shane playing superbly for 84, and we posted an excellent first up 411. By stumps on day two we had four of the South Africans back in the pavilion for only 109. The third day saw a more even contest as Dave Richardson showed great fight in scoring 93 and the South Africans totalled 279, giving us a lead of 132. But, with the pitch really starting to crack up, we sensed that a lead of anything over 300 would be good enough. To get that lead, however, we needed to score another 170 or more, so when De Villiers reduced our batting reply to 34 for five wickets, the game was poised to go either way. I displayed some pretty tired footwork and dragged one onto my stumps to record my ninth duck for my country. So, not only had the century eluded me in this match but so had the test record, with only 22 more to get. I'd have to wait now until after Christmas when the second test started in Durban.

In the meantime Adam Parore gave us back the initiative with a gutsy 49 and, slowly but surely, through the fourth day, we increased the lead to over 300 and finally settled on giving South Africa 327 to win the match. By stumps the game had evened up again, with their chase poised at 128 for two. The pitch was deteriorating, with the cracks now over 5 centimetres wide.

Incredibly, the game was over by lunch, as Simon Doull (four for 33) and Matthew Hart (five for 77) tore into their middle order and we captured eight wickets for 61. What a feeling! The boys were jubilant in victory, as I took the role of popping the corks off the champagne. While playing for New Zealand, I had been involved in victories over every test-playing nation and, according to the media, I'd become the first man in history to do so. To play against them all was one thing, but to be in a Kiwi team that beat them all, was a huge thrill. The missed 100? It didn't bother me at all at this point. We partied long into the night and celebrated a well-planned win. Ken and Geoff Howarth were rightly proud of their efforts, but could we keep it going, keep the standards up?

The test series was now put on hold for a month while four teams — Pakistan, Sri Lanka, South Africa and ourselves — battled it out for the Mandela Trophy. Our major worry, though, was that we had lost the services of Dion Nash and Matthew Hart through unfortunate injuries, which left Chris Pringle as the only bowler with any one-day experience. Added to that was my knee. I had to weigh up whether to go home now and repair the damage with more surgery, or hang in there for a supporting role in the one-dayers before the all-important tests started again. I was desperate both to see the tour out and help us to win the test series, and to achieve my own personal goals. Before the opening one-dayer at Cape Town, I couldn't even jog around the ground but I lined up to play at number five. I really struggled to score at all and felt I was becoming a passenger during the one-day series. But then again, so was the team.

As it turned out, we didn't have the bowling attack, the experience, to cope with the brilliant stroke play of the other three teams. We lost every match quite convincingly, unable to chase the large targets we had been set. Our confidence and form dropped, and the old negative attitudes returned. We didn't practise as well as we had before, and our off field habits focused more on trying to boost morale by being one of the boys, than on rising to the challenge of snatching a win or two.

At East London I knocked on Ken's door and asked if he wanted to talk things through. We were two weeks away from the second test and needed to reassess the whole situation. I had noticed that Ken was getting down, losing his sense of humour a little and starting to spend more time alone, something I'd not seen from him before. I asked him how he was going. He confided in me that he was really battling with the on-field tactics in the one-dayers, that he didn't know what to do. Then he mentioned that he had problems at home that were worrying and affecting him. Ken had never confided in me before so it came as a bit of shock. I felt for him — he seemed lonely and isolated, as I had been in early 1993, unable to talk things out with anyone.

I flew to Cape Town for two days to prepare myself for the upcoming games, missing the last two one-dayers as my knee was getting worse. We were out of the finals by this point, so most of the lads took the opportunity to enjoy the excellent hospitality available, before knuckling down to the serious stuff ahead. That seemed only fair, if it was balanced by first-rate practice sessions and general common sense.

After the one-dayers we had only one first-class match to play in order to get ready for the remaining tests. Ken had planned to have the game off and disappear for a few days, as I had done, but then I pulled a back muscle just before the game and wasn't ready to captain the team at Paarl. Instead of taking a well-deserved break, Ken insisted on captaining the side, rather than Lee Germon, to make sure nothing went wrong in our build-up to the test. Consequently everything did.

First, the pitch was a disaster; as some of the boys said, it was like batting on the moon, and extremely dangerous. Both sides were bowled out for 80 odd each on the first day, with balls flying everywhere. The next morning the game was called off after one over. This was the worst possible preparation and the boys felt deflated and let down by the organisers.

As we now had two days to kill with only sub-standard practice facilities to use, it seemed a good idea to have a team barbecue and relax a little, release some of the tension that was building. During the afternoon a group of the lads embarked on a wine tour, guided by a local cricketer. The rest of us relaxed around the hotel pool, killing time before the barbecue. This turned out to be a fairly quiet affair, with some guys sticking around the bar after they'd eaten, some going off to a pub in town, some just sitting outside, like Shane, Simone and I, Geoff and his partner Kate, sharing a nice bottle of the local Nederburg wine and chewing the fat.

Next morning we went off to practise, using a local club pitch to have an open wicket, when the rain came down and washed us out after just 10 minutes. This only created more frustration. We were gathered inside drinking tea, playing cards, when suddenly I noticed Geoff taking players off, one by one, into a small room out the back of the pavilion to be interviewed by a very upset Mike Sandlant, our team manager. According to Mike, Ken had suspected drug smoking the night before and wanted the management to find out who was involved. Ken asked that every player be interrogated. Apparently he had not actually seen anyone smoking anything, but had heard from someone in the team that something was up.

When it was my turn for questioning, Mike informed me that three players had already owned up to smoking cannabis, and that they would be reported to NZC and probably sent home. I couldn't believe it. I couldn't work out why one player would snitch on his mates and then for Ken to demand an investigation of his own team while we were waiting to practise, and especially when we had a test series to worry about in four days' time.

I walked out of the room and approached Ken on his own. I suggested that this was a crazy state of affairs, especially with the media sitting idly by, and asked why would he want this hanging over his team so close to the second test, when we were one-nil up in the series. If he saw a problem, why didn't he go and have a quiet chat to those concerned and tell them to pull their heads in? He responded by saying that it was in Mike Sandlant's hands and that he couldn't see him changing his mind about reporting the players.

The players were in shock. There were angry mutterings of 'Who told the captain', or 'Talk about the pot calling the kettle black, we could tell some stories about him' and, worst of all, 'Nice fucking team loyalty we have!' From that point on, the whole mood changed to one of resentment and distrust.

The day before the test started at Durban, an upset and disgruntled Ken spoke to the team for the first time since Paarl. He told us that he was sick of everyone's attitude, that he'd had enough and that he felt like chucking in the captaincy unless things changed. Geoff followed him, saying that he was sick of been kicked in the guts with the attitude, behaviour and performance of the team, on and off the field. I couldn't believe what was being said the day before a test match. Was it scare tactics? I don't know. I understood Ken's frustrations after the results in the one-dayers, but this latest outburst had me wondering if he was seeing the bigger picture at all. If the problems he was facing at home were major, then he had everyone's sympathy; it's hard enough at the top without having your own personal difficulties interfering. Ken would have been the first to admit that he was not his usual self.

That night we all got ready for the Christmas party. It was a fun night, full of laughter and hilarity, but underneath you could feel the uneasiness. Mike Sandlant, fortunately, had decided to speak to the three players privately, and fined them $250 each, closing the matter for good. Knowing there would be huge repercussions if an official report went back to NZC, he decided to deal with the situation behind closed doors, and in a firm way that earned the players' respect. Everyone heeded the warning, especially as no one could now trust the team environment since it was obvious that there was a Judas among us. Being one of the boys no longer seemed so desirable.

The second test began with Ken winning the toss again and electing to bat first. It was a reasonable-looking pitch, but I was concerned that the boys had no batting form behind them (and neither, in fact, did the South Africans). We discussed whether it was better to deny the opposition the chance to bowl, especially as they were one-nil down. Nevertheless Ken decided to bat first and we all, except Shane Thomson, let his decision down badly as we crumbled to 185 all out. Shane played really well for 89, but the rest of us were either too reckless or too negative, or just plain out of form. Throughout the innings their quick bowlers bounced us constantly, and we obliged constantly by trying to hook; three of the top order, including me, fell victim to the risky shot. The happy hookers were born.

I needed only four more runs (on top of the 18 not out I had scored before lunch) to go past John Wright's test record but, in attempting to do this in glory, I hooked Steven Jack down fine leg's throat.

South Africa gained only a small lead with their turn at bat, but immediately we were in strife again, losing Darrin Murray for a duck. Amazingly, Ken then decided to strap on the pads and go in at number three, the position where Fleming had been struggling. He was out hooking straightaway.

I marched out determined to knock off the record and then settle in for a long innings. After four singles I finally was able raise my bat as New Zealand's highest test run scorer in history. It was a nice moment but quickly forgotten as I continued to graft more singles until we knocked off South African's small but valuable lead of 41. I then played a loose drive to be out caught for 10, and soon we were looking defeat in the face as our second innings ended at 192, leaving South Africa only 152 to win. We lost convincingly by eight wickets, and you could sense a huge swing in the attitudes of the two teams. We had no time to repair the damage before the final test at Cape Town in two days' time; the wheels now seemed to have come off well and truly. Everyone felt resigned.

I felt down, particularly about my fitness and, because of that, I was unable to find the inspiration, the belief, to turn my form around. I was trying like hell to get positive, but I couldn't work hard enough in the nets owing to my physical problems. Whenever I tried a visualisation session I couldn't hold onto the clear picture long enough, couldn't get relaxed. I found myself jumping from one solution to another, search-ing for the right ingredient to keep me thinking success. The fact that a number of the batsmen were out hooking into clearly laid traps showed how unfocused we had become. It was shattering to watch the whole team crumble so quickly.

I felt that the management of the team, of which I was part, had let the youngsters down badly. I should have done more to help individuals refocus, but I was so upset with some of the management's decisions that I ended up walking away from everything. I couldn't work out why we were looking for off-field problems and making them into major dramas instead of dealing with them privately. Mike did his best but perhaps his inexperience of touring at this level meant he couldn't keep a lid on things. Geoff was fairly quiet all tour, knowing that he couldn't afford to do anything wrong and so kept pretty much to himself, which, for a coach, wasn't ideal. Ken, for his part, was simply down and out.

We lost also at Newlands, Cape Town, on a truly magnificent ground surrounded by tall oak trees and backed by awesome Table Mountain. We became the first side this century to lose a three-test series after winning the first test. Hansie Cronje, the fine South African captain, scored a splendid 100 and showed superb leadership qualities in seeing his side through to a great series win, two-one. For Ken, the hard times continued as his frustrations bubbled over onto the field and he lost his cool upon being given out lbw in the second innings. Match referee Peter Burge fined him 75 percent of his match fee and put him on a two-test suspended sentence for showing dissent towards umpire Barry Lambson, and then, unbelievably, kicking in the umpires' door, while yelling, 'You're fucking useless!' Mind you, some of the decisions Lambson gave during the test did leave him open to criticism; Ken's actions were over the top, but perhaps understandable.

So, by the time the test ended, everyone was relieved to pack up the coffins and prepare to head home. I had further surgery to look forward to upon my return . Although we all knew that we were in for some justified criticism, and plenty of it, we also felt things finally had to change within management. We wanted to get home, put the tour behind us and then go out to do justice to the centenary season of New Zealand cricket. We left South Africa, after a 33-year absence, well and truly high and dry.

CHAPTER 20

Being the Best We Can Be

On 17 January 1995 Geoff Howarth announced his resignation as coach of the New Zealand team. After a meeting that lasted close to two days, Geoff finally emerged to say that, in the best interests of the team, he would resign immediately. This came straight after the resignation, only a week before, of team manager Mike Sandlant, who cited business commitments as the reason for his decision not to continue. The New Zealand team was then selected, with the shock exclusion of Chris Pringle, who had been dropped for no apparent reason; he had been our most successful one-day bowler in the Mandela Trophy series. And now, without any management, Ken Rutherford was on his own, four days from playing the West Indies in the opening one-dayer at Eden Park. I had already undergone another operation for my right knee on 10 January, so Ken was also without a vice-captain.

By Thursday the 19th, both John Reid, the Auckland Cricket Association chief executive, and Gren Alabaster, a former New Zealand player and coach, had been appointed as team coach and manager respectively. Twenty-four hours later, the same three players who had been fined for smoking cannabis in Paarl had been called before NZC and an independent commissioner, and were suspended for three one-day games. Although Mike Sandlant had never reported the pot smoking to NZC, somehow news of the incident had been leaked to the media, and then back to NZC, who were asked for confirmation and whether any action would be taken. NZC then called Sandlant back in to report the incident before announcing that a full inquiry would be made — hence the subsequent suspension.

It was also announced that Chris Pringle was not just dropped but suspended also, for supposed bad behaviour one night before a day's play in Paarl. It was clearly stated that Chris was suspended just for staying out late. This, to my mind, was a ridiculous situation. If Chris had broken a code of discipline in South Africa on a particular evening, then surely it should have been dealt with the next morning. As it wasn't, then one can only assume it didn't add up to much in the first place. If

Chris was our best one-day bowler over there, and he was, then why would you want to stop him from doing the very thing that makes him tick? Chris in many ways is a bit of a character, fond of a few honest beers and a cig over a chat at the bar late at night; sometimes he likes to continue doing that rather than getting all stressed out trying to get to sleep. So why not leave him to be himself? If he's performing in the middle, then who cares? Suspending him was absurd. All it achieved was to cut his heart out, to risk his not performing well again.

The team assembled the next day with three new replacements, mindful that, once again, someone within the ranks had dobbed in his own team-mates, instead of letting what happens on tour stay on tour. Not surprisingly, over the course of the next week the team lost all three one-day internationals to the West Indies convincingly. Can you imagine the undercurrents in a team that was under the spotlight, yet also struggling to be united within itself?

As I recovered at home from my operation while following the fortunes of the boys on TV, I received a fax from the *Sunday Star-Times* asking me whether I would respond to the allegations made in a report by cricket director Rod Fulton that I never supported team management on the tour. I rang Rod immediately, around 7 pm on Saturday, 29 January, and enquired if he knew that his report was with the papers, and what exactly was in it. Rod, expressing surprise that they had the confidential document, told me that he had, in fact, mentioned that I, along with Ken and Geoff, had failed to support Mike Sandlant enough on tour. I admitted to not being behind some of the management decisions and therefore said I didn't have a problem with him reporting it, but why was it with the media? That, he said, he didn't know.

So now we had the débâcle of how a confidential report, containing what appeared to be a fairly blunt assessment of Fulton's views on the problems with our cricket, had been leaked to the media. NZC immediately placed an injunction on the report being printed by the papers, and so the contents were kept under wraps. Ken Rutherford, however, heard that Fulton had recommended he be replaced as captain by Lee Germon, to which Ken replied, 'Maybe it was Rod himself who could have leaked the report. He seems to have a hidden agenda.'

Whatever happened, the whole episode of the leaked report (which probably had some good points to offer) was just another crazy problem for NZC to deal with, let alone the players, who were trying to put it all out of their minds and concentrate on surviving against the mighty West Indies! With all three players back after suspension, the team gave an excellent account of themselves in the first test at Lancaster Park, getting the better of a rain-affected draw.

By Monday, 13 February New Zealand cricket was in one hell of a mess. A record test loss to the West Indies, our worst in history, was just the sickly icing on a hideous birthday cake that had continued to taste worse and worse by the week. The centenary celebrations had become one big fizzer. The public and the media were, quite rightly, starting to give up on the whole sham. So who, this time, was prepared to take the blame, to stand up and be counted? Should it be the 'party on' players, who had been accused of disregarding their responsibility as New Zealand representatives? The administrators for not listening to the players' views regarding the coach way back in September? Or was it that we were always heading to a bitter end because the success of the World Cup went to our heads so much that, when a bomb went off, it divided us once and for all while we hung onto our own personal pride? I never lost the feeling of suspicion that began when I was asked to stand down before the World Cup. In other words, if we were a united front running New Zealand cricket, then why weren't we backing each other, listening to those in the know, and resisting the cries from outside (or inside) when they arose?

Success, of course, is a wonderful thing, a positive thing, but potentially dangerous as well — unless you can keep your finger on the pulse, clear the mist from your eyes and work harder than ever to maintain the standard you've set yourself. NZC made approximately $1.5 million from the success of the World Cup and were therefore poised to take our cricket through another happy era like the 1980s.

As I've pointed out, our dreadful failure of the past two years can be put down to contracting only Andrew Jones and myself for the 1992–93 season, the sacking of Wally Lees for returning home after the Colombo bomb blast, the reappointment of Geoff Howarth two months short of his contracted period with the team performing at an all-time low, the breakdown of my right knee and the sequence of injuries to players thereafter, the continued appointment of Geoff Howarth for the South African tour, despite a vote of no confidence from the team, and the lack of unity and trust within the side after Ken Rutherford reported unacceptable behaviour to the tour management in South Africa, which eventually led to four suspensions.

All these events have contributed to the demise of our national summer game. Why? The answer is not simple, but one factor is critical: the fact that cricket needs to look closely at how it runs its business. The structure of NZC is such that we have a constitution which encourages parochialism rather than doing what's best for the national body. Also the executive team cannot make decisions without broad agreement from a board of volunteers. Instead, we need a chief executive who has the ability, and the authority from a board of specially appointed members, to make decisions for NZC on a day-to-day basis, as, for example, Ian Robson does for the Auckland Warriors. A top businessman or administrator should be given the job, regardless of whether he has cricket experience, with people who do have that experience, especially in playing the game at a high level, on the rung beneath him. The present board should advertise and appoint the best chief executive available now, allowing him to begin head-hunting for top business or sportspeople to be nominated for the board; the six best candidates would be appointed to advise and work with the chief executive to run New Zealand Cricket.

We have to get away from having elected delegates from each major association providing six places on the board when all they do is fight among themselves for parochial reasons, causing disunity and preventing positive action. I also believe that, at present, the minor associations are allowed too much influence within the voting system. For example, each minor inside the Central Districts region is allowed one vote each, on top of the ten votes CD is allowed for itself, so, overall, 19 votes can support a CD move, compared with, say, Wellington's 11 votes (ten for itself, plus one for its only minor association, Hutt Valley). My suggestion is that minors inside majors get no vote at all. This will help everyone in each region to work together in harmony and will create a fairer voting system throughout the country.

As always in a democratic system, there will be a certain amount of lobbying for support, but let's get away from this ridiculous situation where those involved either have no real skills to offer or are more interested in their own futures rather than in the nation's cricket. Let the best independent experts decide our future course. Once the personnel are in position then it's imperative that NZC have the right geographical base, and that, at present, is not in Christchurch. We must move into our largest market areas, as most leading companies in New Zealand do, and begin to work alongside the corporate world. We should also have a marketing arm in each main region, working alongside the local administrations, all these directed by the best marketing manager we can buy.

I would like to see our cricket marketed along the lines of Australian Cricket Board and the Winfield Cup, which produce colourful, up-market, hyped-up media campaigns, especially on TV, promoting their games as something you can't afford to miss. And, talking of TV, why didn't NZC seriously consider alternatives to TV One, such as the Sky Network? Narrow casting — pay TV as opposed to broadcasting — is another way of providing a significant financial influence, and one that could be substantial as the number of subscribers increases up to the year 2000. NZC could benefit from double the amount they have budgeted up to the end of the century. And boy, could we do with that sort of revenue! Cricket is at a low ebb right now, so these ideas may seem difficult to implement if we're always losing, but it is possible to go back to the excitement of the 1992 World Cup and become a great business, if only we are prepared to change and make some good decisions.

These issues have been debated for the last two years, but it seems that only now, when our game has shown all the weaknesses it could possibly show, will we finally make the necessary changes. And if we don't do it now, then our game is doomed to die by the year 2000. This is only stating the obvious.

My way for the future consists of a number of specific — and immediate — changes within NZC ranks:

1. The appointment of the best qualified chief executive. This person does not need to have had cricket experience, the emphasis being on business expertise.

2. The appointment of the best marketing manager available.

3. The reassessment of all other management positions within the present administration — positions such as the cricket director, the national director of coaching, and the running of domestic cricket (which includes women's cricket, junior cricket and umpiring).

4. The appointment of Glenn Turner as the general manager of the New Zealand cricket team and convenor of selectors. This appointment has already been made and is an excellent start. Glenn Turner is ideally qualified to direct the team into the future.

5. The appointment of Wally Lees as the team man-manager.

6. The assessment and appointment of the best-qualified physiotherapist, fitness trainer, sport psychologist and medical expert to co-ordinate all programmes for all national teams, home and away.

7. The appointment of the best qualified person to run the National Cricket Academy (as Rod Marsh does in Adelaide). This person should have a high level of cricket experience.

8. The appointments of a full-time manager, and a home season public relations/business manager to the New Zealand cricket team.

We must move our whole administration to Auckland or Wellington immediately. Surely, too, our administrators should be working out of modern, colourful, fresh offices, not the old wooden building they occupy on Cambridge Terrace. That sort of environment only encourages afternoon naps! The marketing department, especially, needs to feel stimulated and creative if it is to function properly. Give them a view of the harbour, or a lovely cricket ground, if possible. Actually, my ideal would be to see Wellington go ahead with building the new complex at the Basin Reserve for which plans have already been drawn up. Within the building would be the Wellington Cricket Association administration, the New Zealand Cricket administration, a complete indoor facility with six full-length nets, a training room, a lecture room, changing rooms and any number of corporate boxes on the front section for magnificent viewing and entertainment. I would like to see the Basin Reserve adopted as the home of New Zealand cricket, as it's a genuine cricket ground in every respect. There would need to be further seating created to boost the capacity closer to 20,000 than it is now. I would also hope that, if possible, it remains solely a cricket ground. (I have to admit to a certain bias here. I've loved my association with Wellington cricket and have adored playing at the Basin. Wellingtonians have made me feel so welcome and wanted, despite the fact that I have only played nine first-class games for them in five seasons.)

We desperately need to establish, under our own roof, a development complex that is modern and exclusive to cricket in New Zealand. We therefore need to build our own academy either at Eden Park or at the Basin. Although over the last four years they have served a purpose, if not entirely successfully, the facilities in Christchurch are too scattered. We need our own bricks and mortar, as the Australians and South Africans have. The academy should be more of a finishing school as opposed to a place where any number of squads or teams come in for a few days at a time during the year.

We should identify around 15 players in two age groups, totalling 30 in all, and bring them into camp for two weeks at a time. If the cricketers are still at school, then they need to come in during term breaks. The emphasis should be on developing players to fill the élite gaps within the various levels of cricket, teaching them the art of excellence. All the top experts should be involved, with a highly qualified former top player to co-ordinate the whole programme. We don't, realistically, have enough money to accommodate 20 young cricketers for eight months full-time, as the Australians do in Adelaide, but we can adopt the same philosophies in teaching them how to become top players. The Australians have had huge success in producing internationals from their academy and now the South Africans, under Clive Rice, have begun their own. These two countries will continue to move ahead of England and us if we don't take steps to keep up.

We should be following these two outstanding cricket nations as never before. They have set the yardstick in terms of their marketing, development, player support, general excellence and professionalism; we need never again look to England for a model on how to run cricket.

For our own domestic season, I would like, more than anything, to see the internationals play at least 50 percent of the domestic competition. At present we are representing our provinces only around 10 percent, which only weakens our first-class cricket, and doesn't allow the top players to go back to a lower level often enough to work on their game. We are constantly learning about the game only in internationals, which is a very cut-throat and dangerous scenario.

We need to stick to only three tests per year at home, and a maximum of five one-dayers, as opposed to the seasons of 1993–94 and 1994–95, in each of which we had a total of nine tests and 19 one-day internationals. This, on top of all our overseas tours, only puts the players' bodies under huge strain and make them susceptible to the number of injuries we've had. So, by cutting down on the number of international matches in our country, we could go back and play for our provinces more often. We should never have to play back-to-back test matches, but instead have a schedule that sees the touring team play a provincial side in between tests while the national players play for their provinces in the Shell Trophy to prepare for the next test. We don't need to have trophy matches every week, especially when tests are on; instead we can spread the four-day games over the season so as to finish late March. For example, the trophy final in 1994–95 finished on 16 March and therefore could have been played later, particularly if the international season had been over, which it should have been by then.

There are, of course, many complications to overcome when arranging a season itinerary and NZC know those better than I do, but I think we have to stick to a simpler structure of fixtures to allow our all levels of our cricket to link together. Our first-class cricket has been in bad shape through the 1990s. If possible, I would like us to invite fewer international teams to our country, so that we don't risk ruining our domestic cricket, which should be the nursery for our international successes in the future. NZC has made the right move by including four-day matches in our domestic programme, but we've yet to see these scheduled, as I've suggested, to include the New Zealand players, nor have the grounds been able to produce pitches that have lasted long enough for us to see the positive results that this type of cricket has offered Australia. We shouldn't change back to three-day cricket, however, but instead get our groundsmen to aim high and come up with test standard pitches, as Lancaster Park does.

The next issue to deal with is the very important one of the players' needs. We must identify these to ensure the creation of a positive performing environment, we must give the players the support they require and we must provide them with some financial security and reward. The first need, providing an environment that will encourage success, should develop when the right people are appointed as I've suggested. The chief executive, for example, should make very clear to all players their overall responsibilities to cricket in general, including behaviour, image, fitness, sponsors' needs, practice, respect for the game and so on. Glenn Turner, as the general manager of the New

Zealand team, can encourage the development of all those areas, as well as identify the specific role that is expected of each individual. Wally Lees, if he were appointed team man-manager, would then endeavour to ensure that the players were coping on a day-to-day basis, emotionally, mentally and physically, with those responsibilities. At practices, for example, I could see Wally Lees organising the nets, leaving Glenn free to work on individual technique.

The players, from this working relationship with their bosses, can then feel that they are surrounded by a support team. There should also be a public relations manager who can co-ordinate the players' media and sponsor commitments, public appearances, any commercial opportunities and take away any off-field pressures. The team manager's position is also vital, in organising the movement of the team to each venue and ensuring that the players are properly fed and accommodated.

Finally, the players need financial security. Until recently we had a contract system, whereby players on contract were paid a straight retainer on a quarterly basis in return for their availability to play in all matches or tours that were scheduled. Alongside that we had the non-contracted players who were paid a straight match fee or weekly wage for every match or tour week for which they were selected. Two completely separate camps.

The ideal scenario would be to have every player paid exactly the same for each match or tour week for which they are selected, and also have a tiered retainer scheme guaranteeing the players' availability all year round. The reason for securing the availability of all players is to ensure that they train properly on a full-time basis and that they don't over-extend themselves by, for example, playing in the English county season. Rather, they should be fit and fresh to play in all internationals and our own domestic cricket. The tiered retainers should be based on the relative abilities and experience of the players, with a minimum of 12 players being contracted. The scales of retainer could range from $10,000 to $50,000 guaranteed per annum. Match fees would be paid upon selection for a match.

The main area of concern has been that, when a player has been dropped or injured for a length of time, he still gets paid his retainer. Because I have been in this situation with my continued injury problems, the question has been asked often and, unfortunately, this situation has exposed the NZC decision to allow a retainer-only contract system. But a contract is a contract and everyone has to accept that nothing can change until that contract expires. I have desperately wanted to play to earn my money, rather than sit around waiting to become fit again. Now NZC has acknowledged the situation and begun to introduce a fairer system combining both the retainer and the match fees 50-50. This still allows each individual player to be paid his true worth overall if he is able to play all matches or see out all tours. The new system has already been applied to contracts that are up for renewal; mine will be no exception when it expires in April 1996. There are also plans for a financial incentive to be implemented when the team wins matches.

I would also like to see a superannuation fund created for the players, similar to the one the Australians have. Their scheme provides a rising bonus fee for every test or one-dayer you play, which is kept in a fund, can be added to by the player and is paid out two years after retirement. I submitted a proposal to NZC two years ago, based on the Australian Cricket Board scheme, but with only a 50 percent factor. It got thrown into the bottom drawer. In return for this financial security, the ACB stipulates that the players cannot publicly criticise or comment on the board in any way or the money will not be paid out.

All this requires a lot of money, something that NZC claims it doesn't have, but for our cricket to become successful we have to employ the best people, pick the best players and pay them their true worth. If performances drop, then the specially elected board and the chief executive have every right to assess the financial payments of the retainer part, or not to renew the contract. At the moment, because the profile of cricket is struggling owing to poor results, sponsors and spectators are growing wary of spending their money. So, just when we need money to boost our whole business, we find that we are making less than we used to. In fact, we're losing a boatload every year. We not only need to act quickly but we also need to be realistic — it could take at least a year to turn this situation around. I believe we have the people to do this; it's just that we've ignored for too long the issue of who is best qualified to serve NZC. We can change our run of losses, but we need a clean sweep of all who aren't capable of being a successful part of our future.

Finally, we need to build our hopes around the potential brilliance of players such as Stephen Fleming, Dion Nash, Chris Cairns and Adam Parore. We need to ensure that these champions of the future are financially supported and don't have to chase the commercial dollar as I did, that they are protected from excessive media demands and outside distractions, and that ultimately they are directed to become some of the best players in the world. To do this, they need an environment that is professional, organised and motivating.

CHAPTER 21

The Last Boundary,
the Last Run?

> There's got to be a record of you someplace,
> got to be on somebody's books,
> the low down — a picture of your face,
> your injured looks.
> The sacred and profane, the pleasure and the pain,
> somewhere your fingerprints remain concrete,
> and it's your face I'm looking for, on every street.
>   — DIRE STRAITS

It was 8.55 am on 16 March 1995, and I was looking out over Evans Bay as we sat at the end of the tarmac awaiting clearance for take-off to Christchurch. Suddenly it dawned on me as never before — I was finished.

The New Zealand cricket team had just flown from Napier to Wellington the day after suffering what could only be described as our most humiliating test loss for a long time, beaten by the lower ranked Sri Lankans. At the conclusion of the game, for which I had again failed to be fit, I noticed that the team morale wasn't just low, but had actually vanished. So, after failing a fitness test to play in Dunedin, I had packed my bags and flown to the capital, before connecting all the way through to Queenstown.

In the Koru Club lounge before boarding the flight I took time to wish the guys well for the test at Carisbrook, as well as sitting down to read an article my good friend Dave Howman had handed me. Warwick Roger, editor-at-large for Auckland's *Metro* magazine, had written a nice story for the *Evening Post* about his love of watching test cricket at Eden Park, of venturing down to Reimers Avenue and soaking up another day's play. He described how, this time, he had come to see me bat against South Africa, as he sensed that I wouldn't be around to entertain him much longer.

249

Warwick had spent some time with me before the South African tour to write a comprehensive *Metro* story on 'the enigma of Martin Crowe'. Because I respected him as a writer, I welcomed the opportunity for him to write a balanced, thorough piece, and I enjoyed the hours we spent together, feeling satisfied that I'd been given the chance to explain my thoughts. In the final analysis, I agreed with most of what he had to say. It was nice to work with a pro, and an understanding one at that.

So, as I read his *Evening Post* column, I felt that he knew exactly where I was in my cricketing life. He wrote, 'For a little while it looked as though Martin, back on his old stamping ground, might be able to hold the innings together and guide us to an improbable victory, but it was not to be and I really do fear that I've seen the god in the deep twilight of his career.'

Without actually knowing it, of course, Warwick was referring to what was possibly my last innings for my country; the centenary test of New Zealand cricket could be my final appearance wearing the silver fern.

I had struggled through another post-operative period following surgery on 10 January, feeling sore and mentally flat and frustrated. How many times could I be operated on and still come back? I hated the whole thing. Although the knee didn't feel as bad this time, it still seemed a huge effort to get fit again to play international cricket — and do myself justice.

In fact, on 25 January I woke up believing that my career was over. I wanted to retire, call the whole thing off. As I lay in bed, I told Simmy tearfully that I couldn't and didn't want to keep going. I thought she would give a huge sigh of relief and say, 'Finally!', but she was deeply concerned that this was the wrong time to go. She urged me to give it one more fighting effort, to see the season out and think about it over the winter. Jeff flew down to talk me through it. He wanted to see me out there entertaining the crowds again; he stressed that there was plenty to play for. Dave Howman also flew down to lend support.

With all this back-up, it didn't take long to start believing that I would be scoring runs again soon. My training began to feel easier and, with revitalised motivation, I was quickly getting into some sort of shape. I decided to join the Wellington side within a fortnight, intent on going all out to entertain. I aimed to be in good shape for the showpiece of the season, the centenary test against South Africa. I aimed to give 110%, to go all out and prove that I didn't need special treatment because of my knee. I would work like everyone else until I dropped.

I flew to Wellington on 8 February and began practising with great enthusiasm for the next Shell Trophy game. The bat felt so good in my hands and, despite the lay-off, I was timing the ball surprisingly well. I couldn't wait to get to Lancaster Park and start what I called my last mission.

I was ready to play — and play I did! On the most superb batting wicket I've ever experienced in New Zealand, I started with 50 not out, then bowled 20 overs of part-time spin, before launching into a huge run chase of 475 to win, only to knock Canterbury off with eight overs to spare and finish with 193 not out to my name. It was unbelievable. The match produced the most runs in a first-class game in New Zealand cricket history, gave Wellington maximum points and a place in the Shell Trophy final and set me up for a hurried return to the New Zealand team just hours after they had recorded the worst test defeat in our history. I caught the first plane to Napier and lined up to play India, opening the batting with my best mate, recalled batsman Mark Greatbatch.

Next morning, 15 overs into the game, I chased a ball hard out to the point boundary, only to tear the thigh muscle of my left leg — yes, left leg — and limped off once more. Can you believe it? I couldn't speak as Mark Plummer inspected the damage, diagnosing that I'd be out for the next 10 days at least. The cricketing gods, in their wisdom, had spoken again.

I missed all the remaining one-dayers but declared myself fit again just in time for the test. I was preparing to bat at my usual number four position but was very disappointed and surprised to see that Andrew Jones hadn't been selected, especially as he'd been lured out of retirement over the winter by NZC. Accordingly I decided, for one of the few times in my career, to take the number three spot.

Then I tore my thigh muscle again in the first innings and was severely handicapped from that point on. I was now in fairly low spirits, desperate for some luck and inspiration. By the time I was batting in the second innings, though, I could see the perfect chance to score that elusive 100 against South Africa and, I hoped, put the team in a position to achieve a famous victory.

It was the perfect occasion for the perfect celebration, but, alas, the script could not be acted out. Chasing 275 to win after an excellent declaration by Hansie Cronje, we couldn't pull it off. As Warwick Roger said, I was gone for 14, having batted for 29 minutes and faced 19 balls — caught by Darryl Cullinan at first slip off the bowling of Craig Matthews.

The ball I sent to the fence for four to go to 14 was, I must admit, the best cover drive I had stroked for years, and it came on top of two other well-struck fours in Allan Donald's fearsomely fast over.

Interestingly, I was batting at the West Stand end of Eden Park and the ball I drove through the covers for four ended up rolling down the old tunnel from which I walked to face the first ball of my first-class career, 15 years before. In that first innings my first ball was bowled by Dayle Hadlee, and the second ball I faced I drove through the covers for three, although that time I batted from the terraces end. I had also walked out of that tunnel to make my international debut 13 years before when we beat Australia in front of a record-breaking 43,000 crowd.

When I look closely at my test record of 74 matches, 128 innings, 11 not outs, 5394 runs, an average of 46.10, 73 runs per test, 17 centuries and 18 half-centuries, I can honestly say that I feel very satisfied with my return. I have also had great pleasure, and will continue to do so, from helping team mates who have wanted assistance, particularly young players like Adam Parore and Stephen Fleming. Alongside that is the enormous satisfaction I've felt in visiting nearly 150 schools around the country, talking to girls and boys and encouraging them to play the game of cricket.

When I'm not playing cricket, I'm just like anyone else. I have feelings, I like to laugh, to party, to relax with a sexy novel, to cry, to love, to be private, to be a success, to have a pie and a pint with my mates, to enjoy the company of good friends. So am I really an enigma? Or has this idea arisen from the profile of cricket and my desire to get the best out of myself? Or is it simply that I'm difficult to understand because I'm seen to be different?

I guess it comes down to the fact that, in New Zealand, it's unwise to seek and enjoy success, to have opinions and share them, to be high-profile. My biggest regret has been that I spoke out when I should have shut up and kept my thoughts and views to myself. I should have followed the advice of that wonderful quote: 'Life will afford you many opportunities to say nothing — seize them all.' But then that wouldn't be me, would it?

Having said that, I've had a marvellous cricket career. It's been an absolute pleasure, and certainly fulfilling. I'm proud that, as a Kiwi, a New Zealander born and bred, I've given everything I had for my country. I've only ever wanted to represent my nation and to wear the silver fern. That's what satisfies me. Sometimes it even overwhelms me, as it did when I reached 100 at Lords in 1994. I felt utter elation and satisfaction that I had fought my way back to play for New Zealand again.

Soon it will all be over — and that will be a relief. I will be able to enjoy a more settled, stress-free lifestyle. I'm fully aware that certain people will be very wary of some of my criticisms and comments. All I can say is that I've told the truth as I see it. I've made mistakes, many of them, but deep in my heart I know that my intentions have been honest. I pray that our game will grow and become the successful business that it should be.

For myself, I'm keen to get into something completely different when I stop playing — maybe interior design, where my wife Simone is already working, or cricket training and development. I'm interested in sports psychology and also still enthusiastic about helping our finest young cricketers in some way.

But the most important thing for me to concentrate on is Simone and our marriage. It has grown steadily, despite the obvious pressures, and we are keen to raise a family. I love Simone more than anyone in the world, and she is my greatest friend.

The other concern is my health. I must take notice of what my body has been saying to me recently. I've had my fair share of pain and the stress of international cricket has taken its toll, because I've put my body on the line. I need to recharge my energies and regain a strength and confidence that will serve me well in the future. There's no question that I need a quieter life, but the life I've led so far has made me a man rich with memories and wiser from all kinds of experiences. I feel good about what I've done and that makes me think I can continue to live happily in the wonderful country of New Zealand.

Be the best you can be, always.

Career Statistics

by Anthony Boswell

I TEST CAREER

1. Test runs vs each country (home)

		M	I	NO	RUNS	HS	AVG	100's	50's	CT	WINS
vs	ENG	9	15	1	576	143	41.14	2	1	7	1
vs	AUS	9	14	1	385	137	29.62	1	1	4	3
vs	PAK	5	9	1	556	174	69.50	1	4	5	2
vs	SL	2	3	0	365	299	121.67	1	0	2	–
vs	WI	3	6	1	328	119	65.60	2	1	6	1
vs	IND	3	3	0	161	113	53.67	1	0	1	1
vs	SA	1	2	0	30	16	15.00	0	0	1	–
TOTALS		32	52	4	2401	299	50.02	8	7	26	8

2. Test runs vs each country (away)

		M	I	NO	RUNS	HS	AVG	100's	50's	CT	WINS
vs	ENG	13	23	2	845	142	40.24	3	2	12	2
vs	AUS	8	15	2	870	188	66.92	2	5	6	2
vs	PAK	6	11	2	417	108*	46.33	1	2	11	–
vs	SL	6	10	1	262	107	29.11	1	0	2	2
vs	WI	4	7	0	216	188	30.86	1	0	6	–
vs	ZIM	2	4	0	249	140	62.25	1	1	1	1
vs	SA	3	6	0	134	83	22.33	0	1	6	1
TOTALS		42	76	7	2993	188	43.38	9	11	44	8

3. Test runs vs each country (total)

		M	I	NO	RUNS	HS	AVG	100's	50's	CT	WINS
vs	ENG	22	38	3	1421	143	40.60	5	3	19	3
vs	AUS	17	29	3	1255	188	48.27	3	6	10	5
vs	PAK	11	20	3	973	174	57.24	2	6	16	2
vs	SL	8	13	1	627	299	52.25	2	0	4	2
vs	WI	7	13	1	544	188	45.33	3	1	12	1

254

		M	I	NO	RUNS	HS	AVG	100's	50's	CT	WINS
vs	ZIM	2	4	0	249	140	62.25	1	1	1	1
vs	IND	3	3	0	161	113	53.67	1	0	1	1
vs	SA	4	8	0	164	83	20.50	0	1	7	1
TOTALS		74	128	11	5394	299	46.10	17	18	70	16

4. Test runs vs each opposition, series by series (and catches)

SEASON	VS	M	I	NO	HS	RUNS	AVG	100'S	50'S	CATCHES
1981/82	AUS in NZ	3	4	0	9	20	5.00	0	0	3
1983	ENG in ENG	4	8	0	46	163	20.38	0	0	5
1983/84	ENG in NZ	3	4	0	100	148	37.00	1	0	3
1983/84	SL in SL	3	5	1	45	98	24.50	0	0	1
1984/85	PAK in PAK	3	5	0	55	173	34.60	0	1	4
1984/85	PAK in NZ	3	5	0	84	295	59.00	0	3	5
1984/85	WI in WI	4	7	0	188	216	30.86	1	0	6
1985/86	AUS in AUS	3	5	1	188	309	77.25	1	1	4
1985/86	AUS in NZ	3	4	1	137	179	59.67	1	0	0
1986	ENG in ENG	3	5	2	106	206	68.67	1	0	4
1986/87	WI in NZ	3	6	1	119	328	65.60	2	1	6
1986/87	SL in SL	1	1	0	27	27	27.00	0	0	1
1987/88	AUS in AUS	3	6	0	137	396	66.00	1	3	2
1987/88	ENG in NZ	3	5	0	143	216	43.20	1	0	2
1988/89	PAK in NZ	2	4	1	174	261	87.00	1	1	0
1989/90	AUS in AUS	1	2	0	62	92	46.00	0	1	0
1989/90	IND in NZ	3	3	0	113	161	53.67	1	0	1
1990	ENG in ENG	3	4	0	59	96	24.00	0	1	1
1990/91	PAK in PAK	3	6	2	108*	244	61.00	1	1	7
1990/91	SL in NZ	2	3	0	299	365	121.67	1	0	1
1991/92	ENG in NZ	3	6	1	56	212	42.40	0	1	2
1992/93	ZIM in ZIM	2	4	0	140	249	62.25	1	1	1
1992/93	SL in SL	2	4	0	107	137	34.25	1	0	1
1992/93	AUS in NZ	3	6	0	98	186	31.00	0	1	1
1993/94	AUS in AUS	1	2	1	42	73	73.00	0	0	0
1994	ENG in ENG	3	6	0	142	380	63.33	2	1	2
1994/95	SA in SA	3	6	0	83	134	22.33	0	1	6
1994/95	SA in NZ	1	2	0	16	30	15.00	0	0	1
TOTALS		74	128	11	299	5394	46.10	17	18	70

Note: Take away first seven tests and last four tests, and the record reads:

		63	108	11	299	5047	52.03	17	17	55

5. Test bowling

OVERS	MDNS	RUNS	WKTS	AVG	BEST
229.3	52	676	14	48.29	2–25

6. Test captaincy (and batting record)

					TOSS	
MATCHES	WON	LOST	DRAWN		WON	LOST
16	2	7	7		8	8

BATTING RECORD	M	I	NO	HS	RUNS	AVG	100'S	50'S	CT
Non captain	58	97	7	188	3928	43.64	13	14	57
Captain	16	31	4	299	1466	54.30	4	4	13

7. Test centuries by date and venue (as ranked by M.D. Crowe)

NUMBER	SCORE	VS	VENUE	DATE	RANKING
1	100	ENG	Wellington	22/23 Jan 1984	11=
2	188	WI	Georgetown	8/10 Apr 1985	9
3	188	AUS	Brisbane	9/10 Nov 1985	5
4	137	AUS	Christchurch	1/2 Mar 1986	4
5	106	ENG	Lords	25/26 Jul 1986	6
6	119	WI	Wellington	22/23 Feb 1987	11=
7	104	WI	Auckland	2/3 Mar 1987	7
8	137	AUS	Adelaide	11/12 Dec 1987	13=
9	143	ENG	Wellington	3/4 Mar 1988	17
10	174	PAK	Wellington	10/11 Feb 1989	13=
11	113	IND	Auckland	25 Feb 1990	13=
12	108*	PAK	Lahore	20/22/23 Oct 1990	10
13	299	SL	Wellington	3/4 Feb 1991	3
14	140	ZIM	Harare	7 Nov 1992	16
15	107	SL	Colombo (SSC)	8 Dec 1992	2
16	142	ENG	Lords	16/17 June 1994	1
17	115	ENG	Manchester	2/4/5 July 1994	8

8. World record partnership highlights

A.H.Jones/M.D.Crowe 467
Third wicket partnership for New Zealand vs Sri Lanka

Venue — Basin Reserve, Wellington
Date — 3/4 February 1991

Highlights :

1. The highest partnership for any wicket in the history of test cricket.
2. The tenth highest partnership for any wicket in all first class cricket (now the eleventh).
3. The highest partnership for any wicket in New Zealand first class cricket.
4. The highest partnership for the third wicket in all first class cricket.
5. Crowe's 299 is the highest score for New Zealand in test cricket.
6. Crowe went from 126* to 299 on the last day of the test, a record for the number of runs scored in one day for New Zealand in test cricket (173).
7. Crowe's 299 is the second highest second innings score in a test match. The highest is 337 by Hanif Mohammed for Pakistan v West Indies at Bridgetown in 1957/58.

9. All-time top 10 batsmen: centuries per innings

Qualification — 17 centuries

NUMBER	NAME		100'S	INNINGS	CENTURIES PER INNINGS
1	Bradman D.G.	AUS	29	80	2.76
2	Sobers G.S.	WI	26	160	6.15
3	Chappell, G.S.	AUS	24	151	6.29
4	Gavaskar S.M.	IND	34	214	6.29
5	Hammond W.R.	ENG	22	140	6.36
6	Harvey, R.N.	AUS	21	137	6.52
7	Barrington K.F.	ENG	20	132	6.55
8	**Crowe, M.D.**	**NZ**	**17**	**128**	**7.53**
9	Richards, I.V.A.	WI	24	182	7.58
10	Compton, D.C.S.	ENG	17	131	7.71

N.B. Not outs are not deducted from innings calculation.

II ONE-DAY INTERNATIONALS

Table of abbreviations:

WC	World Cup	TRI	Triangular Tournament
WCC	World Championship of Cricket	AAC	Austral-Asia Cup
WSC	World Series Cricket	MT	Mandela Trophy
CS	Centenary Season		

1. ODI runs vs each country, series by series (and catches)

SEASON	VS	M	I	NO	HS	RUNS	AVG	100's	50's	CT
1981/82	AUS in NZ	3	2	0	7	10	5.00	0	0	3
1982/83	AUS in AUS	1	1	0	66	66	66.00	0	1	1
1982/83	SL in NZ	2	2	2	43*	50	n/a	0	0	1
1983	WC in ENG	6	6	0	97	202	33.66	0	1	1
1983/84	ENG in NZ	3	3	1	105*	113	56.50	1	0	0
1983/84	SL in SL	3	3	0	68	106	35.33	0	1	0
1984/85	SL in SL	2	2	1	52*	75	75.00	0	1	1
1984/85	PAK in PAK	4	4	0	67	122	30.50	0	1	1
1984/85	PAK in NZ	3	3	0	59	111	37.00	0	1	2
1984/85	WCC in AUS	4	3	0	22	39	13.00	0	0	1
1984/85	WI in NZ	5	5	1	41	88	22.00	0	0	0
1985/86	WSC in AUS	10	10	0	76	330	33.00	0	3	6
1985/86	AUS in NZ	4	4	0	47	101	25.25	0	0	4
1985/86	TRI in SL	2	2	0	75	79	39.50	0	1	0
1985/86	AAC in SHARJAH	2	2	0	9	10	5.00	0	0	0
1986	ENG in ENG	2	2	1	93*	102	102.00	0	1	0
1986/87	WI in NZ	3	3	0	53	102	34.00	0	1	0
1987/88	WC in IND	6	6	0	72	222	37.00	0	3	4
1987/88	WSC in AUS	9	9	0	52	298	33.11	0	1	5
1987/88	ENG in NZ	3	3	0	18	33	11.00	0	0	1
1988/89	PAK in NZ	5	5	2	87*	196	65.33	0	1	1
1989/90	TRI in NZ	4	4	1	104	190	63.33	1	1	3
1989/90	AAC in SHARJAH	3	3	0	69	115	38.33	0	1	1
1990	ENG in ENG	2	2	0	46	53	26.50	0	0	2
1990/91	PAK in PAK	3	3	0	46	88	29.33	0	0	0
1990/91	WSC in AUS	10	10	0	81	405	40.50	0	4	9
1990/91	SL in NZ	3	3	0	64	98	32.66	0	1	2
1990/91	ENG in NZ	3	3	0	13	24	8.00	0	0	3
1991/92	ENG in NZ	3	3	0	31	66	22.00	0	0	2
1991/92	WC in NZ	9	9	5	100*	456	114.00	1	4	3
1992/93	ZIM in ZIM	2	2	0	94	134	67.00	0	1	1
1992/93	SL in SL	1	1	0	1	1	1.00	0	0	0
1992/93	PAK in NZ	3	3	2	57*	132	132.00	0	1	2
1992/93	AUS in NZ	5	5	1	91*	195	48.75	0	2	4
1994	ENG in ENG	1	1	0	0	0	0.00	0	0	0
1994/95	MT in SA	4	3	0	83	98	32.66	0	1	1
1994/95	CS in NZ	1	1	0	7	7	7.00	0	0	0
TOTALS		139	136	17	105*	4517	37.96	3	33	65

2. ODI runs home and away

	M	I	NO	HS	RUNS	AVG	100's	50's	CT
Home	57	56	14	105*	1884	44.86	3	12	33
Away	82	80	3	97	2633	34.19	0	21	32
Total	139	136	17	105*	4517	37.96	3	33	65

3. ODI bowling

OVERS	MDNS	RUNS	WKTS	AVG	BEST
216	21	954	29	32.90	2.9

4. ODI captaincy (and batting record)

MATCHES	WON	LOST	ABANDONED	TOSS WON	TOSS LOST
44	21	22	1	26	18

BATTING RECORD	M	I	NO	HS	RUNS	AVG	100'S	50'S	CT
Non-captain	95	92	9	105*	2883	34.73	2	20	36
Captain	44	44	8	100*	1634	45.39	1	13	29

5. ODI centuries by date and venue (also ranked by M.D. Crowe)

SCORE	VS	VENUE	DATE	RANKING
105*	ENG	Auckland	25 Feb 1984	2
104	IND	Dunedin	1 Mar 1990	3
100*	AUS	Auckland	22 Feb 1992	1

6. 1992 World Cup scores

Most runs in 1992 World Cup

vs AUS in Auckland	100*	NZ	248-6	A	211	NZ won by 37 runs
vs SL in Hamilton	5	SL	206-9	NZ	210-4	NZ won by 6 wkts
vs SA in Auckland	3*	SA	190-7	NZ	191-3	NZ won by 7 wkts
vs ZIM in Napier	74*	NZ	163-3	Z	105-7	NZ won by 49 runs
vs WI in Auckland	81*	WI	203	NZ	206-5	NZ won by 5 wkts
vs IND in Dunedin	26	I	230	NZ	231-6	NZ won by 4 wkts
vs ENG in Wellington	73*	E	200-8	NZ	201-3	NZ won by 7 wkts
vs PAK in Christchurch	3	NZ	166	P	167-3	Pak won by 7 wkts
vs PAK in Auckland	91	NZ	262-7	P	264-6	Pak won by 4 wkts

	M	I	NO	HS	RUNS	AVG	100'S	50'S
TOTALS	9	9	5	100*	456	114.00	1	4

7. All-time top 5 World Cup runscorers

Qualification — 20 innings

NAME	M	I	NO	R	HS	AVG	100'S
Javed Miandad (P)	28	27	4	1029	103	44.73	1
Richards I.V.A. (WI)	23	21	4	1013	181	59.58	3
Gooch G.A. (E)	21	21	1	897	115	44.85	1
Crowe M.D. (NZ)	**21**	**21**	**5**	**880**	**100***	**55.00**	**1**
Haynes D.L. (WI)	25	25	2	854	105	37.13	1

III FIRST CLASS CAREER

1. First class runs for all teams played for

TEAM	M	I	NO	HS	RUNS	AVG	100's	50's
NZ Test	74	128	11	299	5394	46.10	17	18
Somerset	48	79	12	206*	3984	59.46	14	19
NZ First Class	46	73	20	242*	3617	68.25	14	21
Central Districts	32	55	7	242	3299	68.73	13	10
Auckland	25	45	7	150	1632	42.95	4	10
Wellington	9	16	3	193*	865	66.54	4	2
DB Close/World XI	3	4	1	138*	255	85.00	2	0
Young NZ	2	3	0	47	71	23.67	0	0
NZ Board XI vs Aus	1	2	0	163	179	89.50	1	0
NZ vs Rest	1	1	0	37	37	37.00	0	0
Nth Island vs Aus	1	–	–	–	–	–	–	–
TOTALS	242	406	61	299	19333	56.04	69	80

2. First class bowling and fielding

M	WKTS	RUNS	AVE	5WI	BEST	CATCHES
242	119	4010	33.7	4	5–18	220

3. NZ season 1986–87 game by game, most runs and 100's

	RUNS	MINS	BALLS	6'S	4'S
vs Northern Districts	56	47	39	2	8
	29	49	41	–	4
vs Wellington	160	310	254	1	25
	73	112	111	2	10
vs Otago	73	106	106	–	12
	66	106	92	–	8
vs Auckland	154*	245	230	1	20
	45	102	101	–	3
vs Canterbury	175*	274	230	5	22
	50	98	102	1	5
vs Otago	13	30	32	–	2
	8	29	26	–	1
vs Northern Districts	151	238	194	1	22
vs Canterbury	144	189	175	3	21
	151	205	155	3	18
vs West Indies (1st test)	3	50	37	–	–
	119	385	308	–	15
vs West Indies (2nd test)	10	48	36	–	1
	104	382	264	1	8
vs West Indies (3rd test)	83	213	154	–	13
	9*	39	17	–	–
TOTALS	1676	3257	2704	20	218

	M	I	NO	HS	RUNS	AVG	100's	50's
TOTALS	11	21	3	175*	1676	93.11	8	6

4. 4000 runs in a calendar year

YEAR	NAME		I	NO	RUNS	AVG	100'S
1947	Compton D.C.S	ENG	69	11	4962	85.55	22
1933	Hammond W.R.	ENG	69	7	4445	71.69	16
1930	Bradman D.G.	AUS	52	7	4368	97.06	14
1932	Sutcliffe H.	ENG	62	8	4340	80.37	19
1948	Hutton L.	ENG	69	9	4167	69.45	16
1947	Edrich W.J.	ENG	69	9	4103	68.38	12
1987	**Crowe M.D.**	**NZ**	**60**	**9**	**4045**	**79.31**	**17**

5. All-time top 10 batsmen: centuries per innings

Qualification — 20,000 runs or 400 innings

NUMBER	NAME		INNS	NO	RUNS	AVG	100'S	CENTURIES PER INNINGS
1	Bradman D.G.	AUS	338	43	28067	95.14	117	2.89
2	Hick G.A.	ENG	465	47	24001	57.41	80	5.81
3	**Crowe M.D.**	**NZ**	**406**	**61**	**19333**	**56.04**	**69**	**5.88**
4	Hammond W.R.	ENG	1005	104	50551	56.10	167	6.02
5	Hutton L.	ENG	814	91	40140	55.51	129	6.31
6	Hobbs J.B.	ENG	1315	106	61237	50.65	197	6.68
7	Boycott G.	ENG	1014	162	48426	56.83	151	6.72
8	Compton D.C.S.	ENG	839	88	38942	51.85	123	6.82
9	Pollock R.G.	SA	437	54	20940	54.67	64	6.83
10	Harvey R.N.	AUS	461	35	21699	50.93	67	6.88

6. All-time top 5 NZ batsmen: career average and centuries per innings

Qualification — 10,000 runs or 200 innings

	M	I	NO	HS	RUNS	AVG	100'S	CENTURIES PER INNINGS
Crowe M.D.	242	406	61	299	19333	56.04	69	**5.88**
Turner G.M.	455	792	101	311*	34346	49.70	103	7.69
Donnelly M.P.	131	221	26	208*	9250	47.43	23	9.61
Sutcliffe B.	233	407	39	385	17447	47.41	44	9.25
Dempster C.S.	184	306	36	212	12145	44.98	35	8.74

7. First class centuries

1981–82	150	Auckland vs Central Districts at New Plymouth
1982	104	D B Close XI vs Pakistan at Scarborough
1982–83	119	Auckland vs Otago at Eden Park No.2, Auckland
	108	Auckland vs Northern Districts at Gisborne
	100	Auckland vs Wellington at Eden Park, Auckland
1983	134*	New Zealand vs Middlesex at Lords
	116*	New Zealand vs Essex at Chelmsford
	110*	New Zealand vs D B Close XI at Scarborough
1983–84	119	Central Districts vs Northern Districts at Whangarei
	151	Central Districts vs Auckland at Eden Park No.2, Auckland
	100	**New Zealand vs England at Basin Reserve, Wellington**

1984	100*	Somerset vs Oxford University at the Parks, Oxford
	125	Somerset vs Middlesex at Bath
	113	Somerset vs Lancashire at Bath
	152*	Somerset vs Warwickshire at Edgbaston, Birmingham
	190	Somerset vs Leicestershire at Taunton
	108	Somerset vs Gloucestershire at Bristol
1984–85	143	Central Districts vs Northern Districts at New Plymouth
	118	New Zealand vs Shell Awards XI at Kingston, Jamaica
	188	**New Zealand vs West Indies at Georgetown, Guyana**
1985–86	242*	New Zealand vs South Australia at Adelaide
	188	**New Zealand vs Australia at the Gabba, Brisbane**
	137	**New Zealand vs Australia at Lancaster Park, Christchurch**
1986	100*	New Zealand vs Essex at Chelmsford
	106	**New Zealand vs England at Lords**
1986–87	160	Central Districts vs Wellington at Levin
	154*	Central Districts vs Auckland at Palmerston North
	175*	Central Districts vs Canterbury at Lancaster Park, Christchurch
	151	Central Districts vs Northern Districts at Morrinsville
	144	Central Districts vs Canterbury at New Plymouth
	151	Central Districts vs Canterbury at New Plymouth
	119	**New Zealand vs West Indies at Basin Reserve, Wellington**
	104	**New Zealand vs West Indies at Eden Park, Auckland**
1987	148	Somerset vs Surrey at Taunton
	102*	Somerset vs Middlesex at Bath
	100	Somerset vs Essex at Chelmsford
	206*	Somerset vs Warwickshire at Edgbaston, Birmingham
	105	Somerset vs Worcestershire at Worcester
	148	Somerset vs Glamorgan at Weston-super-Mare
1987–88	119	New Zealand vs West Australia at Perth
	144	New Zealand vs South Australia at Adelaide
	137	**New Zealand vs Australia at Adelaide Oval, Adelaide**
	119*	Central Districts vs Canterbury at Lancaster Park, Christchurch
	143	**New Zealand vs England at Basin Reserve, Wellington**
1988	132	Somerset vs Worcestershire at Worcester
	136*	Somerset vs Lancashire at Old Trafford, Manchester
1988-89	141	Central Districts vs Wellington at New Plymouth
	174	**New Zealand vs Pakistan at Basin Reserve, Wellington**

1989	138*	World XI vs MCC at Scarborough
1989-90	143	New Zealand vs South Australia at Adelaide
	242	Central Districts vs Otago at New Plymouth
	138*	Central Districts vs Northern Districts at Rotorua
	113	**New Zealand vs India at Eden Park, Auckland**
1990	123*	New Zealand vs Essex at Chelmsford
1990-91	105*	New Zealand vs Karachi at Karachi
	108*	**New Zealand vs Pakistan at Gaddafi Stadium, Lahore**
	101	Wellington vs Sri Lanka at Basin Reserve, Wellington
	299	**New Zealand vs Sri Lanka at Basin Reserve, Wellington**
1992-93	**140**	**New Zealand vs Zimbabwe at Harare**
	107	**New Zealand vs Sri Lanka at Colombo (SSC)**
	152	Wellington vs Canterbury at Lancaster Park, Christchurch
	137*	Wellington vs Canterbury at Lancaster Park, Christchurch
	163	NZ President's XI vs Australia at New Plymouth
1993-94	105	New Zealand vs Tasmania at Launceston
1994	102*	New Zealand vs Somerset at Taunton
	142	**New Zealand vs England at Lords**
	115	**New Zealand vs England at Old Trafford, Manchester**
1994-95	124*	New Zealand vs Orange Free State at Bloemfontein
	193*	Wellington vs Canterbury at Lancaster Park, Christchurch